NOAH'S

NOAH'S REJECTS

A MEMOIR

A cautionary tale about life on an island paradise

Rob Kagan

atmosphere press

*To my mother—
who is nowhere in this book
but is all over this book.*

Table of Contents

Author's Note

The adventure you are about to undertake with me is colored by my warped sense of self and community that should be taken with a healthy dose of skepticism. To be clear—everything in this book is factual... except for the parts that I made up.

This book started as a memento to my children, who might not remember everything about their fairy-tale-like existence on Martha's Vineyard. But it turned into a cautionary story for those thinking that nirvana, Xanadu, utopia, paradise, or whatever god you pray to is right around the corner. The grass is always greener... clichés can be true, too.

LEGEND

- (A) The Ag Fair
- (B) Lunch with Sweetie
- (C) Girl's School
- (D) Home
- (E) Bike Accident
- (F) Kiteboard Accident
- (G) Mansion
- (H) Dyke Bridge
- (I) Rescue Jim
- (J) Chappy Ferry

Cuttyhunk

ELIZABETH ISLAND

Sailing adventure to Cuttyhunk

VINEYARD SOUNDS

Tisb

(B)

Marthe

Vineyar

West Tisbury

(A)

Chilmark

Aquinnah

ATLANTI

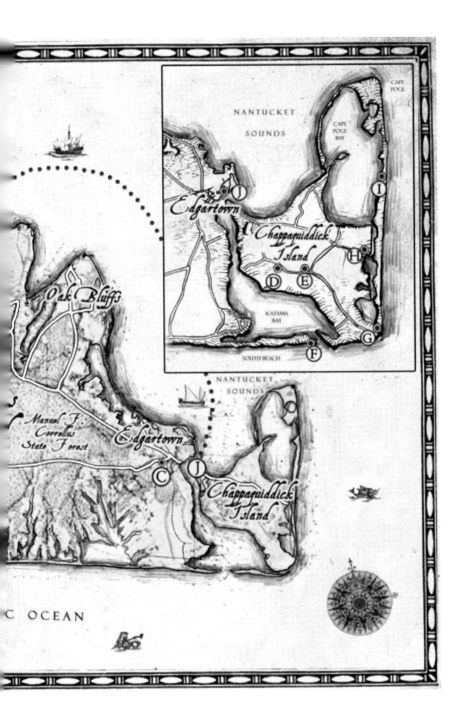

You Can't Make This Shit Up

"Hellooooooooooo?"

I roll away from my wife, Melissa, and look at the clock. It's 11:00 p.m. It's not that late, but for a couple with young kids and a thriving, hands-on business, 11:00 p.m. might as well be the middle of the night. But I'm expecting this call. I get calls like this more often than you would assume. Sometimes it's later or on national holidays. One time, a customer cornered me at the hospital, thirty minutes after my wife gave birth to our first daughter, Ilana. Really! So, 11:00 p.m. isn't a shock. I'm not happy about it, but I'm not shocked. Melissa groans and pulls the blankets away from me in her not-so-subtle attempt to convey she is displeased with the situation.

"Hi, Rob? This is Julie Rodney. I didn't wake you, did I?"

Of course, Julie woke me. She knew she woke me and really didn't care. Julie is one of a hundred customers of mine whose second homes and recreational lives I manage on the tiny isle of Chappaquiddick, off the island of Martha's Vineyard, off the coast of Massachusetts. With my help, these customers get to experience what it must be like to be a resident in paradise for a little while.

3

"Well, Rob, it turns out that when your cleaners were at the house the other day, they didn't stock the side bathroom next to the Blue Seashell guest room with toilet paper."

I'm still trying to wake up, and Julie is hitting me with one of her guest room's made-up names. You know the house is big when they start giving each bedroom a name. It all starts to fall into place in my head, and I rejoin the one-sided conversation already in progress. I stammer out an "Uh-huh," for no reason other than to convey I'm following along. And finally, Julie comes around to why she's calling.

"So, I'm sitting on the toilet with no toilet paper and no way to get to the pantry downstairs. You're lucky I had my phone on me when I went to the bathroom."

I'm lucky? I smile as I mentally take in the scene of an irate, fashionable woman pointing at her phone, talking a mile a minute as she sits with her pants around her ankles on the commode. Julie wants to yell at me, but she's doing it in a controlled way because she has house guests.

I'm now fully awake, circling back to the facts of the situation and Julie's "ask."

"I need you to come over and rectify the situation."

Are you getting this? Let's set aside the fact that my employees were at her house five days ago, not "the other day". Set aside the fact that house cleaners are not stock boys. Set aside the fact that it's 11:00 p.m. This woman wants me to drive to her house and fetch her a roll of toilet paper. Her husband is just down the hall.

You would think I would be yelling. You would think I would hang up the phone. But not me. This is my business. This is Chappy Unlimited. This is me—the toilet paper delivery boy. You might still ask yourself, "Did you go over there?" Hell ya! The word "Unlimited" is right in the name of my company.

I always think there must be a place to draw the line, but I haven't found it yet. In truth, I made a pact with the devil when I decided to live on such an idyllic island where everything revolves around the tourist industry. Of course, this pact came with personal wealth, a good home, nature, and beauty all around me. But it wouldn't be a nefarious pact without its dark side. You have met Julie. Come meet the other animals in the zoo.

Chappy Unlimited: An Origin Story

Chappaquiddick—Are you sixty or older? Well, you're probably picturing an overturned car in a low-lying body of water with a lifeless young woman in it. But that's not Chappaquiddick. That's a news headline, Senator Ted Kennedy's story from 1969. And it's certainly not the story I'm going to tell you today.

My life on Chappaquiddick and my company, Chappy Unlimited, were born out of necessity. I found myself living on the island after moving back to the states from St. John (US Virgin Islands) sixteen years ago when my brother, Andy, and I closed our hand-painted clothing business. It was a wild ride of a business with thirteen stores and a hundred employees of free-wheeling artists in resort areas up and down the East Coast. Crazy that we started it all with only $5,000 and two credit cards. We both had the good fortune of meeting our future wives during those blissful retail days but also had the misfortune of them not wanting to live in a Caribbean paradise. The thought of raising kids on St. John, so far from their New England roots, was just too much. The move was inevitable. An island closer to home seemed like a good compromise.

Enter Chappaquiddick, or Chappy as we call it—an easy

choice as my brother and I had bought a house there to be close to one of our stores. A beautiful island in a quirky and New England kind of way. It's part of the Island of Martha's Vineyard, but in name only. To be clear—Chappy is its own island. Eighteen square miles of sand with one barely paved road that cuts down the middle. Dunes to either side with seagrass swaying in the breeze. And as the land moves away from the water, the dunes give way to sandy soil that somehow allows the most misshaped scrubby oaks to jut out in all directions.

The very nature of the island created challenges for us from the start. We couldn't get anyone to work on our Chappy house. It was a rambling mess that was not suitable for year-round living. It needed insulation. It needed tree trimming. It needed a heating system. I would beg or offer more money to a laborer/tradesman than they usually charged, but they didn't want to come to Chappy. The ferry lines, the lack of a supply store, or even a convenience store to get a bite to eat—all made working on Chappy unappealing to the masses of Martha's Vineyard.

So I decided to start a company to cater to its overprivileged but under-serviced inhabitants. I was already on the island, had a wife for companionship, and food in the fridge. Location, location, location. I always remember that retail mantra.

It was ridiculously easy to start Chappy Unlimited. The town had the names and addresses of every taxpayer on Chappy and was more than willing to put them on a floppy disc for me. A friend created a cute but not too cute mailer. And within three weeks, I had sixty customers. The mailer described all the initial jobs I would perform. Grocery shopping, painting, party planning, lawn maintenance, and cleaning, to name a few. I was not qualified to do most of the chores I advertised. But I was a salesperson, and these chores needed to be done—so why not me? To be clear, I have never had a problem jumping into the abyss.

People would ask, "Can you strip the wallpaper from my walls and then paint them?"

Sure. What could go wrong? Who knew that some wall-paper comes off easily and some wallpaper needs to be steamed off, scrubbed of the glue residue, and then patched with drywall compound where you created divots during the entire process? Not me. But I learned. And people were patient. I showed up. I answered the phone, unlike most tradesmen on the island. And I didn't charge much initially, as even I knew how incompetent I was. It was a win-win situation for both parties. I may have looked like a chicken with his head cut off as there was so much to do and so many mistakes to learn from. But once again, I was my own boss.

Honestly, I believe the possibility of the absurd was a bonus to this new life. A phone call to age a set of new baseball gloves, walk an alpaca whose pen was being renovated, or move a buried time capsule so an ex-spouse wouldn't be able to find it, are examples of amusements I got to participate in. I even received routine calls to rescue people out of locked bathrooms. Ken Cole, the designer, had this same tragedy befall him late one night. Crazy.

I quickly learned that this spit of land off Martha's Vineyard off Cape Cod, where I was putting down roots, was my kind of oasis. My initial choice of location for homestead was based on my circumstance and history. The beauty of my surroundings, the ever-present smell of the ocean and the uniqueness of its inhabitants seemed heaven-made for my being. But it was my new business, helping others when no one else wanted to and having the space to jump off that ledge which is learning a new skill every day, that made this world so enticing. This was my idea of paradise.

Chappy Ferry

To understand island life and Chappy life specifically, you need to become acquainted with the Chappy Ferry—our lifeline to civilization, or at least Martha's Vineyard. Schools, police, food, an office of any kind, or even a public restroom are just a few of the things you can't visit or get on Chappy—hence the importance of the ferry. It's the hub of all activity on Chappy. All stories begin and end there. Have you seen it? It carries three cars and goes 527 feet back and forth all day long between Chappy and the rest of Martha's Vineyard. To look at this glorified boat is to understand New England's frugality and minimalism. There are no flourishes of detail or aesthetic whimsy incorporated in this vessel's design. It's a flat decked boat painted green with wooden railings and benches on either side. And on one side, midship is the captain's wheelhouse. When I say wheelhouse, I really mean a plywood box with a wheel sticking out of it with plastic sheathing for windows. Finally, the name, On Time II (or On Time III), is stenciled on the bow and stern of the boat. The name says it all. The "On Time Ferry" is always on time because it goes when people get there. No schedule. No fuss. Show up, walk, or drive on, and it goes. Unless it's summertime, and then there's an hour's wait or more as everyone wants to go for an excursion at the same time.

The ferry is our Google. We go to it for information about town government, the weather, or inquire if the fish is fresh at the market. Locals and tourists alike are happy to give this advice. The ferry is our Facebook. We see everyone there. We know who's slinking back from a night out. We know the new clothes they are buying, and which relatives are visiting. But more than anything else, the ferry is our lifeline off this rock. I have to go to the store. I have to go to work. I have to go to a gala fundraiser for fuzzy squirrels with limps. Whatever you need, it involves the ferry.

You travel down the main road of Chappy to its peninsula, a windswept piece of sandy dunes with a dirt parking lot, some dinghies lining the beach, and the ferry landing. That's it, nothing more. From this vantage point, you have an unobstructed view of the Edgartown Harbor and the metropolis of tourist shops and whaling captains' houses on the other side of the harbor. You are looking at Edgartown proper and the only stop on the Chappy ferry express. Your eyes always scan the picture in front of you—because it's beautiful and different each time. Is the ferry at the Chappy landing picking up passengers or just arriving to let some off? Is there a blazing red sunset over the church steeple in Edgartown that majestically spreads out over the village shops? Is the lighthouse to your right covered in mist? Do you see big fishing trawlers lined up on the Edgartown wharf, old and weathered but ready for action? The picture is always different, and at the same time, constant—beauty. But just like the ferry, the scenery becomes backdrop as people enter the scene and go about living their lives.

Today I'm at the ferry and leaving my island to help one of my employees, Lorna, sidestep deportation. She is a stereotypically hot-headed redhead from Ireland. And she thought it was a good idea to wallop one of the young summer cops when he tried to take away her beer on the beach last night. Twelve hours later, she's in jail, ICE has been called, and my customers just want to know when their pool house will be cleaned.

I park my car in the dirt lot and walk toward the waiting area to the left of the ferry. There are already groups of people waiting to be walk-on passengers. Day trippers, summer people, workers, and locals all mingle with their own kind as they wait. A group of tanned middle-aged women in tennis whites chats up their counterparts in Nantucket red pants, complete with Vineyard Vines belts. The red pants are so clichéd as to be retro and contrarian. It's a sprawling group but not so spread out as to interconnect with the dusty and unkempt men standing to their right. These workers have had a hard day and are bone-tired but still laugh and push each other around like teenagers. These two groups are on a first-name basis. Jeff, the plumber, with his grease-stained jeans that barely stay over his waist, feels at ease waltzing unannounced into the house of a Wrigley's gum heiress, as he is there to check 'something.' They meet in her hallway and talk about their families like old friends. But here at the ferry, they barely look at each other. That familiarity seems to have disappeared. It's all very orderly. All very high school. Everyone in their clique.

I often get sucked into a conversation with a customer at the ferry who is in dire need of my assistance.

"Rob, I need to have you come over to look at blah, blah, blah."

"Rob, did I tell you that we're out of blah, blah, blah, and can you re-order it?"

I want to talk to these people. I want to remember the important stuff they need doing to make their lives on this rock perfect. Yet sometimes the information comes so fast and disconnected, it seems like just a lot of noise. Noise that is added to the already crowded thoughts in my head. Work, family, businesses, ICE, the airspeed velocity of the common swallow...all compete for attention in my thoughts. I began to bring a notebook with me to the ferry long ago. It helps.

My phone rings and I slide to a stop on the sandy parking lot as I fumble to get my phone out. It's the lawyer I wired $2,000 to this morning to get my employee back.

"Hey Rob, so this is a typical situation. I told you this when we talked this morning. Your employee overstayed her visa and has no real standing to fight this incarceration. At this point, you are in just as much peril for employing her. What do you want to do?"

I'm listening but at the same time trying to figure out which landscaper I will have to move to the cleaning crew, so the wheels of my little empire don't fall off.

"Just be her advocate as much as possible and see if you can get her parents involved. I'll be over soon." Not that I will be able to do anything. But I have to do something. Have to keep moving.

There don't seem to be any customers trying to catch my eye, so I decide to move away from the groups waiting for the ferry, lean against the old bike rack and stare out to sea. Jim, an old, weathered painter I sometimes reluctantly employ, big on promises and short on polish, slams his bike into a slot near me. The bike is mostly rust at this point, with an old, thatched basket on the front. It's serviceable and usually Jim's only form of transportation. Why? Maybe he ran out of gas. Perhaps the police were on Chappy for one reason or another and saw Jim driving and reminded him that maybe he shouldn't be doing that. Perhaps his wife took his keys because he had been drinking or just to piss him off. Whatever the reason, Jim rides his bike and is comfortable with the restrictions it imposes. He takes one last drag of his hand-rolled cigarette that is more weed than tobacco and unloads the paint cans and empty gas container from the bike's basket to his canvas satchel. Ah, the empty gas can gives it away. I wonder what dirt road is now blessed with the wonder that is Jim's old truck?

One of Jim's paint cans tumbles out of his satchel as he turns toward me to say hello. I grab it and wave him off as he tries to get it back. "I'll carry it for you. By the way, how's the Horowitz job coming?"

"I'm almost done. Easy job. I'll be done early. You'll make a lot on this job. But I do need more paint. Guess you didn't buy enough."

Alarm bells go off in my head. I bought plenty of paint. I had a hunch I'd regret subbing a job out to Jim but did it anyway. There are just not enough hours in the day for my crews. This situation seems like Jim Mess-Up 101, but I need to deal with it later. The ferry is here.

I love getting on this floating conveyor belt. It's like a palate cleanser for my mind. It doesn't matter what issue is taxing my brain when I board. The minute I do, the captain reverses the engine's thrust, and we are on our way. It takes two and a half minutes. That's it. That's all it takes for the ferry to make its crossing. My mind clears. I get a reboot. The scene around me makes me smile. The salt air mixes with the diesel exhaust, and I take a break from dissecting whatever problem or drama my little brain was contemplating at the ferry ramp. As the ferry departs its slip, I see the ocean as if for the first time. I see the sun glistening off the little waves in the harbor, the cormorants repeatedly diving down into the water for their umpteenth meal, and countless other images that make my mind spin in a totally different direction—a good direction. I smile and hum. "That's why I'm here." Nature, it does a body good. I'm in the moment, but then, as soon as the trip has started, it ends. In an instant, I'm back on dry land and back to the reality of the day.

My phone rings once again as I walk off the ferry. "Robbie, you need to just walk away. You can't help her now." It's my dad. I'd texted him about my problems with Lorna as soon as I heard. He gets right to the point quickly, as usual, no fuss, no checking in to see how I'm doing. "I keep telling you that you're going to get in trouble with the IRS, ICE, or any number of other governmental agencies. I can't have you going to jail."

Why can't I sustain that cleansing feeling of stepping on the ferry forever? Why can't I compartmentalize the beauty, the non-beauty, my life? I turn to the ferry deck-hand deep in conversation with a summer person about a fish delivery as a distraction from my brain. The safety chain is unhooked, the ramp is lowered, and I'm on my way.

Meet My Supporting Cast

The early days of Chappy Unlimited were chaotic and definitely a learning experience. But I was hungry. The joke was that people could ask me if I could do an appendectomy, and I would say, "Sure, we can pencil you in for next Thursday." I helped an artist create a sculpture out of seagrass and seaweed and then the next day helped with advance work for a congressman visiting the island.

The diversity of customers' requests was fun, a little nerve-racking, as I was working without a net, but definitely fun. One of my well-intentioned attempts at a service offering was catering events for my customers. I was thinking of what people might need, not what I could skillfully accomplish. So, when Sally and Tom Kane, a nice elderly couple living on a stately seaside estate complete with pool and tennis courts, asked me to put together a lobster dinner for her and twenty friends, I said, "Errrrrr, sure."

My meal preparation skills at this point consisted of making peanut butter and jam sandwiches for lunch and mac and cheese for dinner—burning neither one was a treat. After two years of marriage, Melissa's wondrous organic and varied menus still had not affected my eating habits. It would take having children and a documentary on fast food hamburgers for me to see the light of day, and that was a few years off. It's safe to say cooking was not my thing.

What did I do? Who did I turn to? Not my wife. She was still busy with her career in Boston, which she commuted to every week. I knew no one in the catering business, and I had just professed to Mrs. Kane I was a culinary genius.

Enter Jerry. Jerry is my dad. He's the purveyor of free legal advice, as you have already learned. But he's so much more. He followed me to Martha's Vineyard from St. John, where he managed one of our stores after we discovered our manager was stealing from us. He is... Jerry.

He's sixty-four years old, 5'2", and weighs a good 190 pounds. Jerry appears relatively thin for carrying around so much weight on such a small frame. He has muscular arms and legs from walking the hills of St John but nestled in his midsection is a rock-hard stomach the size of a beach ball. It's useful for propping a book on when reading. Meet Jerry for the first time, and somewhere in the conversation, he'll blurt out, "I'm pregnant with twin pink elephants, touch my stomach." There's so much to say about him that I don't know where to start. Let's just say Jerry is Gordon Gecko meets Ignatius J Reilly from *Confederacy of Dunces* and throw in a little Fletcher Reede from *Liar Liar* for good measure. He is a character. This is the number one thing people say when his name comes up.

Regardless of his complicated and sometimes destructive layers—he's my champion, a person who would do anything for me. He's my dad. I ask, and instantly it's done. No task is too big or too small. And now he had agreed to pick up the gauntlet and help me with this catering event.

I have to laugh as the only one with worse eating habits than me is my dad. His apartment is lined with sardine cans, overturned boxes of Cheerios, and Chips Ahoy! Cookies. He has been divorced from my mom since '69, and as a bachelor for life, has become a real-life Oscar Madison. The only difference is to replace stogies from Oscar's mouth and add cigarettes to my dad's. Both are slobs. Both don't own a stitch of clothing without a stain. Both are charming, sweet, funny, and, as I said, characters. No one could really live with them. Jerry would not be anyone's obvious co-pilot for this mission, but he's been my winning choice in any pinch—decision made.

Melissa came down on the weekend, a week before the catering event, and I let her in on my new gig. Finally, she stopped laughing to say, "Oh, you're serious."

Then I laughed.

We put together a lobster, corn on the cob, and salad dinner, complete with margaritas on Saturday night as a dry run, and all went well. It's actually a pretty simple meal. The only twist that Melissa added to the menu was to steam the lobsters in two parts hoppy beer to two parts water. It really adds flavor to the lobster. So, with the menu set, I gave the shopping list to my dad and worried the entire week.

The day of the party arrived, and I called my dad. "Please wear a clean shirt. Actually, bring a few others too. We're dealing with lobsters."

"Good idea, Robbie. I have three that just arrived from Land's End. Anything else?"

I'm sure there were other items I needed, but what did I know? "No, I'll meet you at the ferry in two hours."

"Ok. I'll be there. I'm just dropping off a gift basket at the nurse's station in the hospital. They work so hard. Did you see my letter to the editor about the new Administrator's firing? He was trying to change so much—help the nurses—get rid of waste."

"Yes, I saw it. Island politics and nepotism are ugly. But I have smaller fish to fry... or lobsters. See you in a few."

We met at the allotted time. Food prep in the Kane's kitchen went well. And by that, I mean we washed the ears of corn that fell on the floor and mopped up the splashing water when the lobsters didn't like going into the pot. Good thing I had my dad bring extra clothing since the melted butter made it everywhere but in the bowls.

The Kane's looked in on us a few times. Even gave us some helpful suggestions. They had smiles on their faces, so I wasn't too worried about our lack of professionalism. Needless to say, the dinner went fine. The food was good, the margaritas were strong, and the heavy-duty paper plates my dad had bought at the Stop and Shop were definitely needed. We were not the only ones to drop an ear of corn on the floor.

But if I'm being honest, I would have to say the saving grace to the evening was my dad. He had everyone in stitches with his self-deprecating wit and stories about me as a child. Usually, the help is a non-entity, relegated to the kitchen when not being useful. However, this event turned into the Rob and Jerry show when one of the guests asked my dad if he had ever practiced law in New York City. It turned out the two knew each other. Now the stories came fast and furious. One entailed my dad as a bankruptcy expert on the *Today Show*. What, my dad on the *Today Show*? I learned so much that night, but the most practical thing was that I was not a caterer.

Eventually, I settled on a few profitable divisions for my new business: cleaning, landscaping, caretaking, and construction. All very simple and straightforward. Each day ending with me being tired and sore, but with a feeling of accomplishment. Since those humble beginnings, the company has grown to about fifteen employees working in well-defined categories and a stable of sub-contractors to help take care of my one hundred customers on Chappy. I have a waiting list for our services as I don't want to grow the company bigger than my team can handle.

So, now you have my business in a nutshell. Lots of hard work, but at the same time set in an idyllic location where everyone is striving to relax and enjoy life.

I wish I could be entirely at ease in this seemingly utopian life everyone strives to attain. It's easy to see the appeal of this landscape. The people are all such interesting characters living the local lifestyle that you read about in well-intentioned magazines. But there's an undercurrent here. The fact that life is being played out on a finite piece of sand in the middle of the ocean affects its inhabitants. The struggle to reconcile the inconsistencies of this nirvana is overwhelming to me at times, but then I feel guilty for even seeing the cracks. In rare dark moments, I've thought of leaving the island as a way to quiet my struggles. But that's madness.

"How did I get so disillusioned?" This is what I keep asking myself. I need to take a good look at my life on Chappy this year—into a life less traveled—into my world of Noah's rejects to make sense of my life on this rock.

We start with spring, re-birth, and promise...

SPRING

Winter's Not Over Yet

It's been a long winter. There's no denying that.

I step onto the ferry as the frigid driving rain hits me, and my feet ache from the bitter cold that no layering of socks seems to help. It slaps me awake to the fact that winter is still with us even though the calendar reads March 30th. There's not a soul in town; all the shops and activities that would normally bring people out and about in the summertime are closed for another two months. Hibernation, survival, minimalism—these are all words that describe our winter months.

But there's hope! The sun had been out just the other day. It was warm, and the first appearance of daffodils gave some color to a decidedly brown landscape. We took a drive out onto the beach, watched the seal pups basking in the sun at the water's edge, ate lunch on the bluff above the sand, and thought for a minute about bringing up some of our summer clothing from the basement. It was just a thought.

Now the rain is back. It wouldn't be so bad if the precipitation was light, fluffy snow like the rest of New England is getting. But the warm sea air turns most storms wet and ugly, penetrating our bodies to their core. We always pat ourselves on the back for making it through another winter on this island. Chappy people know they're a hardy bunch. We're proud of it. But we still complain. Come on... another storm—a nor'easter?

Our family hunkers down. 60mph winds means no ferry, tons of electricity disruptions, and probably some household damage at some point. We all have our favorite activities to get us through these storms. Sasha, our ten-year-old buddha baby, heads to a special nook to read a book on fairies. Ilana, who is twelve, somehow knew this storm was coming before all of us and had candles set up next to comfort food and flashlights—always prepared. Melissa makes sure everyone is comfy and settles on the couch with a new book by Geraldine Brooks.

I contact employees, subcontractors, and customers and let them know the next few days are a wash. Some of my guys, who don't live on Chappy, grumble, and I offer to put them up for the duration of the storm. This way, they won't have to worry about getting back home if and when the ferry shuts down.

"Sure, boss. If you are offering that mansion on the point for us to stay in," is their common reply.

I don't blame my crew. The mansion is stocked to the gills with food and has a theater and a bowling alley in the cellar. Obviously, I can't oblige my workers, but I do have the keys to the castle, so to speak. Keys given to me by its owner. It's my official job to check it regularly. Make sure everything is in perfect order. Of course, this includes all its toys.

This mansion is tucked in the farthest corner of Chappy, known as Wasque. It's invisible to anyone who might drive by. A wall of scrubby oaks protects this fortress and makes this piece of land look unremarkable and uninviting. But that's anything but the truth. Sweeping meadows that lead down to four hundred yards of beach come into view as visitors approach the compound. In the distance, you can see the island of Nantucket and little more.

Today I'm glad I have access to this Xanadu. The power cuts out at noon, and the troops can only consume so many s'mores by the fireplace while trying to stay warm.

The ride out to Wasque is stark and desolate. The storm rages on as the wind pushes our old jeep from side to side on the sandy road. We crank up the joyful soundtrack to *The Muppet Movie* as we pass a huge grassy field to our right that slopes down to the shore and barrier beach beyond. Little funnels of rain and leaves whip around the ground. It's otherworldly.

"It's cold," Ilana blurts out. "It feels like we're the only people on the planet." And at this moment, I agree. The summer feels so far away. The people feel so far away. Chappy has the feel of a shutdown carny. And that makes it our own little playground at this moment.

We arrive in the driveway, and there's something about the tires moving from the sand road to the white crushed clam shells that lets us know we've arrived. The crunch of the tires seems more stately, more ordered, and more sophisticated. We drive around the driveway's circular loop, first passing the garage, then the guest house, the pool, and finally resting our car in front of this beautiful monstrosity. I tie a bungee cord from the Jeep's door handle to the rusted running board so the wind doesn't whip it open. It's really blowing out here. The girls are giddy with excitement but wait patiently.

All secured, Melissa and I go through the rules: take your shoes off when you go into the house, put everything back where you found it after playing, and be respectful of other people's personal property. I punch in the alarm code, step aside, and watch a wiz of light that must have been the girls go past me. I don't go in right away as today is a good day to ensure the outside of the buildings are secure and the generator is in working order. Check, check, and check. Very little goes wrong with this house during the off-season. False fire and motion detector alarms are the most persistent problems.

I catch up with the girls at one of the kids' rooms which has about two dozen American Girl dolls in it. It seems kind of creepy with all their eyes staring at me, but Ilana and Sasha are already having conversations with a cowgirl and a ballerina. I tell them to head downstairs after they clean up. I think I see my girls nod their heads.

Before heading down myself, I check all the bedrooms for problems or Goldilocks sleeping in a bed. I used to stop and marvel at each room's workmanship and details as I checked them out for problems. I used to do that in all the houses we oversee. But now, there could be a golden toilet in the middle of the room, and my only thought would be to wonder if it has leaked recently. In the end, it just becomes a job that needs to get done.

I meet up with Melissa and head down to the basement, where I turn on all the lights, fire up the bowling lanes, and check the back-end mechanics. Like an old pro, I oil its joints, re-calibrate the cameras and sensors, and vacuum the entire apparatus to ensure everything is in working order. You would think my job stops there. But I actually am paid to bowl every week. My customer is only on-island sporadically, and this baby needs a workout to make sure it doesn't seize up over time—another passion that has turned into a chore.

I meet up with Melissa in the theater when I'm all done. Music reverberates out of the walls as I slump down in one of the comfy, leather recliners next to my honey. The sounds are deafening and awesome all at the same time. The opening musical sequence tells me all I need to know. I'm in for a treat as cavemen from *2001, A Space Odyssey* fill the screen.

Melissa hands me a bag of popcorn. "Here you go, honey. Compliments of the house."

"Yeah, I forgot to tell you they had a popcorn machine delivered last month. It took me a few hours to put together. Did you like the laminated cheat sheet on how to use it that I wrote up?"

"Silly wabbit. It's not rocket science." We both laugh, grab another handful of popcorn and turn our attention to the Neanderthals on the silver screen.

A text appears on my phone. It's so bright in the darkened theater. Melissa and I sigh in unison as we look at the message. One of my employees with kids has no electricity and no heat. He's asking if I know anyone with firewood. I have plenty at our house, but he's on the main island, and there's no way to get some to him. I text some friends' names who might be able to help. End with a "sorry," and put the phone away. There's really nothing more I can do.

Melissa turns to me and says, "I love being here. Snuggling—watching this epic film. But I worry about this... all this is giving our kids a warped impression of what life around here is really like."

It takes me a second to figure out that Melissa is talking about my employee and not the movie. I rub her hand under the blanket that she has wrapped around her. "Don't worry. One of our friends will bring him some wood."

"No, you don't get it. We are holed up in this cushy place. Our kids are sheltered from the difficulties others struggle with during these endless storms, the monotony of winter, and how it makes them feel."

I'm always just trying to deal with what's in front of me—the situation at hand. Melissa is thinking bigger and wider. All I can think to say is, "Honey, we are getting through it. Every day challenges crop up, and I knock them down. And you hit the nail on the head. We have these things that make life easier. Let's enjoy them."

Melissa sighs. "Sometimes, for me, it's about more than fixing things."

"One day at a time. That's all I can promise or wish for."

Melissa and I give each other a weary smile as a loud crash reverberates and draws our attention back to the screen. We dig down deeper into our chairs and resume watching. We fall asleep at some point but are roused awake by two sweet cinderellas decked out in costumes and glass slippers. It appears it's time to bowl.

We all grab a pair of regulation bowling shoes, a custom bowling ball from the rack of twenty or so, and we're ready to play. I go to the controls and put up the gutter rails, so Sasha and Ilana's balls will make it all the way down the lane to the pins. The girls' faces light up as the balls leave their hands and start their slow, deliberate journey. The balls bounce back and forth between bumper guards before they finally make it down to the pins, where they have just enough energy to push over one or two. Good times. We all laugh.

The troops start to tire and slump on the couch that surrounds the bowling alley. I take this as my cue and start cleaning up. Melissa meets me up in the kitchen.

Our talk is not over. As I'm washing some dishes, she turns me around, hugs me, and says, "Our talk before. It's not just the money or access to all this. Our island has an effect on people. And sometimes not in a good way."

"What are you talking about?" Is all I can think to say. I mean, I kind of know what she's getting at, but it's so far removed from our life—our friends. "Listen. Yes, some people are on the quirky side and let their freak flag fly. We see people who can't get out of their own way. But we are setting a good example for our kids. We are surrounded by good friends and a healthy community." I take a second and then add, "Our kids are growing up in an idyllic and beautiful playground."

"I know, I know," Melissa says in a whisper. "I just think we need to do a better job of making sure our kids don't grow up oblivious to how lucky they are, or worse, fall into the same traps that other kids on this island do as they get older."

I wipe my hands on my jeans and shut off the water to the sink. I hug Melissa. Give her an, "I get it. We got this." Grab her hand and pull her across the floor. We slide to a stop at the head of the stairs and call to the girls that it's time to leave.

We back out of the house, just like we entered—not a figurine or costume or bowling ball out of place. This three-hour tour has been a fun escape from the elements, especially since it's been the umpteenth storm and power outage this winter. Bowling is just one of those activities that gets the entire family laughing. Next time we should all be wearing costumes. We get in our Jeep Wrangler, and the girls wrap a blanket around themselves to keep warm for the ride home. I take one last look at the compound to make sure all is good and draw a deep, cleansing breath of the cold, salty winter air. I put the car in first gear and slowly move along the driveway. The transition from crushed clamshell driveway to hard-packed bumpy sand road brings us back to the present. I check my phone. The ferry is still not moving. Our life is still on hold.

A Few Days Later... A Police Action?

"I've got Edgartown–West Tisbury Road closed off just north of the school, over," says Detective Jason Arbilt as he puts his car in park.

The cars behind him see the flashing lights. They either make a quick U-turn to get the hell out of Dodge before the shit hits the fan or pull over to see the unfolding action. Additional patrol cars get into position, blocking off all the other roads near the Edgartown School and up Main Street.

"Officer Jones, please tell the chief we're all in position, over."

"Roger," says Jones as he sits next to the chief at their vantage point in Memorial Park down the street from the school. I'm nearby with a front-row seat for the upcoming commotion, overhearing their conversation as I watch for my own children. It's 2:55 p.m., and on cue, the bell rings at the school, and everyone waits. The roads are quiet. And then bam, the big metal double doors of the school rip open, and throngs of kids run out, madly yelling and screaming. Running like an alien monster is gobbling them up, and they need to flee at all costs. The crossing guards hastily step aside, their trusty red stop signs at their side.

The kids are not stopping. The kids are not looking both ways or waiting for the OK from the crossing guards. They're just running. It's April 10th, and down the street from the school, about a quarter-mile, the Dairy Queen has just opened for the season. Two hundred or so screaming kids are on their way.

It helps to have some context to understand why this is such a big deal. Imagine living in the center of a festival. One filled with music, your favorite activities, and interesting people. All your off-island friends and the bigger-than-life stars that you see on the movie screen clamor to be a part of your world. And you are spinning, loving this existence. And then it ends. Everything closes down as the summer people move on. The kids know it will be a long time before they feel the high of being the center of the universe again, and feel cheated.

But not today. Today is special—something just for the local kids. This is springtime on Martha's Vineyard. This is how events roll on this rock. Big deals are made of silly events, and they bring a smile to everyone's face.

"Here they come," a patrolman reports on the radio as masses of kids run by him.

By 3:10, the steady stream of students flowing out of the school slows to a trickle, and eventually, my girls peer out of the doors. They're not Dairy Queen kids. The presence of this fast-food icon and its novelty as one of only three national consumer brands on the island is no match for their mother's crunchy granola mantras. Melissa routinely rails against commercialism and poo-poos the chemically concocted and air-infused ice cream that is Dairy Queen.

The girls strap on their way-too-big backpacks and begin to walk away from the eerily quiet front lawn of the school. They usually take the bus home, but today they're meeting me in Memorial Park. We're going to walk into town to go to "our" ice cream hangout, so they don't feel like they are totally left out of the festivities.

I meet up with them on the sidewalk and try to engage the girls in talk of their school day—how it was, what they did, and who they hung with. I get very little information in return. I just shut up and listen to them talk, as that seems like the best way to get the scoop on the day's events. Mostly they are talking about Dairy Queen and how obsessed the kids are with its opening. Everyone watched the clock all day, talking about what flavor or size dish they were going to get. My kids don't get it. Enticing words by ad execs in flashy commercials don't resonate with them. Vegetarian, organic, non-processed, local, present, gender-neutral, and co-parenting are words our girls are more apt to hear in our family's social circle and resonate with. It goes both ways. Many of the kids in Edgartown look at my kids and don't get them either. Their litany of questions never ends. They ask, "You live on Chappy? When does that ferry run, anyway? Is it true there's a haunted junk car lot there?"

Chappy is just a hop, skip, and a jump from this school-yard. But it's a different world for these kids. My daughter, Ilana, sometimes complains, "Why do the other kids think it's so weird to live on Chappy—to live the way we do?"

I try to explain. There are so many boxes our family does and doesn't fit into. We live on Martha's Vineyard like everyone else on this island. We are residents of one of the five towns on the Vineyard, Edgartown, but then we live in a distinct neighborhood of that town that happens to be its own separate island, Chappy. That's one set of boxes. But then we're college-educated off-islanders or wash-a-shores that didn't grow up here. Add to that fact that we are not really working class as our family owns its own business, and we are part of a tiny Jewish population on this spit of land in the sea, and the boxes we fit into get smaller and smaller. I explain to the girls, "It's not your friend's fault. No one understands anyone," I laugh. "Do you understand me?"

Ilana smirks and shrugs her shoulders. Maybe she's getting and not getting at the same time what I'm trying to say. I shrug my shoulders in response to her shrugging her shoulders. We move on.

We're walking toward the girls' regular summer choice for ice cream, The Ice Cream and Candy Bazaar, and the girls break out into a run, gangly legs and arms flailing about as they make for the entrance to "their" ice cream nirvana. They are not so different from the rest of the kids, after all.

"Woooow, yaaaaah. It's open!" Sasha yells to no one in particular. Not a care in the world.

Ice cream. It has the ability to shut off your brain and just yell pleasure to your senses.

The Ice Cream and Candy Bazaar is just how it sounds, an old-timey confectionary with wrapped candy on one side, useless knickknacks that no one really needs hanging all over the place, some handmade chocolate concoctions, and of course, hand-packed ice cream. Truth be told, this shop is no healthier than any other, but the packaging gets us. I think our family feels real in this store. You could say it's our ice cream version of *Cheers*.

I stand back and watch as the girls meticulously look around. They know everything for sale but still take the time to discover it all anew each time they step into this oasis. "Can I try the mint chocolate chip? Thank you. Can I also try the black raspberry?" Ilana asks kind of sheepishly. I give her an eye roll, and she quickly adds another, "Thank you," before devouring her second or maybe tenth sample.

In the end, Sasha picks a single scoop of mint chocolate chip, and Ilana gets a scoop of black raspberry and chocolate chip yogurt in a cup. I throw some dark chocolate-covered apricots in a bag for myself, and we call it a day. All is right with the world. Everyone is smiling.

After ice cream, we walk to the Chappy ferry and give the deckhand our green passenger tickets as we get on board. He's a local Chappy resident and a sweet kid. He works on the ferry as college didn't work out for him, but maybe, eventually, a ferry captain's license is in the cards. Every kid I know who has grown up on Chappy has taken a turn in one role or another on the Chappy ferry. It's a rite of passage.

Two and a half minutes later, the ferry bumps into the ramp on the Chappy side of the harbor, the ramp is lowered onto the deck, the safety chain is lowered, cars disembark, and we're back on Chappy. We wave goodbye to the ferry crew as Milly, the ferry captain, reverses the thrust of the engines to keep the ferry pegged in the slip.

The sound of the metal ramp sounds like an engine revving as the girls slide their shoes along its surface. They jump with a leap off it at the end and run to the left of the parking lot to look for my truck. Ahhh, crap. I forgot. The guys needed an extra truck for debris beach clean-up at a customer's house. I had them drop me off at the ferry instead of going home to grab another car in my rush to meet the girls. The need to deal with each crisis at the moment sometimes clouds the bigger picture for me.

I make excuses and coax the girls into walking to our house as it's a nice warm spring day—for a change. We leave the ferry point walking on the side of the road. The girls kick the broken shells the seagulls have dropped on the asphalt to reveal their daily meal. I attempt to explain this aspect of the food chain to the girls, but another teachable moment about our wilderness is lost as they immediately begin to complain about the walk—and we haven't even gone a hundred yards. I ignore their pleas. I'm being selfish. I want to soak this in. It's nice out, and my crews are set for the day.

The girls eventually settle down into a rhythm of running and exploring the sides of the road. They point out the crane we always seem to see in the shallows of Caleb's Pond as we pass by. And then I spy our sailboat, Noah's Rejects, in the distance past the pond in the harbor.

It's a thirty-three-foot weathered old sloop, bobbing up and down as a passing motorboat's wake hits its hull. To the casual observer from far off, it would appear to be an opulent cruising yacht that one could take on a three-to-four-day sailing excursion in style. But get closer, and you see that it's more like a Winnebago that has seen better days.

Ilana stops dead in her tracks when she also sees our boat. "Tell me again how you picked the name, Noah's Rejects, for the sailboat. I get it. But I don't get it. Does that make sense?"

"Yeah, honey, that makes sense." Hurray, I've broken through, and I'm going to have a conversation with my kids! A chance to tell a story or re-tell a story—just like my dad relentlessly did with me over the years. His tales are legendary. They are known among family and friends as Jerry Tails. They're such a comfort to me now. They bring his Jerryness to the forefront of my mind when anything triggers their memory. It's like having "Here Comes the

Sun" come on the radio or seeing that old episode of Happy Days where Fonzie jumps the shark in his leather jacket. I'm right back in that moment like it's the first time experiencing it. Hopefully, my girls will feel the same way as I tell this story again. Yet, at the same time, I hope it will be a little different. Thinking back, my dad's stories were a little off-base—the result of a vengeful man bitter from his divorce to this day. I take a second to make sure my story will have a more positive effect and then reply, "Well, the original name and artwork came from the hand-painted clothing stores your uncle and I had on various islands up and down the eastern seaboard."

"I get that part, I get that part," Ilana shouts over the noise of the wind. "But what does it mean?"

"OK, give me a second," I say, thinking of a way to make my description kid-friendly and funny. I opt for the easiest and most straightforward answer. "Well, you know the biblical story of Noah and how he had to pick two of each kind of animal to save, right?"

"Yeah, yeah, yeah," Sasha says with a lot of sass that means get to the point.

"The animals that didn't fit the mold of who Noah thought should be saved, well, they missed the boat. So, Noah's Rejects refers to those of us who live exiled, for better or worse, in the island communities where we had stores—free from the constraints of regular society."

The girls start rattling off names of neighbors, friends, and acquaintances they could never see living in suburbia or a big city. Jolene, the naturopath healer, Jim, the painter, definitely Segal, the woman who has goats that sleep in her bed. They keep yelling out names as they run up ahead and leave me behind to wonder whether what I told them was positive or negative.

I believe being one of Noah's rejects is a badge of honor. The mark of an independent thinker, going down my own path no matter how uncommon. Hell, I've started two businesses and still don't own a tie. Sometimes I get the feeling us Noah's rejects didn't have the choice to live in regular society. Our very essence nudged us to this rock in the middle of the ocean like the leper colonies of old. The real question is whether we would be allowed off today, now that we are here, if we wanted to? Who cares, I think to myself. Why would you want to live anywhere else?

My musings are interrupted as the phone rings. I spy the girls in the brush up ahead and decide it's fine to pick it up—bonding time is over. "Hey, what's up?"

"Not good news, Rob. As I told you, there isn't much that could be done for Lorna once the police called ICE."

"Arrrrrgggggghhhh—She's always been a hothead. Where is she? It's been over a month since I've heard anything. Her parents are worried. Why'd they have to scurry her off the Vineyard so fast?"

"That will happen when you hit a cop. I found out she's at an ICE facility in Dover, New Hampshire. Still can't call her. I'll email you the information so you can get it to her parents. They'll probably deport her next month."

We hang up after promising to go grab a beer sometime. Probably never happen. Good gesture anyway.

I break into a run to catch up with the girls. They're starting to get chilly. It's the wind. It whips past us along this stretch of road with the pond on one side and the barrier beach on the other. This very unprotected area changes our nice breezy walk into a forced march against the elements. Storm clouds approach over Manaca Hill, and the rain is on us in minutes. I should have known. Spring isn't really spring on Martha's Vineyard.

It's not a downpour. It's just a steady, cold rain going sideways and hitting us like pine needles—more annoying than painful. But you would think my girls were being shot at by the tone of their voices. They want a ride home. Now! I hear them, but I don't, as my brain is already thinking of my crews' painting, mowing, and building things—all outdoors. I'm sure they're all scurrying for their cars and waiting for instructions—waiting for a call from me that will be delayed as I'm standing on the side of the road in a cell phone dead zone. Ilana and Sasha's complaining turns to tears as the rain becomes steadier.

Their prayers are answered in a matter of minutes as a car stops next to us, and the driver pushes open the passenger door. "Get in, Rob. Looks like your girls are turning on you."

It's one of my customers on his way home from his afternoon coffee in Edgartown. He's a newish customer. Not one I feel close to at this point. Really, I'm not even sure of his name.

The girls jump in the back before the words are even out of this good Samaritan's mouth. I get in the front and move the brochures for various sculpture artists off the seat. Then it hits me. This is that financial guy from New York City. He's always putting some avant-garde stone or metal sculpture in his yard. One time he flew this guy, an artist, I guess, in from Germany. I had to set him up in a hotel. He stacked rocks for three weeks. Boom—art. I could have done that. But I must admit, regardless of the crazy way this uber-rich financial guy throws money around, he's a nice soul. And his wife is always offering my workers and me lemonade. Lemonade always helps.

These types of gestures are the key to creating bonds and goodwill in our small community. The girls even know it's OK to get in the car with strangers who know their names. Everyone knows them on Chappy. I include a new picture of our family on every bill I email to customers. It seems to inspire them to pay faster as it reminds them, I have a family to feed too.

When we get home, the girls run one way and I another. I quickly stop to kiss Melissa, who is sitting on the couch, putting the last-minute touches on a quilt she's making for a friend.

I blurt out as I reach in for a peck, "Edgartown School was crazy as always. But the girls seemed fine not buying into the fast-food nation thing. We had a blast of our own at the Ice Cream and Candy Bazaar."

"Why are you guys sopping wet?"

I grab one of the towels that we leave hanging up to dry off River and give my head a shake. "I forgot. I gave the truck to the guys. They dropped me off at the ferry. Didn't think much of it. Then it was so nice after ice cream that I didn't bother calling you to pick us up—good day for a walk. Even got the girls to open up and talk to me. But then it started raining..."

"Did the girls talk about not running up to Dairy Queen with their friends? Did you think to invite some of them with you guys instead? Melissa is trying to slow me down. Engage me. Draw out the conversation. But in my head, we're home—job done. The girls are safe and dry. I need to pivot to my crews' being idle. There's plenty to do indoors. I just need to get to them before they scatter.

I give another kiss and mumble, "Everyone was gone in a blur. No opportunity. Sorry, Honey. Got to go deal with the crews now that it's raining."

I can hear Melissa sigh. It's a loud sigh. It's for my benefit. I get it. Would it kill me to take a few extra seconds to connect? Yeah. It just might. The closer I get to my desk, the stronger the pull is to my work and other people's needs. I need to listen to my messages and head out to check some houses before my day is finished.

Unwanted Guests

A lot of my time is spent checking empty houses like the mansion with the bowling alley. Some of these houses are older, more interesting homes that have evolved over time to suit their occupants' needs. And then there are the newer ones that are beautiful in a cookie-cutter kind of way. All the homes, old and new, blend together to create a tapestry of summer living.

My first house inspection today is the McCowell's. It's like most of the 400 homes on Chappy, which are hidden down sandy tracks with grassy strips along the center. These passageways give a sense of wonderment about what and who might be down there as you pass by. A sense of stepping back in time overwhelms the senses as nature and little else surrounds you.

This particular house was built in the '70s and for many years was used as a workers' house for summer college kids, or more aptly put, a party house. It's been beaten up pretty good over time. I remember going to a few parties there when I was much, much younger. Cue Barbara Streisand's 'Memories'. Boy, my girls hate that tune. I try to slip it in at bedtime or when they're in the back seat of my car with some of their friends just to see them go ballistic. You gotta have a hobby.

Anyway, the McCowell's bought the house around 1990 and fixed it up by slapping lipstick on a pig, so to speak, and started renting it out to summer vacationers. That's still how it's used today. Not much gets fixed on this house unless it's in dire straits. Once I used the term preventative maintenance with the McCowells, and they looked at me like I had two heads.

The house has been empty all winter long, and my log shows past visits have been uneventful. But, yeah, not today. I walk into the house and pause, taken aback by all the damage. Dirt marks cover the walls. Shades are ripped apart. Someone has had a party in here like the days of old, and they didn't invite me. I walk slowly around and see room after room physically maimed in one form or another. My mind goes numb, and my heart starts to race. I take this personally. I think of these homes as my own. Who would do this?

I take a breath and once again remind myself this can't be my fault, and it's just a house, but it's hard. I want all 'my' houses to be in perfect order. I can figure this out. I pick up one of the overturned chairs and sit. Stuffing spills out of a ripped seam under my leg, and I try to push it back in. I can fix this. But looking at the mess only makes it worse. I put my head in my hands and close my eyes. It's hard to focus when all I can think about is the conversation I'll have with the McCowells.

My mind begins to work again. It feels like hours, but it's probably just minutes. I open my eyes, lift my head, and look around the room with new, unfeeling coldness. Logic is how I'm going to figure this out. Figure out what to do. I look at the room. It's so still and quiet for a scene of such destruction. I look at the violence, and my movie-obsessed brain expects to hear an ominous soundtrack, but only silence. My eyes dart around at random rips, tears, and broken objects. Smudges of dirt on the floor start to come into focus and take shape. Hold on—not dirt. Soot. I turn to the fireplace. I see the overturned grate, and I begin to piece the puzzle together while standing up slowly out of the chair and backing my way out of the house.

I'm not alone. There's an animal in the house. A raccoon must have come down the chimney, entered the house through the open fire damper, and once inside, couldn't get out. It was... probably still is—pissed. I leave the door open as I exit so the little (or big) critter can get home to the woods.

Outside I call the homeowners and tell them the situation. "What?" Yells Mr. McCowell. "You need to take pictures of everything before you clean up this mess. I'll call the insurance company."

Mr. McCowell doesn't ask about anything specific being damaged. This is strictly a utilitarian house, so there's no worry of precious heirlooms being hurt. Rentals, like this one, are outfitted to survive inhabitants who have no vested interest in their temporary digs. Sandy feet, gooey s'mores on the couch, and overfilled glasses of red wine whose contents always find their way onto a carpeted floor, all need to be taken into consideration. The McCowell's have made peace with this fact and outfitted their house accordingly. It's me who always wants more. Always wants a homeowner to keep their place fixed up and as stately as possible.

I love the fact that a raccoon was ingenious enough to find a way in here to stay warm, but it kills me that he wrecked the place. I remind Mr. McCowell, "First things first. I need to make sure the raccoon is out of the house."

"Yes, yes. Of course. Your safety is first. No, I mean take pictures and clean up after that."

I match Mr. McCowell's businesslike demeanor and succinctly state, "Thank you, yes. After I'm sure the animal is out, I'll take pictures of everything. I'll get the cleaning crew over right away and then send you an itemized list of what needs to be thrown away or fixed."

I have not talked to Mr. McCowell since he left last November. A few emails here or there, but no talk. I take his cue and don't ask about his wife, his kids, his life. We end the conversation. I have a plan and move on to the next house to check in on. Thank God the rest of the houses are quiet, tight, and take up one line each in my daily log. Oil tank at thirty percent. Small rip in the corner of the left panel on a screened-in porch. A few fallen limbs on a driveway. Stuff like that. Easy breezy, lemon squeezy.

I go back to the McCowell house to close the doors and chimney flue at the end of the day. At the same time, I put down some baby powder on the floors to see if the raccoon is, in fact, gone. I'll check for footprints tomorrow, but I feel confident the problem has been solved. All that's left to do is the cleanup. "Great news," says the customer.

"Great news," says my wife when I get home. I feel like a rock star as another mess is cleaned up. That was easy.

But things change when I bring my cleaners back to the house the following day. I open the house to the heart-wrenching sounds of high-pitched screams and whines of baby animals.

OK. So the picture is clearer. It's springtime, and the raccoon mother was looking for a warm place to have her pups. She sure found one. But she couldn't feed her pups after I locked her out of her new den. So, what I'm hearing is her pups starving for food and water. Nice. Aren't I the monster?

"What that noise?" Juanita yells out in her halting English.

"It's babies, Juanita. Quaxinins do bebê," I say in Portuguese. I know a few words. Mostly Spanish, but I get by.

"OK. You deal with. We clean," she chirps back. That's it. No fuss. Got a job to do, boom, just do it. And with that, the other cleaners follow Juanita into the house, creating footsteps in the undisturbed baby powder as they go.

"Oh, Juanita. By the way. Thank you for sitting down with Ilana for her project on immigration. She was beaming all weekend about your talk." Turns out Juanita came over the border with a human smuggler years ago. It sounded like a harrowing journey—a lifetime ago. I never asked her about it. I never ask any of my workers about their arrival in this country.

"Sem Problemas."

I don't push, nor get anything more—time to call my customer once again. His response to our new wrinkle is matter-of-fact and gruff.

"Let the babies be," Mr. McCowell tells me. "And they will eventually die." I wonder if the sound of the actual audible shrieks of the baby raccoons would make a difference in his response. It didn't for Juanita. I guess I'm sensitive.

I manage to get him to think better of that idea after I remind him that the inevitable smell will cut into his rental profits. He reluctantly agrees to let me pull up the floorboards where I believe the little creatures are holed up and rescue them. Really, there's no other option.

Next stop, the Chappy ferry—the Wikipedia for this little isolated community.

"Just dunk them in a barrel of water and be done with

it," one guy says. Other locals gather around, telling similar stories of finding unwanted critters and how they disposed of them.

I cut them off. "No, that's not going to happen." We all know each other's soft spots. These guys only asked me to go deer hunting with them once. Just once.

One guy shrugs his shoulders and says, "So, you want to save the world? Fine, call Gus Ben David." The crowd disperses, and everyone goes on their way.

Gus Ben David founded the Felix Neck Wildlife Preserve on Martha's Vineyard in 1969. He's been the key advocate for all things free and wild on the island ever since, and I needed educating.

Gus is out of breath when he answers as he has just come in from brush cutting a path on the reserve. I tell him my story. He doesn't gush over the crying babies or reprimand me for not checking the flue over the winter. He tells me to get the kits, that's what you call baby raccoons, out of the floor, into a cardboard box, and into the woods as quickly as possible. "Wear gloves, heavy ones, Rob. You want to keep your scent off those kits, and God forbid one of them bites you."

He tells me one of two things will happen. One, the mother, hearing her kits crying, will come to them and take them away to a new home. Although, if she smells human on the kits, she might reject them. The second option is that a hawk will hear their screams and swoop down to collect them for an easy dinner. I'm hoping for the former as I grab my heavy-duty leather fireplace gloves and rush back to the McCowell's house.

Everything goes well with the extraction. The cleaners look at me in awe as if I know what I'm doing. Confidence. I'm always exuding confidence. But inside, my brain is yelling, yelling about my ineptitude of getting into this situation—hearing the voices of my family berating me for endangering my health. "Rabies!" It all goes silent in my head as I pull up the floorboards one by one to finally reveal the four cute kits. They instinctively turn their heads away from the bright lights and the smell of disinfectant in the room. I marvel at them. I get lost in the moment. Balls of fur squirming this way and that, cuddling with their siblings to keep warm. How cute is this? And then the screaming comes back to me. It's high-pitched like a hawk but more pleading. They want something. You can hear it. You can hear their desperation as the high pitch cries for help go on and on until they have no more air in their little lungs and then gulp in some more and start over.

The screams snap me out of my haze in an instant, and I get to work, slowly picking them up one by one and placing them in an open cardboard box. They're so adorable. Even Juanita and the other cleaning women take a minute to marvel. Then back to cleaning as if some boss is shooing them away for being unproductive. Some crazy work ethic.

Juanita stops me as I'm leaving the house with kits in tow. "Police stop me in town last night. They want license. They want insurance cards. You know I don't have."

"Oh, wow. Why did they stop you?"

"I think I go too slow. I don't know. But I need money. Lawyers—more lawyers. I'm already paying for immigration."

Immigrant workers like Juanita are always hitting me up for cash. I usually comply as they work so hard for me and always pay me back. They're part of my family and in no way disposable. But the complications of skirting the law stresses me out. Getting involved with Lorna's case was stupid. But it's over. She's home now. Her parents emailed me the other day—Lorna was too embarrassed to contact me herself. My kids, who interact with my employees on a daily basis, and think of them as family, took it hard. I wasn't much better. She was my first employee so many years ago. Now all that's left to do is ship her stuff back to Ireland.

My business brain takes over, and coldly, I know I can't lose Juanita too. My stomach churns at the thought of more sleepless nights.

I muster out an, "I'm sorry. Figure out how much you need. We'll deal with it," before I scoot out the door with my squirming package.

It's late afternoon by the time I get them out into the backwoods of the house, and now all I can do is leave the property with my crew and wait for the next day. Wait to see who will come to collect these adorable animals. Gus told me I would know instantly which of the two possible visitors came calling. After they're gone, the ground and surroundings will tell me whether it was a joyful reunion of mother and kits or a harried pick-and-grab scuffle of predator and prey.

A tired smile is plastered on my face as I drive around Chappy, looking at the sun glistening through the barren trees that have yet to sprout any springtime leaves. I pull down a few more sandy driveways to check on more houses—nothing new to report. But I do note the chirping of birds and a new softness to the ground that reveals which yards have been visited by young fawns. It's good to be here. It's good to be on Chappy during this time of rebirth. This day took so much out of me. The chaos, the destruction, the sadness of nature in the raw, and yet I'm happy. It comes down to the little steps in life. Few people get to see nature up close and are able to affect it in a good way. I take in a full breath of the salty ocean air and slowly exhale. I'm happy. Even the bumpy, dirt road that's killing my truck can't get me down. This place amazes me every day.

I get home late and barely acknowledge my family as I run to my office to go through the gazillion emails and phone messages that await me. The opening of the Dairy Queen a few weeks ago isn't the only event that tells me spring is upon us. Spring equals lots of work.

"Aaahhhh, hey Rob. This is Riley Anderson. Hope you had a great winter. I just remembered our house needs painting and was wondering if you could fit it in before we arrive next month?" Right, he is just remembering.

In an instant, it's 11:00 p.m., my family is asleep (I remember them pestering me at one point to join them for dinner), and I have a list for me and my crews for the next morning. Number one on the list is to check on those raccoon pups. I mean kits.

Island Life

Another day in the life. Island life. Things happen a little differently here. Jerry Jeffers and his little yellow school bus are no exception. He's one of Chappy's elder statesmen. He's seen it all. Jerry is one of those locals who's worn many hats over the years: Wampanoag, local, fireman, tradesman, and town leader.

A bunch of years back, when I first got to Chappy, I bluntly asked him, "Do you have the Ted Kennedy car hidden among the one hundred junked vehicles behind your property?"

He replied quickly and in a deadpan voice as if everyone knew this fact already. "No. Jim Arena, the police chief at the time, had that car towed off Chappy and off the Vineyard so fast it would make your head spin. Never saw it after that day."

These days Jerry's looked at like the nice old grandpa he is. Always there to do what needs to be done, like helping out by being the island's school bus driver. He'll be along shortly to pick up the seven or ten kids and take them to various schools on the main island. The kids love the fact that Jerry gets to skip the ferry line when they are on the bus. They yell with glee as they pass the long line of cars sitting to their left along the water's edge, waiting to get across. Jerry used to come right to our door to pick up the girls, but he's pretty old now, and having him drive down the dirt roads is pushing our luck just a little too far. He's a good soul and means well, but he'll crash the school bus at some point. We all know it. It's just that he drives so slowly I don't think he'll damage our children too badly. Crazy, right? This is Chappy.

I'm blessed with being able to see my girls off to school in the morning. The routine grounds me. Reminds me what's important. Us Jews tend to say, "It gives me such nachas." Don't get me wrong. It's pure chaos in the morning. There're always hair problems or one daughter fighting with the other over some dire slight. But at the same time, it sets my day on the right track. Backpacks filled, lunches made, and we're out the door.

We walk down the dirt road with its washboard ripples from overuse. Instantly I'm smiling—something about a country road. The woods are alive with spring. I hear robins talking to one another, and in the distance, a woodpecker looks for food. I point out some wild, white-flowered snowdrops peeking out on the side of our road as the girls adjust their backpacks and kick random pebbles at each other. They appear in the rest of the state as early as March but don't usually make an appearance on Chappy till late April—like this year. It's like an explosion of life with their bright colors juxtaposed against the stark and barren brown of the forest and sandy roads. I want them to feel the peace and vitality of our surroundings like I do. But today, their agenda is not my agenda. It's hard.

"Dad, Ilana won't let me borrow her hairbrush, and we have school pictures today," Sasha cries, clearly not sharing my moment of springtime rapture. She forgot hers and is now panicked at the thought of a ruined school picture.

I point out that we're all in this together. "Ilana, you might not realize it now, but Sasha will be your best friend throughout life. She'll be the one you turn to in moments of crisis and joy. So if she needs something of yours and you're able to give it, whether it's a hairbrush, or money, or whatever, I would hope you would give it to her. 'What's mine is yours' is the motto of this family. Does that make sense?"

Not to Ilana. She's prepared. She took the time to get her stuff in order for school. And the brush is hers. Arrrrgghhh, where's my *Father Knows Best* moment? In the end, I run back to the house to get Sasha's hairbrush as Ilana will not budge. She doesn't pick up what I'm putting down. Maybe someday. Maybe she will remember my words.

I get to the bus stop just as the girls are climbing up the stairs and toss the hairbrush to Sasha, who instantly smiles. Ilana waves goodbye as if nothing out of the ordinary just happened. I shake my head and sigh—the best-laid plans and all that. My girls are always saying, "Dad!" whenever I lead off or end with a Steinbeck quote or Streisand lyric. Dads will be dads. Clichés have to come from somewhere.

I linger as the bus pulls away and leaves me in a cloud of dust. Ilana is looking out the back window at me. Her hands splayed open on the glass. Sasha is behind her, already deep in conversation with two other kids. There's some type of disconnect. Ilana seems so confident and on top of things. But at the same time, so alone. So in her own head. Recently we learned she has sensory issues. I'm still trying to understand, but basically, the messages her senses are sending her brain are not being delivered in an orderly fashion. The constant mental bombardment is so tiring for her that at the end of school each day she's spent. It takes all our strength and coaxing to get her out of bed to eat dinner. We think this is why she is such a planner. The more ordered her life, the more control she has. We believe she's trying to protect herself from the unplanned inputs that might invade and upend her life at any moment. Sasha just thinks Ilana is a selfish, moody brat. Melissa and I try to explain. But at this point, we don't even understand what we're up against.

I remember the mixed-up feelings I had growing up concerning self-identity and my place in the world. Could Ilana's challenges come from my DNA? I remember discovering later in life that all was not as it seemed when I was in grade school. I thought it was normal to experience panic attacks when plans got upended. I remember trying to talk with my dad a few times about my struggles. His response always turned around to working harder in school and becoming successful. I remember, as a young adult, coming to the realization that my dad's approach was not the best. I vowed to be the kind of parent who helps his kids sidestep those landmines. Well, that was the plan—a plan in progress.

I squint at the rising sun and the girls' bus, which is now no more than a smudge of yellow in the distance. Looking back, I sure needed a do-over for my first school bus experience. Boy, did I get that wrong? The first part of my life was lived in suburbia with my mom, white picket fences, and sidewalks on every street. So, I was unprepared when I moved to my dad's around age eleven to find out my new nouveau riche neighborhood had no sidewalks. No problem, right? Just walk on the side of the road to get to the bus stop. Yet somehow, I thought the people passing me in their cars knew I didn't belong in their town. I was not from a rich enough family or refined enough to belong to their group. I thought they steered clear of me by weaving their car to the other side of the road as they passed to show their displeasure. I assumed they didn't want to get my cooties. I didn't fault them as I knew I didn't belong, and their behavior just magnified my feelings. It wasn't until I moved back to my mom's a few years later that I figured out the motorists were just being safe, so they didn't hit me. There was no playbook or parental guidance for my integration into the life of this rich nirvana-like existence. I was not prepared. And even though I know that truth today, the feeling of separateness has stayed with me.

This story, and others, stick out in my mind when I look at my girls on those walks to the bus. What memories will haunt them through to their adulthood? What random activities, images, and conversations will shape who they are and how they interact with society? Will they have a phobia of all things having to do with eyes because they saw their grandfather pull a hook out of the eyeball of a fish?—The eyeball hanging by a goopy thread from the fish as it's thrown back into the ocean only to float away on the water's surface. I know those eyes haunt me. Lots of things haunt me. I try to make it so my girls aren't haunted by random images, thoughts, and interactions. I worry I'll be unsuccessful.

I clear my head of these thoughts as the girls' bus is long gone. My walk back to the house turns into a jog as my mind begins to swirl with all that's on my plate for the day. All the jobs that need to be attended to and all the employees that need coaching. I begin to sprint. So much for being in the moment. So much for concentrating on what memories stand out in my mind. Running seems to be what sticks in my mind when I remember work. So much running.

The crews are already assembling in front of my shed to get ready for the day's jobs. I jump straight into our itinerary that I meticulously planned out for each of the crews and then catch Santiago's eye. He is my rock—my 6'2" Brazilian rock who has been with me for so many years. His features always stand out to me. The weathered hands and sunken eyes are the look of a much older man. Santiago is only thirty-two, but he could be fifty.

He stops me cold from my businesslike demeanor and says, "Good morning, boss."

He always does this. Just those three words. Short and halting and decisive. It's like a slap in my face. And I deserve it.

I slow down, say, "Good morning, Santiago, good morning, everyone," and take a breath. I promise myself next time, I'll take the time to check in with my crew. See how their lives are going beyond the hours they're tethered to me on Chappy. It rarely happens. I try, but it rarely happens.

I attempt to recover. We talk about family. If nothing else, it gives me a moment to eye the scene in front of me and spot the difficulties that might trip up my day. Is there a broken vehicle? Are the cleaning women fighting with each other over everything and anything? Or is Jonah high at 8:30 in the morning and needs to be sent home? I glean so much new information while I half-listen to the discussion in front of me. I think of Ilana and her difficulties, and my own starting to make more sense. Like how one moment I had the whole day planned out and the next I'm on the ground under a rototiller that's not even being used today and pulling part of some wire mesh fencing from its metal tines. No longer am I connecting with the people around me as the shiny tines caught my eye and distracted me. The agenda for the day is put on hold as I try to fix the problem in front of me.

The fast-paced Portuguese chatter goes on around me as I work to fix the machine. All of a sudden, their language, their presence, their otherness invades my thoughts. I'm now worrying about the $1,500 retainer I just sent off to Juanita's lawyer for her driving problems. There's a simple work-around. I wish Juanita had used it. Some of my other employees have figured out how to obtain legitimate licenses. They set up P.O. boxes in immigrant-friendly states out West, create a paper trail, and drive out for a few weeks to get a license. It's a band-aid solution. It inevitably takes them away from work that I desperately need done—one step forward, two steps back. I think maybe I'll help them all do this in the fall. The fall? That's a joke. I need to get through today.

Alterations in life of any size untether me from my plans and routine. I go down a rabbit hole and fix what's in front of me and hope to get back on schedule. But it never happens. Order is gone. I pull Jonah away from the landscaping crew to be my wingman for the day. Maybe if I throw all the curveballs to Jonah as we work, I can stay right in my head. In the end, I'll lose money by bringing Jonah with me as I can't see charging customers for two people to what amounts to screwing in a new lightbulb. But such is my life.

The consensus of many on Chappy is that I don't charge enough for our services. I remember last summer when a customer stopped me at the ferry with one of my bills in his hand. "Rob, it says on your bill for the 24th—

rewire fan in living room—$100. I know you had a helper and had to leave to get a new switch from town. Don't get me wrong, I love a bargain, but this seems wrong."

I thought about it for a moment and just told him the truth. "Listen, my helper was there because I had nothing for him to do that day. It was a teachable moment. And the switch, well, I knew the switch was bad from my notes over the winter. I should have brought one with me. It's my fault."

I'm my father's son. I want to succeed, to win, to be prosperous. But he was so stingy and greedy that I many times push back on those thoughts. I saw how it affected the lives of people he interacted with. I don't know. Maybe we just evolve as a people. Learn from our mistakes as a culture. No, it's definitely the baggage from my dad.

I can remember sitting with him at a coffee shop as a kid. We knew them all along route 91 in Connecticut from our days of parental visitation trips. I can still picture him sitting at a floral plastic cushioned booth with a faux wooden laminate top at the Parthenon Diner dressed in his pinstriped suit. He always had a cup of coffee and his ever-present Max 120 cigarette between his fingers. The Max 120s were his favorite, I believe, because they were so long, he got more bang for his buck. He would buy them by the carton. The cup of coffee kept him awake, and they were bottomless. Again, money saved. But it was not the thrifty coffee and cigarette binging that irked me. It was his not tipping. It definitely was a thing with him. Sometimes he would leave a couple of dimes on the table when the change came back. But that made it worse in my eyes than not leaving anything at all. As an eight or nine-year-old, I would try to leave some of my allowance money on the table after my dad left for the car. He would catch me sometimes and scold me with some racist or sexist rant, or more often than not, blame an unfeeling God for not ever helping him. The lack of empathy toward others propelled me to be different.

The sound of Jonah throwing tools in my truck brings me back around to the present. I see the teams going about their prep work and dispersing for the day. It's all routine for them. I remember to yell, "Have a good day," as they take off, and I get out from under the rototiller. Jonah is waiting for me in my truck as I add the few items he forgot, and we are on our way.

We head over to the McCowell's house, walk around to the back, and into the woods. I want this to go well. I want a sense of accomplishment that I solved this problem and fixed a situation I helped create. To my great surprise, it looks like I did. The cardboard box sits over on its side. There's no disturbance to the pine needles around it, and about three yards away, I see the paw prints of an adult raccoon in the dirt. I'm no detective, but I used to watch *Law and Order*, and it looks like the mom came for her kits. With a smile on my face and a hop in my step, I peruse the house's interior, where the cleaners are already diligently working. I give Jonah some instructions on replacing the floorboards and go about my day checking small items off my to-do list for other customers.

The smile drops from my face when the phone rings, and I see the Caller ID on the screen. It says Edgartown Police Department. I assume it's about Juanita, but it could be one of a number of issues with employees who have overstayed their visas or never were invited here in the first place. I answer the call and do the dance of trying to be helpful without hurting myself. "Yes, sir. I agree that people need to have a license so they know the laws of the land. I will talk to Juanita about how I might be able to help her."

My dad, always present as legal counsel in my head, will need debriefing.

A Chance to Stretch Our Legs

I try to shake off the mostly benign conversation with the police detective. He was just making sure I was brought up to speed on the situation. Juanita should not be driving without a license. He was just doing his job. Message heard but not received. The rest of the day goes as planned, and I hurry home to get ready for a potluck dinner at the Chappy Community Center. It's one of my favorite places to catch up on my fellow islanders' lives. Potlucks are a big thing on Chappy, and we tend to have them regularly. The community center was built by a bunch of locals who figured out that winters would go by a lot faster and be healthier for everyone concerned if there was more socializing going on.

With the dishes made, the jostling for passenger seat shotgun decided, we are on our way. Each of the girls is holding a dish on her lap. I can hear the clanking of glass container lids as I drive down the potholed dirt road. I put on the brakes just as Melissa opens her mouth to tell me to slow down. I just want to get there and be social.

I recall the first potluck we went to when Ilana was born. I think Melissa had been holed up in our house for a month after giving birth and needed to talk to someone other than me. I had made my wife's famous chocolate chip cookies with a secret ingredient that sends the eater into new stratospheres of gastronomical exuberance. I can't divulge what the ingredient is, but the family motto is 'We'll tell you if you guess it.' To date, no one has.

I remember we entered the community center to find a third of our off-season island neighbors, fifty or so people, milling around talking to each other. Many were congregating around the biggest table, which was dead center in the room and spilling over with various alcohols and hors d'oeuvres. People waited patiently, two or three people deep, to pour one concoction or another. Some looked like they'd gotten a head start before they arrived. One person was generously holding up a thin, older man by the elbow as they got closer to the table. I would learn later that this was none other than Jim, the painter. The two smiled at each other but said little. A big construction guy I had just met on a job was on the other side of the table, throwing an empty underneath the table as he grabbed another brew out of the bowl of ice. As I was taking off my coat, I marveled at his huge winter beard and mustache, and the foam still stuck on the hair above his lip. A fleeting thought entered my head about the warmth he must have felt all winter long with all that facial hair. I put the idea out of my head as I saw his young son clinging to his leg as he slammed the newly opened beer can on the table.

"Tommy, go see your mother for a change," he slurred as he shook his leg.

Tommy thought it was all just fun and games and kept hanging on. The talk of local politics, the ferry's breakdown the day before for two hours, and the jostling of bottles stopped momentarily as the construction guy swung his leg around a little too vigorously as if to get a fly off of him. Everyone tried to ignore it as they would any uncomfortable situation. Tommy eventually got the hint and ran off as the look in his father's eyes changed. Then in an instant, the conversation and drinking went back into high gear. Melissa and I sidestepped the booze train, not realizing at the time how much alcohol was embedded in Chappy's culture and island life.

Sure, I had lived on islands for years with my old business, but as a single, young, and slightly reckless youth. I was never part of the fabric of the communities where I had stores. I was more of an interloper: work, party, sleep, repeat. Seeing adults, family people from all walks of life embrace alcohol as a social crutch was surprising to me. There's a joke about Jews not becoming adult alcoholics by nature because they were subjected to drinking Manischewitz wine every Friday night as a youth. I know it's a cliché and stereotype, but that stuff is rancid!

Bundle in hand, we made our way to the other end of the hall, where there was a fireplace extending up to the cathedral ceiling, blazing with a big fire. Peter Wells, the owner of the Chappy ferry and fire chief, was stoking it, all the while holding court with some new folks who had not heard about the time he rode his bike off the ferry ramp into the ocean below. Needless to say, he didn't make it to the other side.

This guy is such a bundle of welcomeness. Maybe it's his stories or the way he stops to talk to everyone and anyone during his day. He's the one person you're guaranteed to see as you make your way around this little isle. Peter touches everyone's life. He's literally our access to the world via the ferry. He protects Chappy's inhabitants, wielding a fire ax and hose. I would count him as our first real friend on Chappy as year-round residents.

I approached him with a knowing smile and dutifully handed over our bundle of joy to his summoning hands.

And those hands were so big. Peter is tall, thick, but not fat, with a crop of unkempt red hair. He is usually dressed in work clothes or some part of his fireman's gear. A smear of diesel oil or grease seems always to be present on his clothes or brow as maintenance on the Chappy ferry is never done. The sight of little Ilana engulfed by his big mitts, complete with tufts of red hair on his knuckles, was overpowering. Wow, she was tiny. Peter was in heaven, hanging with the newest Chappy member. It's funny that the sight of Peter with my daughter sticks in my mind. It was a random moment but feels so vivid. It feels signifi-cant—stuck in my head.

Melissa and I moved around the room, beaming with pride as we showed Ilana off. Advice was given. Some was good. Most was irrelevant. And a few suggestions were downright disturbing. We made a note to stay clear of one girl as a babysitter. Her laugh sounded more like a cackle as she spilled her drink and told us about the time she took her little brothers driving through the fields of their farm at midnight on their tractor. She was trying to convey the magic of the moonlight, but all I could think about was what was in this sixteen-year-old's drinking glass?

I believe that night was also the first time I got to know Jim, the painter. I had noticed him when we first walked in at the liquor table. His presence and the odd way his hand was all bandaged up with a sock and some duct tape made him hard to miss. We found ourselves both in line at the bathroom, and it gave me the opportunity to peel back this weird onion. I remember him knowing who I was, where I lived, and about my daughter. It took me aback, not realizing how small Chappy was. I tried to cover my shock of the familiarity by asking about his hand.

"Oh, this? I was using an old stump grinder that

someone had thrown away and seemed to have gotten my hand too close to the grinding wheel before I let go of the trigger. Whoops."

He said this all with a sheepish grin like—silly me. And all I could think of was... OK, so why is it bandaged in a sock?

This was the night I decided to become a volunteer EMT. Seeing the colorful people of Chappy up close and personal after the long winter months made it clear I could help keep my neighbors safe. Safe from themselves as well as accidents. I was living on a spit of land where people were making some questionable choices on a daily basis and needed help. But to be truthful, I would be lying if I said it was solely an altruistic gesture. More than anything, I realized I could not or would not rely on anyone else to make sure my family was safe. Having an EMT jump kit in our house with enough bandages to make my own personal mummy was like a baby blanket that let me sleep soundly at night.

Back to the present. A cold mist has been lingering over this entire early May afternoon. But my mood is chipper as always. Because like clockwork, every other Wednesday, we're arriving back at the Chappy Community Center for another potluck. Yet nowadays, we're packing gluten-free cookies and pasta—how life has evolved. I'm not totally on board with the whole gluten-free thing and regularly grumble about it. But Melissa is always trying to figure out what's making her brood cranky, and the answer now seems to be gluten. So there's little gluten in the house these days. Everyone is still cranky, but I remember not to bring that fact up—much.

We enter the center, drop our food on the long main dish table after again sidestepping the central drinking trough, and begin to mill around. My wife goes one way, my daughters fly to another corner where kids are climbing all over the furniture, and I see a fellow volunteer EMT.

We take a moment to talk about the EMT call we went on the other night. One of Chappy's frequent fliers (someone who calls 911 on a regular basis) needed help. It was Tom Kane of my clambake catering days. It seems he didn't understand that marijuana and wine didn't go well with Parkinson's medication. You can imbibe with one of them, but both put you over the edge. It wasn't a big deal—no one freaked out. We entered the house around 10:00 p.m. The dinner party, which included three elderly couples from the neighborhood, sat calmly around the table with a candle flickering, talking, sipping their wine, and waiting for us. Tom Kane was lying nearby on a couch with his eyes closed and a wet cloth on his forehead. There was nothing to be done. Sally, his wife, knew that. He just had to go to the hospital in Oak Bluffs (one ferry and a twelve-mile drive away) to be monitored. We still went through the motions of taking his vitals, as much to keep in practice as anything else, but there was nothing new to be gleaned by our intervention. We were merely a taxicab ride. The Kane's were very appreciative of our service. The only one not grateful for the EMT call was Melissa, who had her scrabble game time with me cut short that night.

I look to the end of the community center hall as we talk and notice Mr. Kane pouring himself a glass of wine. We give each other a look and hope that's all he's having tonight.

While I'm deep in thought, Rich O'Brien runs up to me. He gives me one of his big bear hugs that precede every conversation. Not a light welcoming hug but an over-the-top one that everyone turns to see—one that is loud with grrring sounds. He lets me go and jumps right in with, "Hi Rob, we need to get together and hang. Maybe smoke a joint and go fishing." He always wants to hang, but as of yet, I haven't found too much to talk about with Rich. Seems like a nice enough guy, but the constant reference to smoking, especially when his young boys are around, just doesn't sit well with me. I beg off as usual, and he is gone like a flash to press the flesh with Lyle Hollander—not one of my favorite people.

I still fume at the lost opportunity of creating a construction monopoly on Chappy with him. Lazy, self-centered, and egotistical are some of the nicer words I use to describe Lyle at this point. I see Rich slap him on the back. It spills Lyle's beer, and there seems to be a tense moment between them. But soon they are laughing and look to be thick as thieves.

I continue to watch them and wonder if maybe I'm off base about him—not Lyle, he's worthless... but Rich. He's a young guy and appears to work hard at the high school where he does maintenance. At least his stories of work tell that tale. Maybe it's his energy and eagerness to bond that don't sit well with me. I put these facts in the back of my mind and make a note to attempt to get to know Rich at the next firefighter/ EMT meeting on Sunday.

I run over to my girls to remind them to eat something, grab myself a plate, and take a seat next to Melissa. She's sitting with a couple who have girls roughly the same age as our own. As I sit down, I remember seeing the husband walking through a field with his new metal detector earlier in the day. My boyhood curiosity was piqued at the time, but I didn't want to disturb him. So now seems like a good time to see if I'm missing out on a new hobby. "Hey, have you found any treasure yet?"

He smiles a sheepish grin and proclaims, "I didn't find the treasure at Blue Rock, but I did find some British coins from 1740 and some early 1900s American coins."

"Whoa, whoa, whoa," I yell out with honest bewilderment. "What Blue Rock treasure?"

He tells me the sketchy details of a mysterious rock that marks the spot where some pirates buried a treasure when they were on the run. The story is convoluted and hinges on the ramblings of a secluded old man on Cape Pogue Bay in 1824. But who cares? It's a treasure story. I'm in!

Don't Mess With My Family

Beautiful scenery, an interesting business and clientele, a family life where I get to see everyone throughout my day, a cast of memorable characters for neighbors wherever I turn, and the possibility of finding a buried treasure. What more could you ask for?

The answer is chickens.

We have chickens at our stately manor on Chappy. I feel like we were the last of our friends to get chickens, but now we have them. It's a lifestyle thing. Some locals cultivate crops and livestock to survive. This is juxtaposed by rich summer people who have farm animals brought in for the season and vegetable gardens maintained by expert hands as just one more trophy to show off to guests, never once mentioning the real farmers that do the dirty work. Neither group defines us. My decision to live locally and be part of the farming community is more about being tethered to the island's history. It gives me something to discuss with my friends when we're not obsessed with talking about our businesses. I don't kid myself by thinking that I am a real farmer or that my family lives off the land, but the connection, the toil, and the smells are real. Hard work reaps food. It's that simple.

I dove into the experience as usual with overkill: Reading how-to books and interviewing everyone and anyone on how to create the perfect fowl environment. I built the birds a sixty-square-foot cedar-shingled palace with cozy nesting boxes lined with wood shavings. Every time I scoop a warm egg out of one of those boxes, the smell of the cedar and pine shavings transports me to one of my company's chipping job sites where we reduce mighty trees down to soft, moist wood chips. I'm reminded that our loud, disruptive, and destructive chainsaws have created a by-product that nurtures and comforts a living thing. It all comes full circle. We try to recycle as much as possible from those chipping jobs, including some branches from trees. They look so funky and organic as twisting and expansive perches for the chickens in our coop. The chickens seem to love them, flapping their wings and stepping on each other's feet as they compete for a specific space. In the end, they always settle down, cooing and snuggling against each other for warmth and security for the long night ahead. Below the perches is a small ramp cut into the coop's side, a gateway to their sprawling private grounds. I think if I do the math, I'll find that the delicious, organic, free-range eggs we collect and eat cost about seven dollars apiece. But they are really good eggs, we are living locally, and our kids are learning about something useful. So, seven dollars might just be a bargain.

Our girls named the chickens Cheerio, Bunny Love, Daisy, Rojo, Skunk, and Puffin. We got them almost exactly two years ago, in early May. They're loved, petted, and handled like pets. The thing is, they start out so cute as chicks, living in a box in our house. But boy, they grow up fast and go through a mean, ugly stage before rounding out and looking like their dignified mature selves.

They are truly beautiful birds. Bunny Love, our favorite, has painterly yellow, tan, and brown in her feathers. However, the real reason we adore her is the proud way she waddles around on her feather-covered feet. It's comical, but she makes it work. Skunk has black and white feathers, and Daisy sports mostly white feathers with yellow splotches, of course. And Puffin, well Puffin reminds me of Beaker from *The Muppets* with her "wadda wadda wadda" voice and the scared, halting way she walks around the yard like the world is going to end any minute and she needs to be prepared.

These birds are truly one-of-a-kind. Their eggs are as different as their plumage. Fun fact, the breed of chicken determines the color and consistency of the egg. So, when you get those fine homogeneous eggs from the store, it's because the farmer has only one kind of chicken. And if you ever venture into egg production, don't get fooled by the catalog like we did one year. If they ever offer to give you an exotic breed free with your order—don't fall for it. Our family had visions of majestic plumage, a gait worthy of royalty, and eggs of gold or at least silver in color. We now know exotic is code for male. Amusing side note, we named that rooster Queenie—before we knew Queenie was really a king.

We're home a lot and love to let the chickens out of their fenced-in homestead. Doesn't matter how expansive their coop is. Birds are meant to be free—to feel free. They need more room to rummage and peck. And it doesn't hurt that they look cute walking around the grassy yard without a care in the world. Until one day, while I was sitting at my desk, I heard one of the chickens let out a frightening screech, and then I saw Bunny Love fly by my window. My first thought was I had never seen the chickens fly more than a few feet. Maybe glide, or more accurately, fall from their perches to the ground when I open the coop door each day, but not fly. And then I heard a different, more foreign sound — a loud squawk. Instantly I knew what was up—A hawk!

I ran outside and grabbed the nearest stick I could find. I have to say the huge, red-tailed hawk swooping into our yard for his daily bread was majestic and beautiful. It was definitely beefy with its tell-tale brownish-red back feathers and a white underbelly. The hawk must have had a three- to four-foot wingspan, swooping low overhead like a plane circling to land. As I got a quick flash of its talons, I felt the instinct to duck. The yard resembled a war zone with chickens ducking for cover as this kamikaze pilot nose-dived into the yard, taking swipes at these ridiculously waddling targets. Feathers flew as competing cries of panicked fowls filled the air. But my presence changed the game for the hawk. It was in an angled descent on one of my pets as it saw me with the stick. It immediately swooped around to climb out of the yard but somehow didn't climb high enough and flew through the open door of the fenced-in area of the coop. So now I had cowering chickens under shrubs all around my house and a hawk with a three-foot wingspan trapped in a chicken coop whose sole purpose is to, ironically, keep predators out.

I was pissed and followed the hawk into what was essentially a big cage without thinking. It stopped, and I stopped. It suddenly dawned on me that I was in a cage with a wild, trapped animal with big ass claws.

We looked at each other for a long moment, and I felt I knew what it was thinking. "Really, you're going to come at me with that twig?"

I slowly backed out of the open door and regrouped as the hawk stepped back and did the same. I took a moment to check on the chickens. They were all present and accounted for but scared, literally shaking the feathers off their bodies. With a new resolve, I went back to the hawk. This time I went around the outside of the fenced-in area and poked it with the long handle of a rake. "Get outta here... Yaw, yaw," I yelled.

The hawk's response was to lie on its back. Its long wings flapped open to either side with its white belly exposed to me. It looked like a puppy that wanted its belly scratched. I think it was a defensive measure of some sort, but at the moment, I honestly couldn't figure out what was going on. Was it mocking me? Telling me no stick was going to hurt it, and I should take my best shot? I wavered between astonishment and begrudging admiration for this big, beautiful bird but resumed my assault. Still, the hawk seemed to be taunting me—first hanging upside down from the mesh on the top of the fenced-in area and then strutting around as if it was in its own comfy home. Eventually, and at its own pace, the hawk flew out the door with one flap of its wings. It went to a tree limb, high above the yard, to take in the scene from a safer vantage point.

The hawk stayed on that perch, eyeing me as I slowly collected each chicken from its hiding spot. They were terrified and continued to shiver and shake. But I could tell they were happy to have me scoop them up, cradle them, and deliver them to their now secure coop. The hawk finally flew away, but only after the last chicken was safe inside, and I had latched the door shut. It was not until this moment that I realized the chickens, like my job and my surroundings, told the story of who I was becoming. Crazy person that lives on Chappy—year-round, mind you. Crunchy granola family man. Defender of chickens. Defender of our lifestyle. I like what I have become. I like the definition that is me. This is paradise.

The Bike Path Saga Begins

It's Saturday, mid May. The chickens are back to their old routine of walking around the yard. Short memory span, I guess. Ilana and Melissa are baking some concoction, and Sasha has decided to ride her bike to Anna and Scott's house to play with their daughter, Emma. Sounds good. Actually, it sounds adventurous as the first half-mile of Sasha's journey is on a dirt road. She will probably get off her bike at some point, say a bad word like "damn" or "hell", and walk the rest of the way until she gets to the main paved road. Then it's another half-mile to Emma's house. I see her take her bike out of the shed and don't think about her again until my EMT beeper goes off twenty minutes later.

The jarring noise is always the same—lots of beeps at different intervals. It seems to go on forever. Why can't the dispatch just start talking and tell me where I need to go to help a person in need? The beeping finally does stop as it always does, and the dispatch person rattles off who needs to listen to this announcement.

I listen for the word "Chappy" and little more. It's not like I can do much for anyone on any other part of Martha's Vineyard. First, there would be the Chappy ferry to contend with and then the fact that the rest of the island is one hundred square miles. The patient would be dead before I got there. But today I hear the word "Chappy"; I run down the stairs to grab my jump kit. It carries all my first aid supplies, and as I throw it over my shoulder, I stop—dead in my tracks. The call sounds too familiar. It's right around the corner. I don't even stop to tell Melissa. I just run.

I'm the first EMT on the scene. People are already huddled around Sasha, trying to help her stop crying. Tom and Sally Kane, who still remind me of the scrumptious clambake that my dad and I put on for them, are patting at her wounds with a handkerchief. Jim, the painter, has just run back from his bicycle with what looks like a painter's drop cloth to put under Sasha. Another woman, only known to me as the bird lady, as she has over one hundred bird feeders in her front lawn trees, is peppering Sasha with questions—not really waiting for replies. I'm taking this all in as I lay my EMT jump kit on the ground, open it, and get out my equipment: stethoscope, BP cuff, flashlight for the eyes, and gloves.

I go through the motions of getting in EMT mode. I concentrate on the ritual to keep calm. I'm ready. Everyone clears away as I approach. Sasha has scrapes and dirt everywhere, but she is alive and intact as far as I can tell. I kneel, and all goes silent other than the sounds coming from Sasha. I don't know if it's because the people around me have stopped talking or because I have blocked them out. Concentrating on my routine as an EMT is all that's allowing me to keep it together. I put on a stoic face and begin my rehearsed dialog with my patient—more to keep myself from crying than anything else. I ask her probing questions as I take her vitals. I'm gentle but firm, and

Sasha calms down and stops crying. She talks about the accident and says the words "sorry" over and over again.

I tell her to hush. "Let's just concentrate on your pain. We can deal with the other stuff later." I'm fuming inside as I spy Jason Arbilt, an Edgartown detective, talking to a man next to his car on the other side of the road. But there's plenty of time for that later. Slowly, the voices of those around me begin to register in my head again as I get better control of the situation. I feel the crisp, breezy air of the island around me. It's like a movie just taken off pause. The action starts up again as if it had never stopped. My daughter is hurt and scared, but I got this.

I feel competent in most situations, but emergencies are my jam. Life with Jerry as a child got me ready for anything. Who drops a boat in the ocean on the first day of the season and goes for a spin with no communication or safety equipment? It's as if God sent the fog rolling in as an answer... no one!

I'm able to block out the nonsense around me and home in on the few things that will make a difference. And really, no one is going to die today. I can see in an instant Sasha is battered but not broken. This kind of EMT situation is the norm here, and my main job is being calm. This, above all else, will calm everyone around me. I can feel Sasha's pulse slowing down to normal as I talk. Feel her breathing modulate as I slowly, with no sense of rush, wash away the dirt from her bloody scrapes. I continue to ask her very professional and unemotional questions to set the mood of our interaction. I've got this. She's going to be OK.

"Tell me, where do you feel pain?"

I get the "all over" answer and tell her I'm going to feel her body from her toes to her head. "Yell if it hurts."

She gives me a look like—yeah, I'm going to yell.

I probe her body, squeezing each part as I go. Sasha is being very brave, and I believe I'm not doing so bad myself. I mark some notes down with a sharpie on my gloved hand next to her latest vitals and wipe my forehead. A smile crosses my face. I actually put rubber gloves on before I treated my own daughter. Pretty robotic of me. I never thought I had this EMT thing down. I always find myself taking the backseat to other more experienced EMTs off the Edgartown ambulance. There are just not enough runs on Chappy to get in a rhythm or for me to feel confident, but I'm doing OK.

Sasha is lucky. Besides her superficial wounds, it appears she might just have a sprained wrist or maybe a broken bone in her forearm. I'm still cleaning her wounds when Melissa comes running up to us. I can tell she doesn't know whether to yell at me or hug Sasha. Somehow, she does both at the same time. I have no excuse, but instinct took over at the time of the call, and time wasted talking to Melissa was time wasted not helping Sasha. At least that's what I'm telling myself. The crowd had made room for me when I arrived. They now part like the red sea for Melissa.

"Why didn't you say something when you left the house?" She yells as if no one is around.

"I didn't know. I just thought it was a call."

"You're full of crap. You ran so fast out of the house I thought one of your employees must have been hurt. And besides, they would have told you. If I find out they told you, I'm going to..." Melissa's words become a mumble as she locks eyes with Sasha. She crumbles to the ground and hugs her with so much fury and so much gentleness at the same time. I marvel at how she does this.

Sasha melts into her arms, and it's only the random

movement where Melissa brushes against her wrist that elicits an, "Owwwwww, Mom!"

"Sorry. Sorry. I didn't know. Rob, is she OK?"

Normally, we are not supposed to give a diagnosis as we are not doctors, but I think if I pulled that bullshit with Melissa right here and now, there would be another victim on the scene. So I tell her what I think about Sasha's wrist and how brave she's been. Melissa takes in the information and seems to calm down. Now confident Sasha will be OK, Melissa transitions into a mother hen, and the fireworks really start. Melissa makes a beeline for Detective Arbilt, who is still talking to the driver of the car that forced Sasha off the road. The driver is a summer resident with a house down the road. He took the turn a little too wide. He should have known better. He hit some sand and fishtailed a little. He was going too fast. This is for sure. Sasha was probably around the blind curve and too far out on the road as well. She knows to stay to the edge as there are no sidewalks. I hope she was not playing around. Jason sees Melissa coming and meets her halfway before she can get to the driver.

"What the hell were you thinking?" Melissa yells as she approaches.

Jason catches her as he says, "OK, OK, Melissa. We were just talking about the situation. I'm getting all the facts. Francis Collins here has been telling me about the sand and how he lost control on the turn in the road. Do you know Francis?" I think Jason is trying to diffuse the situation by making it more familiar, but it doesn't work.

"Yes, I know Mr. Collins, and he knows me. We all know each other. And I know he drives too fast. People know to get out of his way as he barrels out of his side road, phone in hand, without stopping."

"I most certainly do not. I'm so sorry about your daughter. It was an accident," Francis tries to say with an air of emotionless control, but something about the scene gets to him, and he wells up with tears.

Maybe it's Melissa throwing a grenade when she says, "I'm sure you would have a different stance if it were your daughter. Where is Talia? Playing tennis? At the beach? Somewhere safe?"

Francis continues to try to convey to Melissa and Jason he's a good person. He's a member of the community—a person that drives safely. Jason issues a citation for speeding anyway—maybe as a gesture to our family. I don't know. Melissa is still not appeased. She wants her pound of flesh, and this blubbering summer person is not giving her any satisfaction. We all know he's only partly to blame. There should be a sidewalk here. This serpentine road is no place for pedestrian and bicycle traffic. Melissa has bigger fish to fry.

The real cavalry arrives in the form of an ambulance from town, and they take over from me. I turn my attention to Melissa and Jason now that my patient is in good hands. I get to them just as the driver in the accident is pulling away. Melissa is still fuming and wants answers Jason can't give her. "Why is there no sidewalk on Chappy? Why doesn't anyone care about this situation that keeps happening over and over again? Do we need to wait for something worse to happen to one of my kids before you start doing something about it?" The questions keep coming. I put my arms around Melissa and tell her she's right but that Jason isn't the enemy. Jason gives me a look that says thank you and extricates himself as quickly as possible from our conversation. Melissa breaks my embrace and rushes toward the waiting ambulance with her baby inside. As I said, she has bigger fish to fry.

Chappy is treated like the stepchild to the main part of Edgartown. Good for all its property tax money but an after-thought when it comes to town services since only 179 year-round voting residents live here. I can't tell you the number of times I've heard a townsperson say, "Why spend money over there. We never go there."

I can't remember how many times I jokingly brought up the idea of seceding from Edgartown at one of our fire station meetings. Today I rethink the joking part.

Is it Still Called Kidnapping When it's Your Father?

The ER is an exercise in hurry up and wait. Sasha is calm but bored. Melissa smiles up at one of the nurses when she gives Sasha some fun activity books. Honestly, the books will probably distract Melissa more than Sasha.

Dad's passing the time at the nurse's station chatting up the 'girls'. He had just finished his dialysis treatment in the hospital when I called him about the accident. It's all so random.

I get up and go over to him as my own way to pass the time. Dad looks over at me. He shakes his head as a patient goes by on a gurney with an oxygen mask on his face. Dad's next words come out so naturally, fresh and whimsical—as if he's thinking them for the first time. But I've heard it all before. I believe I first heard this particular request when I was eight. It's warped, but it's comforting to feel the consistency of his words. "Never put me in a nursing home. If I'm doomed—get me a hotel room, two hookers, and a carton of Max 120s. If I'm alive in the morning, repeat until I'm dead."

The nurses smirk and tease my dad as he says this

seemingly absurd wish. "Oh Jerry, don't go. I'll marry you any day."

I'm not listening to the nurses. Their banter will play out like countless other meaningless encounters. But for me, my dad's words elicit memories echoing from each time I heard them. The conversation goes on around me, but I'm no longer present. I'm back in 1976 thinking of one of my other Dad memories.

Jerry speeds down I-91 in his new Opel GT Sportster. An advertisement for the Tall Ships armada in New York Harbor for the Bicentennial is playing on the radio. He wipes away the ash from a Max 120 cigarette that has fallen onto his wrinkled business shirt. All the while balancing a Styrofoam coffee cup against the steering wheel with his other hand. The stains, spills, and litter around the car tell the story of who my dad is or at least how he lives his life.

In Jerry's eyes, his two children sitting next to him are all that seem to matter. Andy, fourteen, and me, ten, are smooshed together in the passenger seat next to him with lots of questions, but we know to wait. We know our dad has a plan. He always has a plan. Jerry has just literally kidnapped us. We didn't bat an eye when he showed up at school toward the end of the day and signed us out without notifying our mother.

Jerry is a lawyer. He knows the courtroom he will find himself in the next day, the judge owes him, and let's just say the deck is stacked in his favor. Andy and I knew a court hearing was set up, but we didn't know what for, and thought our mother would be bringing us. Oh well. Plans change.

Tomorrow seems so far away as we speed down the highway in this little roadster. Dad hits the gas as he stubs out yet another half-smoked cigarette. He looks over at us and seems to make a mental note that he needs to pick up a bigger car before tomorrow's court case. "How we doing?" He asks with a forced grin.

"Fine," says Andy with an equally pained expression. Being the older brother, Andy knows our dad's history and is leery of this 'excursion'.

I, on the other hand, have no trepidation and am always ready for any adventure. Damn the risk or fallout. "Will we have time to go to a show before we head back?" I ask.

Dad quickly replies with his well-planned offensive that he's been concocting for this very moment. "No, I'm going to show you your new home in the wealthiest town in the country." He pauses and glances over at us to gauge our reaction. "The town has a private minibus system to take you wherever you want to go, including the marina where you can grab your motorboat whenever you choose. Oh, and you have to meet Marilyn, your new governess."

Andy slumps deeper into the seat as my eyes almost explode—my mind whirls with a million questions. This plan is all news to us. We knew nothing of the move, the new house, or that our mom was on board with this plan. Of course, she wasn't. And what's a governess?

With the bait firmly hooked into at least one of his son's brains, our dad delves into the real reason he abruptly absconded with us boys. We need to be prepped for tomorrow's court case. What to say, how to say it, when to cry. It's all calculated. The directions are all on a cassette tape to be played back over and over again until we know our lines and cues.

"Your honor, my mother would often chase us around the house with a ruler. There was this one time when she was tired from work and didn't get home until..." The car speeds on as the tape is rewound, and Andy and I perfect our performance.

Andy reluctantly plays his part, mostly because I'm so enthusiastically diving into the performance. He's always stuck close to me as a lifeline. This could be because he's seen more of the carnage of our parents' divorce. Andy readily admits he has no recollection of the first seven years of his life. Lots of baggage. It's tough being a pawn, but we all have our parts to play. This might all sound above a ten-year-old's grasp, but seeing all this courtroom drama up close and personal ever since I could walk, and my dad holding nothing back with details or commentary, has made a man child out of me.

The study session is interrupted by the sound of clinking cans attached to the back of an old sedan we pass on the highway. A sign that reads, 'Just Married', is pushed up against the car's back window. Andy slumps down in the seat even farther, if that's possible, as he knows what's coming next. "That poor schmuck," Jerry yells. Andy and I are now going to be subjected to the preachings of a committed man. "Don't ever get married! It's better to date women. Once you marry them, the sweets become scarce. If you want a fuck, you'll have to earn it. Wait till that guy forgets an in-law's birthday or doesn't want to go out to dinner one night. His wife will simply say no that night. That'll teach him!"

Andy doesn't want to bait his dad to elaborate, so he keeps his mouth shut. I'm different and love to egg him on and proceed to ask the familiar question. "Dad, aren't you going to marry again?"

"Of course I am," my father replies. Andy quickly turns his head in shock but then settles back in the seat because he soon realizes what lies ahead. "I'll get married... but it must be a double wedding with the Pope."

I break into laughter.

"Or when the Statue of Liberty sits down or when pigs fly." And the little Opel GT flies on toward nirvana, or at least what a judge will hopefully perceive as nirvana when he views it in a glossy report with pictures, stats, and fictitious quotes from adoring neighbors waiting to meet Jerry's boys.

We're duly impressed with the trappings of our dad's wealth. The choice of guardianship isn't really fair for boys our age. Either live a middle-class existence with our mother in a nowhere town in a small ranch-style house and, of course, with lots of rules and balanced meals. Or live in a fairy tale world of a modern house on the water, a governess, which we learn is just a fancy word for a nanny, a boat, and close proximity to the playground that is New York City. You might think this is all ridiculous. No judge is going to fall for this circus show. Boys belong with their mother, in a stable home. Not with a single, jet-setting father who works in the city from 6:00 a.m. to midnight each day. Not with a man who unabashedly is using his children as pawns to get back at his ex-wife. But Andy and I have no illusions that our dad will have any trouble with the task at hand. Our dad once brought our mother to court because I protested, she served fish too many times a week. It cost our mother money she didn't have, time she couldn't afford to take off work, and in the end, she was ordered to only feed the boys fish once a week.

So, this is going to happen. Andy and I know it, and we get ready to play our parts.

We ride back to our mom's the next day in the sedan that our dad just bought this morning. The drive is full of last-minute briefings on what to say and how to say it. Jerry seems to relax as the final pieces fall into place. There's still a little more time to make some jabs at his ex-wife and her new, financially unsuccessful husband. I put my hands under my lap and squeeze my legs as he talks on. I love my dad but his hatred makes me anxious. It helps that I've learned to forget things soon after they're said.

The topics of money and success rule Jerry's world, and the fact that his ex-wife's husband has neither fills him with joy. "You know kids, remember that when you're looking for a career in life, you have three choices: You can be a doctor, a lawyer, or own your own business. This is the only way to make money in this world. Working for a company leads you nowhere. Especially as a Jew."

Andy and I dutifully nod along with the familiar refrain—sounds right. All our friends' parents back home are wealthy and fall into one of those categories. It never dawns on our dad or us that this conversation repeated three or four times every time we get together will haunt Andy and me for the rest of our lives. They don't call it brainwashing for nothin'.

Lunch With My Sweetie

I feel like I'm in a fog the next morning as I try to make sense of the past weekend. I drive onto the main paved road and pass the scene of Sasha's accident. The sand is sprayed across the road, and its contact with my tires sounds unusually loud in my ears. It's uncomfortable, and I want it to stop. And it does as soon as I exit the turn. "All is good," I keep telling myself. It helps that Sasha is doing fine. She didn't even miss school, but the scene up ahead puts this all out of my head.

Never a dull moment is what I'm thinking as I spy the upcoming carnival in front of me. Three Arabian Stallions and one border collie are spread out, cantering up the road. So stately, so calm in their gate. They trot as if they are the only creatures on earth. Penelope, a stately English woman, rides the lead horse. She canters with her nose high in the air, riding clothes impeccably tailored, and oblivious to the world around her. Directly behind her are two Arabian military personnel costumed in official garb. Green field uniforms, medals, and swords create a comical air for everyone but the participants in this farce. My girls refer to this sideshow as "Penelope's Chappy Parade Extravaganza."

I believe she hired Frick and Frack when she went to Saudi Arabia and purchased these stallions. I see them around all the time in different locales, but they never break character and are never out of uniform. The horses walk in the fancy way that only obnoxious well-trained horses can. The sole wisp of chaos and whimsy is the border collie running back and forth across the road behind the horses. I know to tread lightly. There's never any easy way around this spectacle.

I creep up slowly on Penelope and company as I don't want to spook the horses. The collie is well aware of my presence and yelps at me to stay back. Penelope knows I'm behind her but makes no move to bring her entourage to the side of the road. The middle of the road is where she likes to be. Finally, five minutes later, with no warning, no change in the road's topography, Penelope rides her stallion to the side of the road, and her military guard follows suit. I slowly pass and give the horses a wide berth. Penelope looks over for a second with a scowl and nothing more. The guards never break rank. The dog chases me on.

This circus delays my rare trip off Chappy to meet Melissa for lunch and catch up on her rage against 'the man'. She has gone to Edgartown to find out how to get sidewalks for Chappy.

We decide to meet at the Scottish Bakehouse in West Tisbury, one of five other towns on Martha's Vineyard. It's our go-to meeting place even though it's fifteen miles from Chappy, which feels more like forty-five miles for Chappy folks. But we love this place. Crunchy granola atmosphere, check. Gluten-free options, check. And picnic tables outside to watch the world go by, check. Melissa and I meet up on the restaurant's deck, which is little more than a small stand-alone, old cottage with a dirt parking lot. Melissa had less of a drive as she was already up-island for a power yoga class after her investigative trip to the selectmen's office. She looks drained. I wonder which activity took more out of her?

We wait to order our meals and bide our time reading the many flyers that adorn the restaurant walls. Yoga, 12 step programs, writing groups, and concerts of all kinds are the subject of these colorful leaflets. If you're looking to live an alternative lifestyle, then you've hit the mother lode on Martha's Vineyard. Sometimes a funky ad will hit me. Today, I see nothing new, and my attention returns to the people behind the counter.

They really seem to believe in their mission with this food thing. They take pride in describing the curry and bean salad to an undecided customer and point out that the greens are from Morning Glory, a local farm in Edgartown. I concentrate on the woman's work clothes as a way to pass the time until I can order. She's wearing a black t-shirt, a long skirt that reminds me of a Japanese warrior robe, a wampum bracelet, a little bead nose ring, a wooden stick in the middle of the hair bun on top of her head, and Tevas round out the ensemble. I get the sense this restaurant counter person came to the Vineyard to be herself—let her personality scream out to the world through her clothing, job, and just being here. She is so different from me. I guess she would be the first to profess this fact. But our journeys both lead us here. The ethos of this island is so welcoming to all stripes of life. I sometimes wonder how we all found this place.

The woman behind the counter is on the phone talking about the Monday night drum circle on State Beach as we stand in the corner and wait for our food. I marvel at how long it's been since I've been to one of those. I laugh to myself—way before my time with Melissa. The visceral enjoyment of the percussion sounds wafting through the still night air competing with the crashing of the surf was always so enticing. But my younger self was better at dealing with the sand fleas and being able to go out after a long day at work. Another time. Another person. It turns out our journeys might not be that different—just another part of the timeline.

The counter attendant is now off the phone and brings our food out. I take it and head to one of the old, weathered picnic tables where Melissa is already sitting. I brush away the pine needles that have made a nice bed on the tabletop as Melissa heads back inside for the napkins I have obviously forgotten.

As soon as she returns, Melissa begins complaining, which she calls sharing, about the town selectmen and their pass-the-buck attitude. "I really don't understand it. This seems like a no-brainer."

"I know, honey, but this is politics and money."

"What politics? A windy road—a dangerous road—lots of people riding bikes with no protection... this was our daughter!"

"I know, I know." I pull Melissa close and try to tread lightly. "Everyone gets it. But there are unfortunately more important things to some of these people."

"It's stupid. It's all ridiculous subterfuge. I looked in the town archives. The arguments that everyone put forth the last time this issue came up are so transparent. These people don't really care about the Barrens Buckmoth and whether it's endangered. No one really believes sidewalks are less safe than driving lanes. It's all just an easy excuse. I bet that stupid moth never comes up when they clear acreage to build one of their houses!"

Melissa is fuming but in control. She knows she needs to be intelligent about this and be prepared before she strikes next. This sounds like a war to me. I'm glad I'm on her side on this one. We make a plan to sit down with Peter. He knows the town's political construct as the fire chief and, above all else, knows where all the bones are buried as he's lived on Chappy forever. Peter will know what to do.

Today's lunch is meant to help us connect as we go about our hectic lives. It's good to be off of our rock. Getting to West Tisbury is only up-island, but it still feels like a world away from Chappy. I sincerely want to take a break from work and our Chappy life and just hang with Melissa.

I switch topics to save my fantasy and begin talking about Melissa's yoga class as a way to get, well, more grounded in our conversation. You can't throw a stick on Martha's Vineyard without hitting a yoga class. It's a big part of the island culture. Melissa goes to the Yoga Barn up-island to relax and reconnect. She goes there to be present. She goes there to get centered.

Unfortunately, she frequently comes away from a yoga class with more stress due to her friends' gossip mentality. Melissa relates her attempt to lie on her mat in Shavasana pose, eyes closed, and forget her morning of bureaucracy.

"I was rhythmically breathing and calm until Ann nudged me. She just starts in, no pleasantries. 'Is Sasha OK? How do you live over there? It's like the wild west.' I just smile, you know, what am I really going to say? I don't want to get into it. So I just say, 'she's fine.' What I was really thinking was about how Ann's off-island sister asked her the same question about how she could live in Vineyard Haven when we were over her house for book club a few weeks back."

Melissa goes on to recount whispered stories told from mat to mat around her as she tries to focus on preparing for her practice. She doesn't get specific. She doesn't want to feed the beast but gives me the gist of the vibe. They are all eager to talk about the accident and tell her the newest gossip about one of our friends, one of our neighbors, one of the many Noah's rejects before class begins.

The sheer volume of the gossip. How close it all comes to our lives. Hell, the accident is about our life. We think of ourselves as above all the craziness on the Vineyard—the stories. It's all there on the outskirts of our lives, but then it appears to get closer and closer as tales erupt about friends of ours. Real friends. Maybe we're not immune. It turns out we're not immune.

We eat in silence for a while. The breeze is so nice up here. Different from Chappy. I forget I'm on an island as the wilderness around us is lush, and the trees are straight and tall. I feel like I'm in farm country. I take it all in, even the squirrels that scurry around our table who have never bothered to migrate to Chappy. Melissa, I assume, is taking in the change of scenery like me until she blurts out, "Can you imagine living off-island in a random city and having the luxury of re-inventing yourself—no one knowing your business?"

I'm caught off guard and can only think to say, "Huh?"

"Shit happens. Life happens. Baggage is collected. But off-island people have the luxury of changing jobs, changing friends, heck, even changing homes. They can sidestep the pigeon-hole their troubles put them in and re-invent themselves."

"Yeah, the island can be a fishbowl. Are you sorry I dragged you here from Boston to raise our family?" I ask, not really wanting to know the answer, not wanting to deal with this shit—our shit.

"I love it here. I love our friends and the beauty and the sea. It's just too much information. Sometimes I just want to be anonymous. Do you get that?"

"Of course. But I think we are doing a good job of balancing the crap in our life. The bike accident notwithstanding." I don't know how else to answer. The alternative, taking up roots and moving, seems absurd. We live in paradise.

Melissa puts her fork down, slides closer to me, and puts her head on my shoulder. "I hope so."

As we sit and the discussion is fresh in my head, I see a guy out of the corner of my eye, coming out of the Bakehouse with his tray of food. We nod as he walks to a table far from us with his new girlfriend. I think about how this woman is an interesting choice for a girlfriend. How I know she likes sucking on toes; I don't know. Could have been talking to her ex, a bartender, at a barbecue. Or I could have heard it from the younger guys at the fire station. Hey, this woman is a performance artist, and it could have been in one of her pieces. I just don't remember. But unfortunately, I know it. The dating scene is one long game of musical chairs as one partner moves down the line in this fishbowl to their next partner—already knowing everything about them. A person's drug preference, rap sheet, child support issues, and even their membership in a secretive swinger's club called the Silk Sheets is public knowledge.

Melissa and I always have a good laugh about the infamous Silk Sheets Club and wonder if they have membership cards. It's good to laugh. It's good to see the humor in the craziness that is our life and revel in it. Today is nothing new. Life happens. The seasons happen. It's springtime, and we're starting to shake off the winter hibernation feeling. That which doesn't kill us makes us stronger and all that. Right?

Our lunch ends. Melissa still has more errands to finish, and I have to get back to Chappy and the business. We hug and plan to touch base with the doctor about Sasha's wrist injury. It was, in fact, just a sprain, and we count ourselves lucky. We end our rendezvous by agreeing to walk the beach the following day with the family as our lab, River, has been jonesing to go swimming.

Spring, like all seasons, is defined by its routines. It starts out jarring because it's so different from the one before it. A sense of urgency on Chappy takes hold as everyone suddenly remembers the jobs they promised to get done back in September. All of a sudden, there are actual cars and trucks and tractors on the road. But before long, we're running on schedule. We remember to check the Chappy ferry webcam before we drive down to the point to see how long the line is. All the various companies jockeying for entrance to a customer's house fall into line and wait their turn. Eventually, we get to a place where we feel able to take a breath and relax. We've got this. We've done this before, year after year. I think of River chasing her tail. We're both running too fast to consider more than the task at hand, and it's entertaining. It's tiring, repetitive, and maybe useless, but it's entertaining.

I Love This Place

Our dog, River, is like all labs. She just wants to run, fetch a ball, swim, and then lie down with one of our family members and snuggle when it's all said and done. We know the image of a black lab is a cliché: Martha's Vineyard = The Black Dog. I have never been on a trip anywhere in the world without seeing a Black Dog t-shirt at some point. Most people wearing those shirts don't even know it's associated with a tavern on Martha's Vineyard. An old-school restaurant with wide wooden pine planks for flooring, a working fireplace, and windows that line three sides of the place that look out onto Vineyard Haven Harbor. Winter is the best time of year to take in this piece of Vineyard history. There are no rushing crowds. The smell of simmering fish chowder mixes with the sea air. Plenty of time to gaze out at the sea. The Black Dog's clipper ships, the Shenandoah and Alabama, sitting silent and alone, framed by the tavern's windows, bobbing up and down in the harbor. The place feels comfortable—like a black lab.

River is the embodiment of love. Look into her eyes. There's no judgment, no animosity, and no understanding of evil or trepidation. She only sees goodness and longing for good times ahead. I think she loves her home on Chappy more than we do. What a playground—few dangers. Skunks are really the only critters that spook her, and in the end, River can't wander too far—it's an island. So, it's not worrisome that I have not seen her for two hours since I let her out this morning.

Then a white truck pulls into our driveway. This one-of-a-kind island silliness has its roof sheared off to make it a convertible pick-up. Obviously, with this particular truck, it must be Aaron Weeks. It screams of its owner. "I want a functional truck, and I want a convertible while I'm on vacation at my summer home—so rip the top off that thing." It's good to see Aaron for the first time since last fall, but I'm a little worried. I don't have any work lined up for him at this point and am already feeling overwhelmed with all that's on my crew's plate, and Memorial Weekend is only two weeks away.

"Hey, Rob. Look who I found in the surf in front of our house?" River jumps over Aaron's lap and out of the truck before Aaron can even get the door all the way open. She is wet, with twigs and seaweed plastered to her shiny coat.

"Oh wow, sorry for your pants... and dealing with this monster. Can I get you a towel?"

"Hah, no thanks. I'll live. It's just water. I watched River for a good twenty minutes in the surf in front of our house and was tempted to join her. She was having a ball. But that water has to be fifty degrees. Finally, I called her to the house with a big meat bone from our dinner last night. I've got to say; your dog was conflicted... which was more interesting... the waves or the bone?"

"Well, thanks. I'm glad she gave you a good show." River slides up to me as I say this, using my leg either as a scratching post or a towel or both. Then she gives a big shake between Aaron and me for good measure—we both laugh.

"Anyway, this gave me an excuse to stop by. Can you come over to start a view clearing job at some point? You know the drill. A few trees at a time to increase our view of the ocean. Nothing to alert the building inspector or our neighbors on the conservation land where the trees tend to live."

"Yeah, I get it, Aaron. We can schedule some drive-by cutting over the course of the year. Mostly in the off-season, so prying eyes won't get alarmed—doesn't bother me. You know I'll end up making double as the set-up and dumping of chips always takes time—and billable?"

Aaron's good-natured smile seems to quiver for a second at my deadpan retort, but he recovers quickly. "Yeah, I get that," he says. "It is what it is."

Homeowners constantly want to push the envelope with their land to get a better view or build a more comfortable house—even if it does go against the town bylaws. I take a laissez-faire attitude about the whole situation. But Aaron's situation is a little different. It's not even his land! Good thing I like him.

We shake hands as I stare a little too long at Aaron's big bushy mustache. I love that stache. The combination of this big guy's wavy silver hair, cargo shorts, and that mustache driving around in this absurd truck makes him— one of a kind. Aaron and I talk a little longer about the steamers he just collected in Caleb's Pond and the pilings being put in at the Chappy ferry—small talk. And then we make a plan to meet at his house later in the day. The scene is ultimately broken up when I notice River bounds for our open front door. I need to run her down before she brings half the Atlantic Ocean into our home.

River is very happy to be rubbed down with a towel—such joy. The wag of her tail is infectious and makes me want to just run back outside with her and go exploring. But then I hear the vibrating "Beeeeeep, Buuuurp, Beeeep, Waaaaaa, Peeeep" of the EMT pager in my pocket. The annoying rhythmic sound goes on until finally, a dispatcher announces, "Chappy Fire Department, Chappy EMTs, Edgartown Police Department, Edgartown Rescue, please proceed to 15 Sea Avenue on Chappy for a 20-31." The dispatcher attempts to give directions to the emergency, and then the entire process repeats itself.

I click off the still blaring beeper and phone the com center. Many of the roads on Chappy only exist on a map, and directions are futile. I understand why they don't broadcast people's names over the airwaves, but I need some context. It makes my job harder to get to a scene when they go on and on with directions with roads that just don't exist.

The 911 operator comes on the phone and is all business until I say, "Hello, this is Rob Kagan, EMT on Chappy. Can you tell me whose house the call is for?"

The dispatch operator becomes more congenial and replies, "Hi Rob. The 20-31 is at Doug Fizzer's house. Do you understand that?"

Sure, I know Doug. He's another Chappy volunteer EMT. I wonder why the operator would ask me that? I don't think much of the question or the silly codes they always throw in the page. I never learned them. Why can't they just speak English? I have enough on my plate without buying into these nonsense codes. The simpler it can be for my brain, the better. There's an emergency. I need to grab my jump bag, find out the location, and get there. Simple. The rest is window dressing. I thank the dispatcher and hang up as I rush to the scene.

Doug's house is a ramshackle mess in what is known as the Enos Lots. This area of Chappy was subdivided into small parcels in 1900 to create a vacation bungalow community. The plan never took shape, but the zoning put in place at the time makes it the only place on Chappy with suburban-like streets and a dense group of houses.

I drive over the bumpy roads of the Enos Lots and think of Doug. I don't know much about him, but he shows up at EMT scenes with confidence, a no-nonsense demeanor and joins in wherever he's needed. Physically he doesn't stick out from any of the other older EMTs or firefighters. They all seem to have the same big barrel chest, scruffy beard, and weathered fishing derby hat from years gone by. But Doug's always smiling, always quick with a story of a recent adventure on his motorcycle up-island. Everything he does seems to be in a slow-moving, no rush kind of way. His essence puts me at ease. I think about this as I'm first on the scene. I grab my jump kit out of the back of my truck and run up to the door. I open it up and yell, "Hey, Doug. What's up? You don't feel well?" No answer. I walk right in and continue to call to Doug.

I see the red flashing lights shining in the windows, hear a "Wop, wop," and know an Edgartown Police Cruiser has arrived. They're really on the ball today. Usually, I already have first vitals before the police show up. I make my way to the second floor to what looks like it might be Doug's bedroom. My only thought is this place is a shithole. I try not to judge as I step over some laundry and newspapers on the stairway but can't help it. People are so different when you see them up close. Doug's room is dark and quiet when I enter. I cross over to the windows and open the shades as I don't see any light switches. Suddenly

I stop short as I look out onto the yard and see the group of emergency vehicles on the lawn. There are a lot of vehicles here—more than usual. That's strange.

There's a smell of smoke in the air—definitely not from a woodstove or fireplace. But it's definitely some type of smoky smell. I turn around before my mind catches up with my senses, and there's Doug on his bed. There isn't much of his head intact, but I assume it's Doug. There's a splatter of blood and what I assume is brain all over the wall. A gun is on the floor directly beneath his big, meaty, lifeless hand. I can't look away. I can't comprehend what I'm looking at for the longest time. I don't react. I don't cry. I don't yell. I just drop my bag and walk out of the house.

Outside there's a lot of rushing around. Everyone is talking to me at once, but I can't hear them. My brain is just trying to comprehend what I saw. Why would anyone do that to themselves? What is so terrible that this is the answer he came up with? Peter is helping me sit down and asks me what I saw? He's asking me why I went into the house? He yells and gets my attention. "The call was for a 20-31! Shots fired. Why would you go in the house?" It all slowly sinks in as I put my head in my lap and throw up.

I say to no one in particular what I saw as someone hands me a rag to wipe my mouth. The tone of the scene changes as people file into the house and get to work. I become a patient. My vitals are taken, and after a while, Peter drives me home. Another EMT follows in my truck, so I don't have to come back and get it.

No one is home when we get there, and Peter offers to stay with me.

I tell him, "Don't worry, I'm fine."

I'm not fine. How could I be? But it's the kind of not fine that I'm going to have to work through alone. There's nothing for Peter to do.

He puts his hand on my shoulder and tells me, "I remember my first body." And leaves.

Life is complicated. I get that. But this island should be able to trump all of that. The island vibe—community—nature—beauty everywhere you look. These things should make life here easy. I don't understand. This is Chappy. This is an oasis. I love this place. How could Doug not love living here—not love living? I start a mantra as I sit on the porch, rocking back and forth on my old swing hanging from a rusty chain.

"I love this place. I love this place." I begin to mumble. The words mix with the sound and melodic rhythm of the creaking porch swing as a gentle breeze brings the smell of lilac to me. My senses are rebooting, but I need more.

I need to think of the positive. Doug's choice has rattled me. I need a minute to get back on track. This island life is so wondrous, and I need to remind myself how lucky we are to live here. I see on my phone Julie is calling for the third time today. The first time was about a light bulb in a lamp that went out, and she is having a dinner party tonight. The second call was about the pool cover being wrinkled on its stand. All are emergencies to Julie. All need to be attended to now. But I don't care what this third call is about, and I do the unthinkable by putting the phone into 'Do Not Disturb' mode.

I close my eyes and try and relax. But my body is numb. There's static noise ringing in my head, like a TV that has lost its signal. I fight it all and attempt to concentrate on Melissa and how she calms Ilana at bedtime.

"Squeeze and breathe. Squeeze and breathe—first squeeze your toes and breathe out, then your ankles and thighs and hips, all the way up to your eyelids. Soon, Ilana, you will be drifting off to sleep."

The method works. We live by it as a family to get us back on track, calm us down, and ultimately sleep. Within minutes, I begin to have feeling in my body. I lift my legs off the ground as I get the porch swing going at a good clip and begin my mantra and remind myself of the beauty that surrounds me.

"I love this place." It doesn't matter where I'm standing on this little isle of Chappaquiddick. I can walk down any road, take a random right or left turn, walk a little while, and eventually, I'll come to a clearing. Maybe it's marshland. Maybe it's a hayfield. Eventually, there will be a pond of some sort with a wooden bridge or dock jutting out from it. So old and weathered that I might second guess if I should walk on it. But I have to walk on it. It's part of the journey. It's part of the landscape. I think as I walk, how do the ridges in these boards get so pronounced? How do people avoid stubbing their toes on the rusty nails that have popped up and loose from the slack and weathered wood? Is that a box turtle that just popped its head under the water and left a never-ending ripple of circles expanding slowly outward till they hit the shore? So many questions. Good questions. Ahhhhh, nature—it does a body good.

Without much effort, I once again squeeze my eyes shut, slowly open them, and another memory washes over me. "I love this place." Entrain is the de facto house band for our island. The soundtrack to our soul. What a band. Every Thursday night when Melissa and I were dating, we drove off Chappy to Oak Bluffs to see them at a place called the Atlantic Connection (The AC). It was a scene, and alive, and sweaty, and there were drums. They had two drummers that went off on this world-beat kind of thing. It was exhilarating. At the end of each concert, we fell out into the streets. We would beg for donuts at the back of a bakery, making them for the following day. It became a whole separate thing. It became 'Back Door Donuts'. But that was later. When we went to hear Entrain, it was just begging for donuts.

The porch swing has slowed to a standstill. These images are soothing and wondrous, but I need more time. Doug is still crowding my thoughts and leaving me questioning. It's like when someone tells you to smile. You can't just smile. Or rather, you can, but a muscle reflex doesn't change your thoughts. The mess on the walls, thinking about the patterns Doug's brain formed, and the contrast to the dark paneling on the wall—it's all so distracting from my attempt to right my ship. I need my mantra a little longer. So I push off with my feet once again and think of more stories, more good in the world, more good in my little world. Creak, swoosh, creak, swoosh, creak, swoosh— the rocker does its work of clearing my brain.

"I love this place." The Martha's Vineyard high school football team must travel off-island to compete. It's a big-time constraint for high schoolers. It's a big commitment. Families get that. The town gets that. We're all proud of these athletes' strength and pride for their island. So, it doesn't seem like a big hardship to meet them at the ferry when they return from battle with the fire engines blaring their horns and the townspeople cheering their arrival.

"I love this place." It's Ilana's birthday. What to do? What to do? There's no Chuck E. Cheese on our island. We have to make this stuff up. And I feel like I have to go big or go home. So, we're going to have a fire at our house. Or, more specifically, a non-fire—a soaker. I put on my fireman's gear, which incidentally looks ridiculous on me. I'm

5'4" and a twig. This ten-thousand-pound fire retardant suit, complete with a big ass metal helmet, makes me look like a kid playing dress-up, and it takes all my energy just to walk around in this thing.

Once suited up, I grab the biggest and shiniest fire engine from our fleet of two fire trucks at the Chappy Fire Station and drive it to our house. The lights blazing and horns blaring as I go. Everyone checks out the commotion. There's a quizzical look on most Chappy residents because their police scanners are quiet. Just me playing with a town toy. It's Chappy.

I turn down our road, and the squeal of the old air brakes alerts all to my arrival. The engine bounces to a stop, and the partygoers are on it like flies. Kids try on helmets. Melissa dons a suit off the back of the truck. I stare and wonder how she makes that suit look so cute? I hook up some two-inch hoses and start spraying everything that moves. Lots of screaming. Lots of running. Then, the hose gets wrestled away from me, and I take off running. Needless to say, I got soaked that day. But it was worth it.

Once again, the porch swing comes to a halt, but I don't set it back in motion. I'm certainly not healed. But the weight in my head and the unusual static that has filled my senses has dissipated a little. The world, my world, the green of nature around me is coming back into focus.

I'm certainly thinking clearer now. This is also helping me remember why Doug might have had a harder time with his path in life. Doug's ramshackle house reminds me of his wife's heroin overdose a few winters back. The off-season is so raw and isolating. He must've been lonely. I didn't think much of it when I was at Doug's house, but now I remember the scattered collection of empties everywhere. He certainly has had his share of benevolent taxi rides from people like Detective Arbilt. We all try and help our neighbors, but sometimes it's just not enough.

It takes me a minute to realize the weight on top of my foot is River's head resting on it. How long has she been there? Did she know I needed her? She looks up when I look down. Those eyes are so big. I believe she understands. And then she is off and running. The connection is gone. Melissa and the kids are home.

Melissa bends over and kisses me. "Hi, sweetie. I saw the ambulance leaving Chappy. Everything OK?"

"Sure. I was the first there as always. But then they didn't need me, and I left."

Melissa smiles but in a sad way. She already knows about the suicide and my presence at the scene. I find out later that three people made a point to voice their concern for me as she drove onto the Chappy Ferry. Milly, the ferry captain, cryptically says, "Give Rob a hug for me. He's had a hard day." She can be so quirky and socially awkward. But she means well. Others were more detailed and gossipy with their helpful information. There're no secrets on an island.

Melissa doesn't push me for details. Maybe for her own self-preservation. Maybe she thinks it didn't affect me as a seasoned EMT. It doesn't matter. I sense she knows. I appreciate the space. But on some level, it disturbs me even more. Life is so fragile. Our perspective protects us. I want to believe Doug is just an anomaly.

Melissa breaks the tension by telling me to get up and help with the groceries. As we walk down the porch stairs, we both look over our shoulders at the girls screaming with delight, running with a stick, and River bouncing right behind them.

A smile comes over my face, and I put Doug and the

image of his lifeless body out of my mind—a defense mechanism in place for many years. Deal with the immediate to get through it. And bury the implications and ramifications down deep as if the situation never happened. Life is so much sweeter by concentrating on puppy dogs and children playing.

Back On Track

Back to summer prep. The conversation about Aaron's view clearing job seems like a month ago, but that and five other new jobs on my answering machine need to be looked at. It never occurs to me to say no to a customer. Just hunker down and take more. Erase lines on the schedule and add more items. This is what consumes me—creating a new schedule that makes sense. Makes me feel calm. Makes me feel in control. The control is the drug that pushes me further and puts unhappy things like Doug out of my head. Saying no to more jobs wouldn't give me that feeling.

Schedule, re-work schedule, work, help save the world, smell the beach plums, and if there's time, be there for my family. Rinse and repeat. This is spring on Chappy. It's a good life. It's certainly a full life. And as it gets closer and closer to Memorial Day weekend, the island's pace and vibe gets more frenetic. No one has time to talk. There are frankly not enough hours in the day, but you find them anyway. No one has time to help you as they need help themselves. Summer people are imminent. Get off the road. Grab your loved ones. Hide. Here it comes.

SUMMER

Memorial Day Weekend

It's like a fire hose being turned on. The lines in town at the post office, the traffic on the road, the restaurants that a week earlier had one table filled are now packed to the gills. The big weekends during the summer are like New Year's Eve. The amateurs are on-island and are fucking everything up. These interlopers are coming into our house and touching our stuff. They want to do things their way. This is how it feels to a jaded local population who has seen this scene play out year after year. We had a vibe going all off-season—an island vibe. Now it has changed once again. People come to this wilderness, zoo, refuge to be part of this fragile, beautiful, and funky ecosystem. They want to shed their busy conventional lives to be part of this colorful existence, but it's hard. It takes time. And right now, at the beginning of the summer, there are a lot of bumping elbows as everyone jockeys for position.

"Seriously, you're going to honk your horn because that old man isn't turning fast enough?" Melissa yells at the windshield. I hear this and a lot more since she has me on speakerphone as we attempt to talk through a survival plan for Memorial Day weekend. "I got to go—a space just opened up in the parking lot." And with that, the phone goes dead.

When Melissa and I finally touch base again that evening, she is no less harried. She tells me about the rest of her day, including the trip to Stop and Shop, where they have just jacked the prices up for the summer season. We call it Fort Knox. She tells me it was fun to see people out and talking about their weekend plans but also tiring. By the time she got to the checkout, she just wanted to come home.

But apparently a woman behind her in white capri pants and a striped sailor shirt made the grave error of saying, "Excuse me, we're having a barbecue tomorrow, and I have to meet the tent people, and you know how it is. All I have are these four items. Could I trouble you to let me go ahead of you?"

Well, Melissa isn't a confrontational person. She is pretty level-headed, but according to her own assessment, she completely lost it... In a controlled rage, she retorted, "No. I imagine I have just as many things to do as you do, if not more. Should I list them?" Melissa tapped her index finger to begin the count. "I just went to the doctor with my daughter because last week some stupid summer person had to get to town in a hurry for his coffee and hit her. I had to mail some packages back to Amazon and sat in line for thirty minutes just to hand the postal clerk the pre-stamped boxes. I then waited twenty minutes in traffic to go all of 300 yards to get to this lovely place, and I still have to drop off some clothes at the Boys & Girls Club before I get home to meet my kids—sounds boring—sounds mundane. But it's life, and I'm living it. I know your party seems more important, but it isn't. You can wait an extra five minutes while I purchase my food."

"I wish I had been there," I tell her, but I don't mention that I already heard some of this from Milly as she was letting people off the ferry, and even Jason, the police detective from the bike accident, both of whom expressed how proud they were of Melissa. It's usually August before the locals start turning on the summer people and losing their shit. Melissa is off to a momentous start.

Just the fact that Melissa went off of Chappy the day before Memorial Day weekend makes me shake my head at her. But she doesn't have the luxury of hiding out on the island like I do. Real-world errands make leaving Chappy inevitable and ultimately make her irritable. My crews and I have plenty to do sitting tight on Chappy, which suits us just fine.

My customers have arrived and seem to be settled in their houses by Saturday morning. For many, it's been ten months since they've been on-island. I let out a long sigh of relief and tell my family they have me for the entire weekend. What do they want to do? I'm very excited! I seriously believe this weekend is going to be different from summer's past. This is where I'm delusional. It never works out, and my family never falls for it.

The calls start coming in slow and steady. They always begin the same, "I'm sorry to bother you, Rob, but..." I take them in stride. It's hard for me not to jump when my customers call. Is it my retail background yelling in my subconscious that, 'Customers are king'? Or is it my sense of always wanting approval from an upper class I felt shunned by when I lived in that hoity-toity town with my dad? Probably a little of both. Most times, the calls are dispatched quickly and painlessly. It's as simple as telling my customers something about their house they don't remember, like their Wi-Fi password or where they keep the spare propane tank. In the end, it disrupts my family time, but we're paid well for the disruption, and the bulk of it only lasts twelve weeks a year.

There's a lull in the phone calls, and I re-group with the family about our potential for a good day. I pitch an idea of our first boating adventure of the season that will have a little bit for everyone. I get a big thumbs-up from the crew. Melissa packs a healthy lunch with gluten-free snacks, fruit, goat cheese, crackers, and a peanut butter and jam sandwich for me. I look in on the girls as they pack for the adventure. Ilana has three piles on the ground. One with two water bottles, snacks, and books. Another with pillows and comfortable blankets and a third with changes of clothes, foul weather gear, and multiple towels.

"Sweetheart, I don't think you will need all this stuff," I say in the most non-confrontational and off-handed way I can muster. I try to make a joke of it. "I just saw an Armageddon movie last night. The family had three minutes to grab the essentials before the streets opened up and swallowed their house. Grab your bathing suit, a towel, and we can be on our way."

Sasha rolls her eyes at me, grabs her one bag, and hightails it out of the room as Ilana begins to implode. "I need everything in here. I might need this towel after swimming, and then I need another to lie on. You know I need water and..." This has the makings of a disaster before it even begins. I backtrack. I tell another joke. Ilana isn't hearing it. She begins to cry and kick the wall. Her world is coming apart. This packing was her control. A way to feel OK about changing her weekend routine at the last minute—packing made her world make sense and be manageable. (I'm an idiot and don't get it.)

This is supposed to be fun. I mean, I get her challenges with sensory issues. The control thing that allows her to better deal with the information coming at her in a foreign and garbled manner into her brain. Her control also lulls me into a sense of thinking she has everything organized. Looking at her—I see a regular kid. Then bam, Ilana's world falls apart as I unconsciously rip at her plan that she set in place to feel comfortable in her own skin.

Melissa strides into the room and motions for me to leave. "Hey, kid. I'm here."

"Get away," Ilana yells back as she kicks at her mom, and my heart goes into my stomach. I don't know what makes me feel worse—that I'll not get a fun, simple adventure with my family or that I upended my daughter's world.

"I'm just going to sit here and be with you," Melissa calmly states. I hear her say this a few times, and Ilana's exasperated outbursts become less and less and quieter and quieter. Soon Melissa has her in the kitchen packing food and loading bags in the car like nothing happened.

"Hi, Daddy," Ilana chirps as she runs by me with her bags on either shoulder. The whiplash-like mood change never gets easier for me. I smile and tell her how excited I am for our boating adventure. "Do you have everything?" She asks, and it feels like a trap.

Cautiously, but with as much enthusiasm as I can muster up, I list off my accomplishments. "I've got the life jackets, the inner tube, the keys to the motorboat, and my Tevas. I'm all set."

I see Melissa on the porch as she heads out to the car, hug her, and thank her for once again cleaning up my mess. "Just try harder to understand her and be with her, OK?"

I shake my head and half hear her, but my mind is elsewhere. The water feels close.

I want to get away from home quickly before another

customer calls with a request. Once I'm out on the boat, well then, all bets are off, and it will take a septic tank blowing up all over a lawn to get me back onto shore. So, I grab bags from family members to 'help out' and fishtail a little as we turn out of our dirt driveway. I need to get to the water.

Our little thirteen-foot motorboat is moored fifteen feet off the rocky beach a half-mile from our house. Sometimes we walk there to throw the ball for River, but today, the SUV is needed for all our baggage. There's no parking at this beach, and you usually have to park way up on the hill and walk through a poison ivy-laden path. But a caretaker for the mansion that abuts the beach lets me park under a big old oak tree, which is just twenty-five feet from the entrance. The spot is hidden by a fence and a big group of beach plum bushes. Luckily, no one gets the inclination to steal my shady spot.

Ilana already has our kayak off the wooden cradle that stores all the dinghies and has it at the water's edge. A new fight erupts about who will paddle out with me to get the motorboat on its mooring. Sasha is the little sister, but at times she has enough of tiptoeing around her volatile, older sister and takes a stand. This is not the day for that. In a rare moment of parental competence, I pull a lesson out of my learnings from *Sesame Street* when I was a kid. "Ilana will paddle out with me, and when we bring the boat back—Sasha will get her turn."

Sasha starts to protest, but I give her a pleading glance, and she gives one back that says, "You owe me, big time."

Once the motorboat is onshore and supplies stowed, the girls hook up the line to the inner tube to start the day with some excitement. The girls scream and give the thumbs up to go faster, but as they get bored with mere speed, the pantomime of a lasso being swung gets furiously imitated by both of them. They want the whip! I smile as the salt air whips through my hair, and I bounce up and down with the rhythm of the waves passing beneath us. Melissa has been holding on to me and the railing. She also sees the girls' sign, and her knuckles go white as her grip gets a little tighter, and she holds on for dear life.

I begin to make a slow circle with the boat, and then another and another. This goes on until the waves from the boat's wake start piling upon themselves, higher and higher. All the while, the girls and their blown-up rubber tube exit the outside wake of the boat and are hurtling along at an obscene and unsafe speed. One of two things typically happens at this point. First, the girls can't hang on any longer and slip off the back of the inner tube, and their bodies skip along the surface like a flat pebble thrown from shore. How many times do they skip before they crash below the waves of the harbor? That is the big question.

The other option is they hold on, defy gravity and physics and give me that look. You know that look from your kids. It says, "Bring it on, old man. This is nothing. I know your games, and I can take it." Today I get the look and begin to straighten out the motorboat, so I can get away from my man-made tsunami of circular waves. Then I turn back as quickly as I can and drive the boat directly through it. Ilana then Sasha takes a direct hit by a wave, bounces straight up into the air, and lands with a thwap in the ocean. I sometimes get nervous; I might have taken things too far. Melissa always thinks I have taken it too far, but she knows this is my turf and concentrates on holding on and counting survival on the boat as a victory.

The girls live. They are screaming and slapping the water as their laughs echo in the bay around us. All is good.

I'm not thinking about my customers or their houses. I'm not thinking about EMT calls that bring me up close and personal to the challenges of Chappy life. I'm not thinking about the tantrum that almost derailed this happy moment. I'm not thinking, period. The girls yell, "Again, again." And for twenty minutes until they can hardly breathe anymore from yelling and gasping for air as they inhale saltwater, time stands still. Life is good.

There's a break in the action as the girls are clearly spent. I turn my gaze to the shoreline for a second, and instantly Chappy Unlimited becomes my focus. The houses dotting the horizon are mostly my customers. I squint my eyes and can see the cleaners' car at one house. I take a sigh of relief as I remember Juanita's police problems are finally behind her for the moment. Money, community service, and a promise not to drive again without a license is all it took. But our troubles are just muted and never finished as Juanita continues to drive my car full of immigrant cleaners from job to job. Happy this is Chappy. Good thing the police presence on this little island is nonexistent. Good thing I am present with my family and not thinking about this stuff.

The girls barely have the energy to swim to us. It takes all they have just to grab the guardrail, put one foot on the engine casing above the idled prop, and haul themselves up onto the boat.

"You guys were awesome out there. I'm just glad you have all your limbs. Did anyone get hurt?" Melissa says in a sing-songy voice as she vigorously rubs each of them down with a towel.

Ilana and Sasha talk over each other about the different aspects of the chaos they just lived through. "Did you see me kick off the tube that last go-round and do a crazy backflip into the water?" Ilana screams out way too loud now that the engine is off.

"Crazy is right. I saw your leg fly by my head, and that's the last I saw of you. By the way, I stayed on."

Ilana doesn't hear or understand the jab and continues rapid-fire about the entire excursion. "The whip was intense, and those waves built up so high. Could you guys hear us scream?"

Melissa steps in to calm the situation down and brings it all back to how cool they looked. At the same time, she gives me the look that tells me it's time to move on to the next phase of our afternoon. Lunch.

We head for the barrier beach that protects Edgartown's inner harbor from the unrelenting pounding waves of the Atlantic beyond. I anchor in the shallows, the girls jump off the boat, and run away with no word of bye or anything. I know where they're going. No worries. It's only one hundred yards to the other side of this tiny strip of land, and it's always their first stop to see the raging ocean and the salt spray that whips off the tops of the waves as they make their way toward shore. Five minutes are spent running toward the crashing waves, screaming and retreating, only to do it over and over again. This gives way to exploring the rest of the long stretch of beach for possible friend sightings. Today they find an old schooner ship that has washed ashore and grab me to check it out. It's pretty wild. It's pretty old. Maybe two hundred years old. Only the boat's wooden gunnel is visible above the sand, but it has bronze spikes sticking up that were probably used for tying off lines from the mast. It will be gone tomorrow or the next day, like all the treasures that wash ashore. The pounding of the waves and the violent tides bring treasures to the beach and just as quickly take them away. But it's cool to see history up close and personal. I make up a story about pirates, treasures, and point out where a cannonball had clearly pierced this vessel's side and sent it to a watery grave. The girls run screaming back to Melissa as I get a little too graphic with the sword fight descriptions.

Melissa is lounging in the sun, reading a book, when the girls arrive back from seeing the remnants of the schooner. She somehow gets them to stand still long enough to put some food in their bellies before they're off again. I sit down with Melissa and look at my watch. The activities so far have been fun but are just a prelude to my real reason for today's adventure. I want to get out on our sailboat. It's the one place I'm free—where my mind feels free. The constant attention needed to sail a boat, the wind whipping through the air, and the rhythmic splashing of the waves against the hull occupy my spirit and is cleansing. And for maybe the only time in my life, I feel in control.

I make some excuse about the tides, or maybe it's a straight-out bribe to get the girls back in line with my vision of the day. Anyway, we pack up and shove off from the beach like we've done it a million times. We *have* done it a million times.

The ride to the sailboat is quick, but enough time for the girls to pepper me with questions about my customers and their houses we pass. I point out the putting green we're installing on the waterside of one house, talk about the possibility that Lady Gaga might be the owner of another house, and then my gaze stops on our neighbor's house, Thomas Hawthorne.

He's a very old and wealthy landowner who lives at the end of our road. He's known for buying up land around his house whenever possible to decrease the number of neighbors he has to deal with. He would love to scoop up our house. Thomas was once a friend, bought shirts in my store back in the day... before I opened Chappy Unlimited... before I was deemed working-class and sullied our neighborhood with a lawnmower trailer and other equipment.

The girls point out the rock wall on the sides of his property. They saw him yesterday extending it near our house.

"Yes, I saw him. He was nice enough to mention that the stately grass strip going down the middle of our dirt road can't grow in front of our house because we have so much traffic coming in and out."

Melissa gives me a look—not appropriate. I gun the engine, it gets loud and drowns out the conversation, and in no time, we arrive at Noah's Rejects. The animals' images and the boat's name on the stern, while still funky, are old and faded. What once gave me a sense of joy and nostalgia for my old company where the design came from is replaced with the dread of another chore that needs doing. I need to repaint the image of Noah's Rejects. I shake the thought off as we get busy with our task at hand. It's amazing how efficient we all are on Noah's Rejects. Everyone has their job. Everyone knows what they need to do to get us on our way.

I deal with the mooring lines. Ilana takes off the mainsail cover and stows it below. Melissa gets out more sunscreen and the winch handles for good measure. And Sasha concentrates on getting all of our stuff stowed below. We use the motor usually only to get the sailboat on and off the mooring. Sometimes not even then. It's good practice to sail old school and be ready for those inevitable mechanical emergencies. But not today. Today we use the engine.

This is our first day on the sailboat this season, and besides, I have another surprise in store for the girls later on. At least I think I have another surprise planned. The meltdown earlier in the day gives me pause, but that was so long ago. We'll see.

Ilana keeps the engine throttled down, and the boat pointed into the wind as we move off the mooring, and I raise the mainsail. I take over the helm from Ilana so she can slather some more sunscreen on her shoulders, and I edge the boat off the wind. The sail fills with air, and we're on our way. Crosby, Stills, and Nash becomes audible as I cut the engines. This is the sign for the girls to unfurl the genoa sail, which will give us more speed. It turns out to be a tricky task today as their hands are still slippery from the sunscreen. They deal with it. The genoa billows out and fills with a big thwap.

It takes only one tack to turn up the harbor and slide past the Chappy ferry and toward the outer harbor. The girls strain their arms, waving crazily and yelling at the Chappy ferry captain and deckhand as we go by. The rituals of our summer sails are once again upon us.

I love that the ferry captains are friendly enough to always wave at the girls. They have enough to do and have competing beckoning hand gestures from all the tourists and summer people vying for their attention without worrying about acknowledging my kids. Some captains wave more vigorously than others as their personalities dictate. Milly is definitely one of those old, salty captains that makes a good show of it. She's a natural performer. Gives a quick salute as we glide by. She swings her rutter to starboard at the same time to skirt around us as she makes her way across the harbor. It gets me thinking about the bond between the ferry crew and us. We're in this together, stewarding passengers, tourists, summer people along on their way to enjoying this paradise.

We both have our challenges with our roles. The ferry crew even came up with an inane list of questions they get on a day-to-day basis. I thought it was so funny and sad that I made it into a t-shirt for them. Everyone loved it. The summer homeowners and day-trippers alike all bought one. The captains got a kick out of the irony of that. The list goes as follows:

TOP 10 QUESTIONS ON THE CHAPPY FERRY AND POSSIBLE ANSWERS

Q: Where does the Chappy ferry go?

> **A:** Chappy.

Q: Do you need a reservation?

> **A:** NO.

Q: Where is the town of Chappy?

> **A:** Chappy is not a town. It's part of Edgartown.

Q: How long does this trip take?

> **A:** 2.5 minutes – just look, you can see the other side!

Q: Where is the shopping center?

> **A:** There is a junk car lot that might sell snacks today.

Q: Do you charge for dogs?

> **A:** Next question, please.

Q: Do you serve drinks on the ferry?

> **A:** Drunk people think they are so funny.

Q: What is the schedule for the ferry?

    A: It goes when people get on the ferry.

Q: Where is the bridge that used to be here?

    A: AAARRRGGGH – The Dyke Bridge, which is the only bridge on Chappy, is on Dyke Road.

Q: Where is the Kennedy bridge?

    A: You mean the Dyke Bridge? They don't name a bridge after you when a woman dies in your car.

My mind returns to sailing as the town and ferry become smaller and smaller to our aft, and it's time to tack once again. Trim the sails, adjust my seat cushion, grab a Coke, and I'm in heaven. "Thank you, Dad," I think but never say out loud. In the 1970s, he was a newly minted lawyer with no boating skills, no sense of direction, and no love of nature. But he determined that all the accomplished people in his town had a leisure boat, and so he went out and got one. My brother and I were the hapless guinea pigs that survived squalls, pea soup mists, and engine failures. We eventually racked up enough sea miles to be able to take on any calamity. And we loved it. The bigger the calamity, the more excitement, the more chaos, the better the adventure. I don't think it's a coincidence that our childhood boats were called, 'Chaos', 'Chicken of the Sea', and 'Calamity'. My bravery in the face of chaos and the ability to deal with any emergency our dad could get us into stays with me today. Life skills created out of a sense of insecurity about his place in society. Go figure.

Thoughts of my dad disappear as I hear happy screaming. The girls are running around the boat like it's a gymnasium. Opening hatches, climbing through them, and perching themselves on the bow spreader like they are characters in the movie *Titanic*. Not that they have ever seen it. I think it's just an instinctual thing to spread your arms and feel the sensation of flying as your legs are curled safely around the metal railings that surround the bow of a boat. I'm very loose with discipline on board. Partly because of my upbringing and partly because of that mantra I often repeat. "That which doesn't kill you makes you stronger."

I think of this mantra as Ilana runs behind me and almost slips off the boat's stern. Time for my surprise. I slowly take my phone out of my pocket along with my wallet and hand them to Melissa. She knows something's up. She isn't always happy with my shenanigans but knows the boat is my domain and silently sits back and waits for the mayhem. The sails are full, and we're going along at a nice clip, but not too fast. I see the girls emerge from the hatch above the v-berth and begin to make their way toward me. They walk as if they are on dry land with balance that only comes after years of boating. I smile at them, they smile at me, and then I pitch myself off the stern of the boat.

I hear screaming as I surface on the water and watch the boat moving away from me. I resist the urge to call out directions to the girls and watch with great pride as Ilana drops all the sails, all the while yelling at me, "Are you kidding me? Are you kidding me?" She barks orders at Melissa and Sasha. "Mommy, go below and put the batteries on 'ALL' and then start the engines. Sasha. Sasha! Throw anything that floats at Daddy as we come back toward him. Tie a line around that seat cushion if you can." Ilana, a twelve-year-old, mind you, could do this all by herself but controlling others, I think, helps her feel in control of the situation. Sasha fumbles with the knot on the line to the cushion, and Ilana grabs it to tie it herself. Sasha switches gears and goes down below to grab the long hook in case I need to be pulled closer to the boat during the 'rescue'. The Keystone Cops comes to mind as I watch the action unfold, but my family is actually rising to the challenge.

The sails are down, the engine on, and everyone is in the cockpit steaming mad as Ilana turns the boat around to come collect me. I don't think it's even in her database to consider running me over. The job is to save Dad, and she is going to do it. She has a plan. She's got this. There's no time for emotional thoughts. Although, I don't believe the other two mates would have any compunction sailing right by me and back to port. But Ilana is the one in charge, and she expertly idles the engine and puts it in neutral as Sasha begins pummeling everything that floats at my head. Good thing she's a lousy shot.

The whole time there's plenty of screaming still going on. I try not to laugh as I collect the floating debris and make my way to the ladder clamped to the boat's stern. My crew refuses to fetch me a towel as I land on the deck. I deserve that. I stand freezing as the seawater and random pieces of seaweed drip off my body. I thank them for saving me. "I must have slipped," I say. No one's buying it, and everyone's mad at me. But I still tell them how proud of them I am, and we continue on our sailing ways.

It's been a good day. I don't say this out loud for fear of jinxing it, and instead, just smile. But the smile quickly goes away because as I'm drying off, I spy my phone. It appears to have a gazillion messages on it. I assume from customers that need hands-on help—yesterday—no doubt. I resist the urge. I've been resisting the urge all day. I'm so proud of myself for resisting that urge. I don't want to pick up the phone. It's only going to ruin my day—this perfect day. I'm present. Melissa gives me a wary look. I return the look with an I'm sorry look and pick up the phone. Message after message is about something I could fix if I were not on this boat. The sound of disappointment from my customers, real or imagined, pulls at my sense of commitment.

Ilana is calling my name, but I don't hear her. She has independently decided that our sailing adventure is over for the day and is heading Noah's Rejects into port. Good call. But the wind is coming right at us, and she needs help tacking into the wind so we can get past the Chappy ferry and into the harbor. Finally, she resorts to yelling, "Dad, Dad, Dad!"

Melissa irritably calls out her tired refrain. "Don't you hear your daughter calling your name?"

I shamefully answer, "No," and throw the phone down in the corner and take over the helm from Ilana.

We expertly tack back and forth in the quieted wind of the harbor and slip past the Chappy ferry. The girls get their much sought-after wave from the captain once again, and all is good in the world. We then turn a corner and go down harbor for the last leg of our journey. This final tack signals to everyone it's clean-up time. Bags need to be packed, cushions stowed, food put away, hatches shut and latched, etc., etc. Family members scoot by each other with a sense of purpose, and like a well-oiled machine, we're moored, everything stored away, and the skiff loaded for our journey home.

In no time we are on the dirt road back to our house. We are all exhausted—a fun exhaustion. Melissa announces that her plan is to chill out and watch the last four innings of the Sox game. The thought of melting into our couch with maybe a bowl of popcorn and a glass of lemonade in our lap's whirls in my brain. I look around for reactions. Ilana is all smiles. Sasha doesn't react. She seems to be sacked out in Melissa's lap as we bounce along on the bumpy road. An abrupt and deep pothole puts an end to her short-lived nap. Now awake, she takes great effort to lift her limp and tired arm to turn up the car radio volume as Bob Marley begins to play. It seems to rejuvenate her, if only for a few moments. "Reggae, Baby," she lethargically yells. It's sweet to see her mimic one of my favorite expressions. We all start singing, "One love. One heart. Let's get together and feel alright." We're home before the song even gets past the first verse.

First World Problems

Settling in on the couch after half-heartedly putting away supplies from our boating adventure, Melissa and Ilana yell to me, "You're missing it!" Sasha looks away from the TV in disgust and slinks off to her bed with an iPad and a Disney movie. She never got the sports bug and gladly proclaims, "I would rather watch paint dry than watch a Red Sox game."

Where did I go wrong?

I hear Ilana yell and the cheers from the crowd in the background, but I'm stuck in my office returning calls I have been putting off all day. Most people offer apologetic pleas for forgiveness for bothering me on Memorial Day weekend. That doesn't stop them from calling. They still want help. I talk most of them down off their own personal ledge. Tell them how to work the gadgets in their own house or promise to meet with them the following morning—Sunday morning. I'm well aware of the day. The customers are too. They would still appreciate it if I could stop over. I'll stop over.

I already leave the family Sunday mornings for the firefighter weekly volunteer roll call and bull session at the Chappy Fire Station. I'll have plenty of time before then to stop by some houses and still make it back home for more family time. At least, this is what I always tell myself. Two customers feel they can't wait until Sunday, so I run past Melissa on the way out and tell her I'll be back in a few minutes. Melissa pulls the blanket tightly around her and Ilana as Big Papi hits a slammer to center field. I hear them both scream as their hands slap in what I assume is a big high five.

I listen to the game on the radio as I drive to my first customer's house. I need to make things right. Not having a house in perfect order for a customer's arrival gets to me. The Red Sox end the inning with another two runs on the board as I pull up to the Jones's house. I park my old yellow Jeep Wrangler next to their shiny blue Range Rover. The difference in cars says it all. But I love that old Jeep, especially since summer is here, and the top and doors are off. It's impossible not to have a good time in a stripped-down Wrangler.

I knock and walk into the house. I rarely wait until a customer comes to the door. I feel a sense of entitlement with the houses under my care. I definitely spend more time in them than their owners and have grown to feel like the house is mine as much as it's my customer's. I know the place inside and out, what it needs, and what makes it happy. Today, even though the house might be happy, Mrs. Jones is not. I ask about the weekend and the family running around the backyard. Mrs. Jones asks about my family, also. Lots of pleasantries while we're making our way toward the basement and the 'problem'. Mrs. Jones stops mid-sentence about how pleased she was to see the picture of my daughters horseback riding that accompanied my last bill as she points to the huge puddle of water on the basement floor; it's touching cardboard boxes and cans of paint. I turn off the water pump to the entire house and move the boxes away from the puddle as I tell her how sorry I am about the situation. All the time thinking to myself, "Why didn't they do this before I got here?" I get the sense these customers believe I'm the dog that needs his nose rubbed in the poop that has ruined the living room carpet. What do I care? It makes them feel better.

This situation, which barely registers a two on the shit-storm meter, could have been avoided. It will be avoided in the future with new procedures, but it was no one's fault. You see, the plumber turned the water on in the house for the season just a few days earlier. I know because I was with him. I dropped off my cleaning crew, who immediately got to work, scrubbing mold off the walls that had built up over the winter. I even checked the entire house one last time while the plumber and cleaners were doing their jobs. All good. All manageable. I left with the plumber to go to another house because we had seven houses to turn on that day. I trusted my cleaning crew after fifteen years to make sure the house was in tip-top shape for the Jones's arrival. Everything inside and outside was on track to be perfect. One of my other crews, the landscapers, was due to touch up the lawn and beds the next day. I had the same confidence in them.

My crews didn't let me down. So, what happened? It turns out the water line to the fridge got tweaked when the plumber reconnected it and pushed the fridge back into place. The bad connection only produced a slight drip, but over the course of a few days, that little drip became a big mess. It doesn't take much. I'm happy the basement below the kitchen is unfinished, or this situation could've been a whole lot worse. I modify the water line's connection so the plumber doesn't have to come back out to the house. The

Jones's thank me, but they're still mad at the plumber. They intend to fire him and not pay the plumbing bill. I talk them down off that ledge. I explain that no plumbers on the island are taking new clients. It was a miracle I got them 'The Plumber of Last Resort' when they bought their house a few years back. Seriously, that's what is printed on the plumber's bills right at the top after his name. I talk about checking their house right after the plumber is done with his work in the future. This should never happen again. I also point out that I'll not be charging them for this visit, mopping up the puddle, or carrying the cardboard boxes upstairs to their porch for airing out. I don't mind. I play the long game, and usually, my going the extra mile ends up creating new business and new projects from my grateful customers. I still can't get over the fact that no one thought to turn off the water or move the boxes that the puddle was encroaching on. God forbid the croquet game on the back lawn gets interrupted for thirty seconds. The game reminds me I have a family to get back to. After a rushed wave goodbye to Mrs. Jones, I'm on my way.

The only other customer I need to visit this weekend has a car with some sort of problem. Again, I'll learn another lesson today to never forget. A big part of my business is the accumulation of random facts about the unlikely but possible things that can befall a property when left unattended. I ran my business for fifteen years with over one thousand water turn-ons and never once had a refrigerator line leak after being pushed back in place, until now.

Next random fact to learn—why the McCarthys' car has no lights. The car was safely stored in their beach house garage all winter long. A few weeks ago, I tried to charge the car battery, but it wouldn't take a charge. No problem.

Many times, we find the battery has frozen over the winter from non-use and needs replacing. So, we replace it and test to make sure the car starts. I'm anxious to find out where I went wrong.

Again, there's a lot of hugging and talking about families when I first arrive. I'm offered lemonade and some cookies. They don't want to be rude before they rip my head off. But I need to get back to my family, and the Red Sox, who I see on my phone, are losing 4-6 in the eighth inning. What the hell, Kimbrel?

I move the conversation along and purposely point out the great things we did over the winter and the problems we headed off before their arrival. The dead pines killed by many winter storms are nowhere in sight. The Armenian flag, Edgartown Yacht Club flag, and US flag are all flying high, and none of them is intertwined with the others. This is a feat unto itself. Lastly, the pool is crystal clear even though the well water was copper-colored last month. It didn't clear up until last week when I bought the water filtration company owner a beer at a preschool fundraiser then begged him to come to Chappy.

I felt really proud of myself. Thought I would get a pat on the back for all of our good work. I was wrong. The issue—the car started and drove fine when I tested it a few days ago. However, I didn't do a full ten-point inspection.

Yet this is what the McCarthy's thought I should have done. The problem isn't that the car doesn't start. The problem is that the lights didn't work last night when they drove back from their dinner in town. "All the lights were out! Not just one. What did you do to our car over the winter, Rob?" They ask.

I have no idea. I'm not a mechanic. It's amazing how fast these people can go from hugging me to not understanding why I let them down. I rarely take it personally.

On a more philosophical note, I believe from experience that most customer tantrums have nothing to do with me. Did they fight with their child the day before? Did they lose money in the market last week? Is their company being investigated for malfeasance? More often than not, the reason for their reprimand is overstated because of some other life crisis, and I just happen to be in the crosshairs.

I know I'm working hard for the McCarthys, and so do they. I have been on the payroll for eight years now at an average billing rate of $3,000 a month. There's no other alternative for my level of services on Chappy. It's Good to Be the King plays over and over in my head.

I attempt to look professional and open up the hood of the car. Fortunately, or unfortunately, I spot the problem immediately. Mice. They gnawed on the wires of the lights where they came out of the fuse box. My guys should have caught this, and I should've told them to inspect the car more closely when they replaced the battery. I learn so many lessons in my travels as a resort caretaker. I just hate it when it's in front of a customer.

The McCarthys, upon learning this new information, revert to sweetness and pleasantries. They thank me for stopping over and tell me to go home as they will call the exterminator next. I shake my head as I pull out of the driveway, give the exterminator a heads up in a text, and rush home to catch the rest of the game. Again, I make a note to make sure exterminators put mouse poison in all cars left on Chappy over the winter and do a full inspection of them the following spring. Hey, I get to master another skill—auto mechanic trouble-shooter.

Melissa and Ilana don't even look up as I enter the house. I don't try to explain why I have been gone for an hour. What's the use? Same old, same old. I should take solace in the fact that out of one hundred customers, only two needed hand-holding this weekend. I grab a Coke, some chips, and watch half an inning before I fall asleep on the couch.

A 'Real' Fire

I don't know if it's been ten minutes or ten hours, but Melissa is shaking me awake as Sasha runs toward me with my beeper blaring off its telltale set of beeps. I must have been exhausted because I usually jump when that thing goes off—even if it's the middle of the night. The particular pattern of beeps, I believe, tells me the message is for a house fire. I have been 'on the force' for sixteen years, and I finally get to fight a fire—a real fire. Not one we start in a car wreck brought over to Chappy on a flatbed from the big island. Not a house about to be demolished to make way for a mega-mansion. But a real fire in a real house—a dwelling with belongings in it that people cherish, near other structures that need protection. This is what I trained for—my adrenaline is pumping.

I'm one of the first at the scene and set up my EMT jump kit away from the action as Engine 460 rolls up. I run over, grab my bag out of the back of the engine, and don my firefighting gear. I feel as ridiculous as ever in this oversized, heavy costume. But you got to be safe, right? I look around, and no one is laughing at me, so I put my insecurities aside. The Chappy Fire Department is on scene and on task. Two guys on traffic, four guys getting the hoses in place and coupled up to the pumper truck. Even Lyle Hollander is on the scene, and I begrudgingly admire his knowledge of the firetruck apparatus.

Lyle tests the pressure in the lines. No pressure. I sigh as we know we're the poor stepchildren of Edgartown, and our old engine doesn't get the love it deserves. Lyle tries to get pressure again. It takes a few minutes, but he succeeds. Yay for the old engine! Yay for Lyle—for once. Everything begins to flow, just like a drill. It's kind of exciting. Finally, I'm in position. I'm actually fighting a fire. I'm on the nozzle with another volunteer, who is younger and stronger, behind me—steadying the hose. This big 3″ hose has a flow rate of 250 GPM (gallons per minute) and is hard to handle. It's a lot of water!

Spray to the right. Spray to the left. The fire heats up, and I adjust the spray. Seems like I'm really knocking down this fire and fast. I'm proud of myself. Peter comes my way. I can see him out of the corner of my eye. He was talking with the homeowner, who happens to be one of my customers, and other chiefs from Edgartown. I'm ready for a good pat on my back, but then he's in my ear and yelling at me to slow down. Contain the area, and don't concentrate so much on the structure.

Huh?

Peter explains as he sees the crestfallen look on my face. "The house is a goner. It's a total loss. It became one within minutes of the outbreak. The more we put the fire out at this point just means more expense to cart the debris away to the dump."

I was so proud of myself. We train and rehearse scenarios week after week at the fire station. Is it weird to say I have been looking forward to helping someone in such a primal way where teamwork and courage wipe away all the bullshit of life? Now I learn that it all comes down to money. I get it, though I'd never thought of a fire that way.

I feel like Steve Martin's character in *The Jerk* when he finally realizes his job's true cynical nature at the carny 'Guess Your Weight' booth. His bosses don't care if he can't guess a carnival goer's weight. The prizes are worth less than the price of the attraction.

A lightbulb goes off when his bosses let him in on the scam. "It's a profit deal. Takes the pressure off... Get your weight guessed... take a chance and win some crap."

Now I, too, know why I'm here and can look at the situation in a new light. This summer house is dispensable and replaceable. It's relatively new, rarely used, and looks to have been furnished with Restoration Hardware and Pottery Barn furniture. There's none of the emotional baggage of a family home used for countless years. There are no door frames with children's height stenciled on them. The walls are not adorned with artwork and ribbons of honor from the local agricultural fair. There probably hasn't even been enough time to accumulate a bookcase of old weathered books read and reread as the homeowners sit and look out at their beautiful view of the harbor. I have a new swagger in my spraying. I shut off my brain that thought I was making a difference in someone's life. I have more fun with the situation. It's fun playing fireman... for the day. 'No pressure'.

My family has me recount the fire story over and over when I get home. I promise to show them the black stained earth scene first thing the following morning. But it's been a long day, and all I can think about now is sleep. I'm so exhausted that I'm lucky to make it to the station for the 10:00 a.m. roll call the next morning, where there's a swirl of activity already in progress. Lots of back-slapping, a little washing of our truck, and for the guys that actually know what they are doing, fixing the equipment that didn't perform up to snuff at the fire.

I stick to wiping the mud off the front bumper and talking to the coms center on the radio. Rich O'Brien sees me doing the weekly engine check on Engine 460 and comes over to talk. Well, it starts with his bear hug and then talk. I think back to our interaction at the potluck and make a note to stick around long enough to get to know him a little better. Give him a chance. He's so eager to please and make a connection. For some reason, I feel like a snob snubbing Rich's desire to connect with me, and I don't like it.

"So Rob, when are we going to get together and go crazy," Rich blurts out as he lets go of me.

I tell him about my days. Talk about the responsibilities of my business and family life. "You know how it is with kids, Rich. I need to make time for them at the end of the day. I fail miserably at it but still try. How are you able to fit it all in?"

"Well, you know, Rob. Gabe and Neal had the fishing gear all lined up on the porch and worms dug from the backyard when I got home from working at the high school the other day. When I leave that janitorial job each day, it's just family, family, family. Missy," that's his wife, "is the same. She has a picnic basket all set each weekend so we can go to the jetties or some other beach to have fun. But I want to cut loose with you. You are like the mayor of Chappy."

It turns out Rich is just another guy trying to connect. Trying to be a part of something bigger. Our talk turns to his troubles with housing and never having enough money to live on Chappy the way he wants. And then there's his son, Gabe. He's on the spectrum and having difficulty staying in the public elementary school. Rich doesn't go into detail about this, but I know it all the same. Sounds like he has a lot on his plate. Young guy, cute family, no money, no permanent housing, and me pushing him away when he clearly wants to be my friend.

I feel bad. So, I decide to throw him a lifeline. "Rich, why don't you moonlight working with my company to make some extra money. I'm sure it could help put some savings in the bank for a future house on Chappy." Another bear hug comes my way and a lot of thank-yous. It's kind of embarrassing. All the other guys look our way.

Rich immediately runs around and tells everyone the news. "Rob and I are going to take on the world. Me and him together. Bam. We are an unstoppable team." There's that enthusiasm again. I tamp down the urge to tell him that Chappy Unlimited has already grown as big as it needs to be. I make enough money. I just need more bodies!

Lyle comes up to me with a smirk. "Finally found someone your own size to play with. Good for you."

I don't want to bite at his remark but can't resist getting my own jab in. "Thanks. It will be refreshing to work with someone who shows up on time and doesn't wander off for four-hour coffee breaks." He's rattled me, gotten under my skin once again, and it pisses me off. I slunk off before our words escalate. This is still a very small island, and I need to deal with Lyle from time to time for business.

After the fire meeting, I run to the ten customers' houses I intended to visit earlier in the morning to assure them we're on the job and their small problems (which we agree at the moment are huge) will be addressed after the weekend. New lightbulbs for the Sniders. Cut the grass shorter at the Cohens'. Don't cut the grass so short at the Millers'. Mrs. Skoler tells me to disregard Mr. Skoler's instructions to skip cleaning the kitchen cabinets each week—and clean them. The list goes on and on and on.

The rest of Sunday is a blur of non-activity, which is nice, but then Monday morning of the holiday weekend arrives, and I am antsy. No family projects on the agenda and no work to do—time for a bike ride with River. I run into Peter Wells on the way out the door. Melissa has been waiting for him since the crack of dawn. They're starting their plans to tackle the bike path situation on Chappy. Melissa has every state and local statute about bike paths laid out on our dining room table in neat stacks. There are also color-coded files and folders on accidents. It's safe to say Melissa is ready, motivated, and eager to help make Chappy safer.

Peter lumbers into the dining room with his weathered satchel that contains information of another type. At one point, he was a surveyor, and the bike path as a project excites him on two fronts. The people of Chappy's safety is always on his mind, and getting back in the saddle again as a land investigator feels like coming home. Peter lays out pictures of the entire island on the floor—there's not enough room on the table. The pieced-together puzzle picture of Chappy in eight-and-a-half by eleven sheets of paper takes up a third of the dining room when all is said and done.

At one point, Sasha slides through the menagerie, and papers go swirling. "Sorry," she says as she backs up and giggles all at the same time. Ilana peeks her head around the corner five seconds later. She must have gotten the low-down from Sasha and has to see for herself what's up.

Peter stops his re-puzzling of the floor long enough to give Ilana a high five, and then she is off like a rocket. Dance party in the playroom trumps paperwork in the dining room any day of the week.

Sweat and dirt are dripping off my legs as I walk in the door with River panting behind me. It was a good ride. The sight of Peter coming out of the bathroom startles me as I forgot he was at our house. "Come see what we're up to," he says as he grabs my arm with his big mitt of a hand.

The sight of all these papers in the dining room is daunting. The task before this gang of two is overwhelming. But unfortunately, all I see is one customer's property abutting another's throughout the papers on the floor. Driving the back roads of Chappy, even I forget how connected all these properties are. My business seems bigger and more complicated as I see the scope of it all on this room size map. So many neighbors with so many interconnected issues. How many of them will I lose as they begin to talk and feel threatened by my wife's plans? I put this thought out of my mind and blurt out, "Wow! You guys have done a lot of work. What am I looking at?"

Melissa goes through the setback regulations the town has set in place. Points out the green lines on the pictures where there's room to put in a bike path and a red line where the road has to be moved so one can be put in place. Seeing the efficiency and thought that went into the work so far, I smile. It's been thirteen years since Melissa was in the corporate world, but she's still as organized as ever.

Melissa eyes their work so far and frowns. "Why do we need to go through this charade? Every roadblock put in the way of this project in the past is stupid and blatantly self-serving."

"I don't disagree," Peter says. "But to win this game, we

need to play the game. And we need to play it better than anyone has played before."

"I think things have changed," I declare with conviction. "There are so many more year-round working families with biking age kids than the last time this issue came up. We can make the summer people see how important this is to their workers' families' safety. The loud minority in this fight is mostly comprised of the old guard of Chappy summer residents. They remember how Chappy has been since the '40s or '50s. But there are many new homeowners. Probably over a hundred since the last time this issue came up. Nouveau riche that expect certain amenities at their summer homes. They all have kids riding their bikes to town for ice cream or out to the beach. They'll want this." I repeat in my head, they'll want this, all the while secretly unsure of myself and half believing the acronym NIMBY will rule the day.

The rest of the day is spent reversing course and thinking about getting back into our family routine. Memorial Day weekend is a head fake to the summer. You think it's the start of craziness but come Monday afternoon, the only craziness left is at the ferry in Vineyard Haven, where the lines to get off our island are endless. The next three weeks will be quiet, with most summer families' children still in school. It's not until about June 20th that the frenetic energy of the off-islanders settles in for the duration of the summer. So we wait, but not calmly and not without purpose. The island is in overdrive. This test weekend only shines a spotlight on how much everyone has to get done before the season really starts. The real chaos begins now.

Workers, Help!

It's only been a few weeks since Memorial Weekend, but I'm already overwhelmed with the pace of summer. I head to the Chappy ferry after getting my kids off to school and my crews off to their appointed rounds. The crews are going to be busy putting out the fires our customers lit over the weekend. This is on top of all the regular chores already on our agenda.

The seven-day work week has officially begun. And that's why I'm heading to the ferry. Today I have fifteen interviews set up for new employee hires. My lead workers for each division have been with me for years, but I still need many new bodies each summer, especially since I lost Lorna on the cleaning crew to ICE.

We're busy all year round, but there's busy, and then there's Vineyard-summer busy. Usually, I advertise in the paper and put a notice at the Chamber of Commerce, but lately, most of my hires have been coming from a Facebook group dedicated to island jobs. I arrive at the ferry upbeat and excited to get some extra help—conveniently forgetting my experiences from years past. The reality of who shows up for job interviews, if they show up at all, infuriates me. Don't these people want to work?

I take the ferry to the Edgartown side and place myself on a bench overlooking the harbor. My dad drives up on his moped as I'm waiting for the first interview. "Hi, Dad. How's your day going?" I say with genuine pleasure to see him. I was not expecting this encounter. I never really expect to see him, but then there he is, in my presence, in my life.

He's always popping up around the island. Jerry sightings are common and a tracking hobby of our family friends. It takes him a few minutes to get himself off his beast of a moped and put it on the kickstand. It's a big fancy one, and he's very proud of it. He's also proud that he manages it himself—hence the reason I don't jump up and steady it on the kickstand for him. It's all tricked out with every accessory you can buy for this model. Maybe just a few too many accessories. His breath is labored and shallow as he moves his body around to lift the moped onto its resting place. My dad is getting old. He shuffles over with his Velcro sneakers, never lifting off the pavement. It has become a telltale sign that Jerry is around. You always hear the shuffle before you see the man.

Looking at him, I realize I take my dad for granted sometimes. Always around. Always there to help. The shuffling gets louder as he is right in front of me and rouses me out of my thoughts. "Hey, Robbie, what are you doing in town?" He calls me Robbie. Everyone pre-college calls me Robbie.

"I'm off Chappy to hire more help. Everyone is over-worked, and I hope I can get some reliable employees this year."

Dad proclaims a little too loudly, "The Jamaicans are lazy, the local kids couldn't be bothered to get a job, and everyone else is a drug addict. When I was young, I had three jobs. One delivering papers in the morning, one with the town roads department, and one serving ice cream from a Ding Dong truck. Now everything is handed to everyone. No one wants to work hard or get their hands dirty."

"Dad! Those are stereotypes. You know that."

His diatribe makes me self-conscious, and I look around to make sure no one's listening. I try to curb his language and show him how people are people. The struggles they go through today. Definitely different than the past but still valid. It almost worked when he lived in St. John for a minute. He lived and broke bread with people outside of his comfort zone. But then a Molotov cocktail was thrown at his home in the middle of the night. It wasn't racially motivated. It was about a parking space. But that didn't matter—West Indians on one side of the issue and white ex-pats on the other. He has many stories that describe the same outcome. These sad stories most undoubtedly had many nuances and shades of gray. But to Jerry, they were black and white situations, and he, at some point, gave up seeing the nuances.

I safely bring the conversation back around to his presence in Edgartown at this moment in time. "What brings you to Edgartown?"

"Oh, I was at the docks in Oak Bluffs and saw the Patriot ferry come in. I got to talking with a deckhand who I am helping with a legal matter when I saw a package being unloaded for Soft as a Grape. I know the store owner is short-handed, so I just put it on my moped and am going to drop it off to him."

I nod my head, remembering my days working in our t-shirt shop. "I'm sure he will appreciate it."

"Anyway, got to go. Say hello to the girls."

Our conversation is short. Short questions. Looking for short answers.

As he shuffles away with the box under his arm, he turns back and brings it all back home by saying, "Really, Robbie. Sidestep those problems with ICE and just hire Americans."

And then he's off. I always want to handcuff him to a stationary object when I see him. Just so I can get a little more time with him. Understand him a little better. Sitting with him is like seeing a caricature of a jaded man from the depression. There's so much of that angry onion to peel away and discover. And at the same time, there's a kindness in him and a desire to help others that I can't explain. But because it's my dad, it's that much more difficult to question and challenge. I want to understand and push away the hatred and keep the kindness, thus doing the same for myself.

But Jerry likes snippets. He wants to tell a story, be entertaining, help a stranger, and then be off before he actually has to be authentic with anyone. He's loved by so many because he swoops in, is charming and engaging, and then gone. I think the interlude today was all of five minutes. That's about right—five minutes of Jerry.

I look back at my list of potential workers as my dad rides off. I sit, my pad of paper in hand. My list of candidates all written out with their promised skills next to their names. And unfortunately, 9:00 a.m. passes as the first candidate, Susie, is a no-show. I call the number the potential future rock star for my cleaning division gave me. The woman answering the phone is groggy and sounds a little hungover. I'm still optimistic. This can't be the woman I talked to just four days earlier with the sing-songy voice, impeccable credentials, and a wish to work year-round for me. But it is.

Susie grunts, "I guess I don't get the job, right?"

I hang up without answering, slump down into the bench, and console myself that at least I have a good view of the harbor while I waste my day. The second applicant spits tobacco as we talk. One woman comes with her boyfriend as she doesn't speak any English. She looks like she'll cry if I look her directly in the eye. Two brothers didn't understand this was an interview and walk off when they're not going on a job immediately. A veteran can't lift anything on the job or work long hours because she was run over by an armored vehicle when she was on military duty in Afghanistan. Oh, and she can't pay taxes because it would mess up her disability. I thank her for her service and tell her I'll call the next day.

Time passes. Some hold it together long enough to get through an interview, and I'll take a chance on them, but my hopes are not high. My best candidates are the ones new to the island, and I usually hire them on the spot before someone else snatches them up. Most of the ones I don't hire have been on-island for years, jumping from job to job as they burn one bridge after another. Maybe getting married a third time, like many islanders do, and having a fifth child isn't the best move, right? Americans, locals, or Islander—whatever you call them... they got some baggage.

I walk away from an exhausting day with four new employees. I needed twelve. I jump on the Chappy ferry, barely looking up from the chicken scratch of notes about my new hires. No looking at the lighthouse to my left or seagulls circling the Memorial Wharf to my right. Just tired and bummed things didn't go better. I take a seat at the far end of the ferry. The rumbling of the diesel engine barely clears my head. All I can think of is how much worse it would've been if I'd actually made the prospective employees come to Chappy for interviews. Then I would have zero new hires. It's only as I'm getting off on the Chappy side that I remember to say hi to Milly as she is waving cars off the ferry. She smiles but barely waves back. She's got a forty-five-minute cue for the ferry stacked up on either side of the harbor. So much to do. So little time.

My only thought is to speed home and email my new hires. I want them starting tomorrow. But then I see my cleaning and landscaping crews' vehicles at a house near the ferry. The owners are big on parties and not so big on tidying up. I'm sure the cleaning crew has plenty to contend with. So, I stop to check it out. Walk into a mountain of maybe twenty or so towels at the entrance to the mudroom. I shake my head and walk on, looking for Juanita. I find her furiously cleaning the oven while simultaneously motioning some of the other girls to move the laundry along in halting Portuguese.

I blurt out that I have hired some new cleaners to help the crew out, and she stops cold in her tracks. Juanita doesn't like anyone working on her crew who she doesn't pick from her friends at the Brazilian church that encompasses her life outside of Chappy Unlimited. "Non-Brazilians are too slow. They don't work hard and talky, talky, talky, all day long." This is the reprimand I get from Juanita each year when I try to hire new employees for my own company. It's true that Juanita is possibly the best cleaning person I have ever known. She is one-of-a-kind, and expecting new hires to work as she does isn't possible.

"Juanita, please give these women time to learn to clean. You've been doing it your entire life. The women from your church have been doing it their entire lives. I need some employees who are legal and pay taxes."

"Fine," she says. "We'll see."

I know this tone. Juanita is so passive-aggressive it's scary. I have wanted to fire her many times. Did it once, but it only lasted a week. The rub of it is that customers love her, wouldn't have any other crew in their house. They claim they'd fire me if Juanita were not on my staff. That's a lot of power for one little five-foot woman to wield on this little rock off of a rock. But I still try each year to hire some new blood—some legal blood.

I still have hope. But within days of a new person starting, Juanita is already grabbing rags out of their hands to show them how to do it right—how to do it faster. American women just don't want to put up with that shit. No job is worth working at breakneck speeds, sweat pouring down your face, and being yelled at that the toilet you just cleaned isn't clean enough.

I implore Juanita to ease up. Flattery is a useful tool, and it usually buys me a few more days. "Not everyone can clean like you. You're the best. It takes time." But Juanita will still only give them a week at most and let them go without even telling me. The first I'll hear about it is the following day when a new Brazilian is working in place of the nice American co-ed who was trying her hardest but just had not spent her entire life picking up after others.

Juanita has no tact, but she has mad skills, and I'm stuck with her. The drama, the crying, and the constant employee turnover on the cleaning crew kills me. I have calculated many times how much money I'm making off their backs, what other service business I would lose if I got rid of the cleaning crew, and in the end, I need to suck it up and breathe.

There's a lot less drama with the landscaping crew. Or let's say there's less crying on the landscaping crew when there are fights, so I can fix the problems more quickly. I tell Kyle and Santiago, who have been a reliable team of ten years, and Jonah, who's just recently been hired, about the new employees when I come back outside.

Santiago shrugs his shoulders, and Kyle responds, "Whatever."

Jonah stays quiet as I think he senses the jury is still out on him and his staying power.

They appreciate the extra help but also know the odds of a new employee working out. They hate wasting time training new help only to have them not put in any effort, come to work stoned, or not show up at all—predictable behavior in the land of misfits and underachievers. I guess the real difference is that the new landscaping hires fail themselves by not living up to their potential versus the new cleaning hires who never get the chance to succeed.

Bull in a China Shop

It's been a long day already, but the girls have a half-day of school, and I want to rush home to meet them at the bus stop. Well, they could walk home themselves, but you know, any excuse to see the girls. It was different with my dad. He was a workaholic. I don't remember ever seeing him during daylight hours. Sometimes there was a hired hand to scoop me up from school, but rarely. I vowed to be different. I'm different.

So I park the truck, lean against it with my back nestled in one of the many dents, and wait. I'm scrolling through my phone for relevant emails when I hear Melissa approach from down the road. The tell-tale creaking of our SUV's floorboards gives her away. She stops, and I duck in the window for a peck on the cheek and a nuzzle to River's head. River is getting way too amped up in Melissa's lap as I pet her.

Melissa can barely get the words out. "I didn't think you were coming for the girls, so I brought River to walk them home."

"I'll take her from here," I say as I open the car, and Melissa gets trampled. "Sorry. Where are you off to?"

"Getting a jump start on the bike path and finding out

who owns what and where boundaries are."

I tell her to expect resistance and dragging feet. I coach her to be a bull in a china shop and demand the help she'll need. Jerry, the short lawyer with the Napoleon complex, would be proud of my words.

Melissa will have none of it. She thinks positively and is only going to put out good energy in the universe. This is how she thinks things get done. "I've got this," she says.

I can tell when Melissa returns home from town that all didn't go well. Slamming doors is her way of saying, "I'm upset."

I leave the girls playing dance party in the playroom and approach the closed bathroom door. "Hey, honey. Tell me about town. How can I help?"

Melissa doesn't come out. Her muffled reply indicates she's probably sitting with her head in her hands. "I walked in all prepared. I had my one hundred applications for land survey information fully filled out, and Tyler, you know, John and Sheila's daughter, told me to come back with the request in the fall. She said the sheer volume of paperwork would put her back weeks, if not months. I talked about our project and the importance of the safety issues. But Tyler already knows all about our project. Knows about Sasha's fall, too. How does everyone know? Why does everyone know?"

"Come on out. Let's take a walk."

Melissa agrees. We walk in silence for a few minutes. Her eyes dart back and forth as she clenches and unclenches her fists. I let out a big sigh. Our change of scenario does not appear to have dampened her rage. Suddenly it bubbles to the surface once again. "I tried appealing to Tyler's sense of motherhood. No go. I'm not getting anywhere. Finally, I gave in to the Kagan way of thinking and raised my voice. I basically said, 'Are you saying that you refuse my requests for public records? Here are my applications. Here's my check. I expect my request to be filled. I won't take no for an answer or be put off. The courthouse is right across the street.'"

I squeeze Melissa's hand. "Sorry, I know how much you hate the Kagan way." We talk more and half convince ourselves people will come around once the facts and plans are laid out in front of them. Our mood changes for the better, and we once again feel positive about the project's prospects by the time we turn down our road.

This is when Thomas Hawthorne pulls up, stogie in hand. Melissa steps back as she hates the smoke.

He starts out all nice and friendly but in a backhanded kind of way. "Hi. Your yard looks good. I see that there's less stuff on it."

"Thomas, it's the middle of the day, and my crews are out. My equipment will be back tonight."

"Oh, is there any way you can create a driveway that goes behind your house and park the stuff back there? I know your neighbors would appreciate it."

Melissa, at this point, gives a lethargic wave and scurries to the house. She just got back in a good mood and knows where this conversation is going.

The fact is there are only four people on our street. Me, a customer of mine who loves me, and then there's Hawthorne and another guy, Grommel. Grommel actually has an empty wooded lot across from our house. He's on Hawthorne's team. One day he berated me endlessly for putting a gouge in a tree on his side of the road. I asked around. My employees knew nothing of it. Finally, the UPS driver told me he backed into it on the way out of our driveway. We went over to Grommel's and let him in on the facts. He thanked the UPS driver and told him not to worry about it. No apology for me—just a scowl. Thinking about it and this idiot in front of me puts me in the mood I believe Melissa was just in.

"Thomas, my home is kept in good order. You know I don't have any more land to do what you are asking. You own all that land."

"This is true. Why don't you just move? I think Oak Bluffs is more suited for people like you. We don't want that kind of clutter on Chappy."

I think of a lot of retorts. Want to throw his NIMBY attitude in his face. Ask him where he would be without people like me who volunteer as firefighters and EMTs. But in the end, I just say, "Leave me alone, Thomas. Go back to your comfortable castle in your comfortable world and leave me the fuck alone."

Town Hall, Town Politics

By late June, the season is in full swing. Summer people are here. Tourists are here. Cue the barbecues, the crowded streets, cars driving slowly, as every day is now Sunday. The transient homeowners forcibly take control of the narrative as if they believe the island's lights were just turned on for their amusement and folly. They've arrived for the season now that the sun is warm and are already strutting around like peacocks. Locals, lulled by a long off-season of lax rules and mores, forget their 'place' and sometimes get a scolding. "How long have you lived on the Vineyard?" A summer person will inevitably ask me to validate that they have the authority in a dispute or point of fact. The question bites to the quick as these summer people puff up their chests, talk of lineage, and scold me about some unspeakable atrocity I have committed.

Just yesterday, I was walking River down the dirt road near our house, and a runner approached. Not thinking much of it, I stepped aside so he didn't have to disrupt his run. River wouldn't be a nuisance as she was rummaging in the woods off the side of the road for some rodent, no doubt. This guy looked in the woods as he passed, stopped directly in front of me, pointed at River, all sweaty and out of breath, and told me to put my dog on a leash. I ignored his comment, as Chappy is one big dog park, and chose just to enjoy the site of River being River and take in the simplicity of a dog on a mission. The jogger was visibly upset and about to react to my lack of response when he recognized me from a town meeting where I was in favor of putting a cell tower on Chappy. In a breath, he segued into berating me about it and questioning my motives. I was polite and told him of the countless EMT calls where people suffered because they could not get cell reception and sometimes had to wait for hours for someone to figure out they needed help.

The runner stammered and tried to tell me the problem was not that bad. "You're going to ruin the rural nature of our island," he said with authority. "I like that I don't have cell service here. I have a phone in my house. We all do. We don't need cell service."

How could he spew this crap with a straight face? The real reason was, like a bike path, a cell tower equates to a more convenient and tourist-friendly environment. This guy doesn't want more tourists on Chappy who are not homeowners. He has his piece of paradise and doesn't want to share it with any more people than absolutely necessary.

The runner got flustered by my calling him out on the facts and relied on that old trope by telling me how long he'd lived on Chappy and asking how long I'd lived here? I never proudly proclaim twenty-five years. I hate pissing contests. And anyway, this guy knew how long I'd lived here. But he was still implying that because his family had had a house on Chappy for fifty years, he and people like him should call the shots. These people come to the Vineyard for two to three months each year and claim to be locals. Survive one week in February on this rock, and then tell me you are a local, asshole.

I was a little crankier than usual with the jogger as the fight for a bike path, which seems like a no-brainer, is picking up steam. The conversations at the ferry are getting more heated, and each side has rehearsed their talking points with their brethren ad nauseam. It will all come to a head tonight at the Edgartown Town Selectmen meeting, where the issue is on the docket.

Some customers I thought were rational human beings are acting like I'm ruining their summer existence by supporting a bike path, saying things like, "Rob, I love you, but having a bike path crossing all those roads and driveways will make for more accidents."

A well-educated financial planner tells me one afternoon, "Who will stop? The car? The bike? No one will know, and so there will be more collisions."

Another customer, a lawyer, found that old statute about the Barrens Buckmoth that Melissa mentioned and brought it up as a reason to kill the project. "It's on the endangered species list in Massachusetts, and their habitat should not be disturbed." He bellowed with authority.

"But they're not endangered here." I retorted and instantly regretted it. They're on everyone's land. Construction, in general, would grind to a halt if this lawyer's argument was upheld. My defense only egged the lawyer on, and I was stuck in a useless back and forth for the next hour.

Inane conversations like this make me double down on the cause. I conclude that level heads will ultimately prevail. The loud minority will be shot down by the many summer people who have homes on Chappy and have not yet weighed in on this debate.

At 6:00 p.m., my family heads to the meeting. We're all dressed in clean clothes after a long day of work for me, playing for the girls, and meeting prep for Melissa. We're not wearing items that we would wear to a party or graduation, but the clothes say, "Hey, we know this is a special event, we take this seriously, and we respect everyone involved." The girls are not happy about going. It seems like a lot of effort. But we're going.

My dad taught me to push to be heard. Melissa continues to help me see the toxic nature of that strategy. Watching small government in action and seeing their mom succinctly and passionately state her case for the bike path will be a good lesson for our daughters and me. It's communication that sways minds, not yelling.

We arrive at the Chappy ferry in time to see the throngs of summer people and locals alike file on board. Anytime there's a selectmen's meeting, and the word Chappy is mentioned in any of the agenda items, you'll see a huge uptick in the audience size. Everyone knows who's on which side of the 'argument'. And to exacerbate that point, two groups of whispering folks form at each end of the ferry, carefully going over their 'points' to be brought up at the meeting. Melissa knew the issue would draw attention, but not like this. She asked to be put on the docket merely to inform the selectmen of her intentions to thoroughly research and present a plan at a later date. I believe she has gotten everyone's attention.

We enter the town offices single file through the side door and travel to the meeting room down the hall. We take some seats toward the front of the room. Everyone is very cordial and says hello to one another as they take their seats—fake smiles all around.

"The selectmen will sit across from us at the wooden

desks positioned in a semi-circle," Melissa explains to the girls. They're already fidgety and don't know why they had to come. They get that this is all for them and the other children of Chappy, but no one else brought their kids.

"Look Dad," Ilana says. "There's Jim. He's still in his overalls with every color of paint under the sun on them. His daughter, Katie, isn't here. Peter didn't even bring his granddaughters. This is so unfair."

I try to explain the chess game that is about to unfold. I try to describe how the conversation will be shaped by the fact there are young children in the room. I tell them their very presence speaks volumes about our intent and resolve on this issue. We want a human face to symbolize our cause. We want the recipients of our message to know by not acting on our query, they are affecting the lives of our children.

The gavel is banged, and the meeting comes to order. The first item on the docket will be the bike path. The town routinely puts Chappy business first because the meeting starts at 6:30, and the ferry shuts down at 7:30 for the ferry captain's dinner break. Actually, this is only the case in the offseason as the ferry runs straight from 6:45 a.m. to midnight in the summer. But habits are habits, and we're glad to have our discussion first and get the kids home to bed at a reasonable time.

The chairman of the selectmen talks a little about the bike path discussion history on Chappy and then gives the floor to Melissa.

"Hi everyone, I believe most of you know I'm Melissa Kagan, and I live on Chappy year-round with Rob, who owns Chappy Unlimited. These are our kids, Ilana and Sasha. Sasha is sporting a wrist brace from the bike accident this spring where a car pushed her off the road."

A few chairs can be heard moving around as well as some grumbling at this last statement. Melissa looks at me quizzically but pushes on. "Peter Wells, sitting to my right, is what I consider one of the most level-headed, no-nonsense people on our little island. As everyone knows, he's the Chappy Fire Chief, ferry owner, and a past land surveyor. He is uniquely qualified to help us navigate the question of how to make the roads of Chappy safer for all travelers." Again, grumbling from pockets of the audience break out and are louder this time. Melissa is getting a little red as she speaks.

I know her and what's going through her head. I'm waiting for her to say the sky is blue to see how many people object to this fact. But instead, Melissa takes a deep breath and lays out her intentions to research this situation with Peter and, frankly, anyone else who wants to get involved. "Listen, I have not come to any conclusions. My baby was injured while innocently riding her bicycle on the side of the road, and I want to see if there's a safer alternative to the status quo. Currently, we don't have any of the logistics planned out or the answer to how a bike path could even be paid for. This is why we're here asking for the selectmen's guidance and help. The only thing I know for sure is that I don't feel safe having my children ride their bikes in our own neighborhood, and that's not right."

A hiss is audible to our right, and I can see Lila Hawthorne, our neighbor, isn't happy with the presentation. Melissa sits down and buries her head in her bag, looking for a tissue. It's quite evident by the way her voice was wavering at the end that she is close to tears. She comes away from her search with a few tissues and dabs her eyes as she stares straight ahead and tries to regain her composure. The chairman bangs the gavel and thanks Melissa for her comments.

A board member of the CIA speaks next. This isn't the real CIA, but the Chappy Island Association. The games both organizations play are suspect, but the local CIA has not stooped to overthrowing governments. Not yet. The CIA representative is an older fellow whose family lineage on Chappy goes back generations. He gets up slowly and methodically as his barrel-chested body doesn't fit in the schoolroom like chairs in the selectmen's meeting room. He smiles at some of the old guard on Chappy before he expertly and with less emotion than Melissa begins to speak of the poor woodland creatures that will be disrupted if we bulldoze more land for a bike path. He brings up the asphalt that will be needed for the project, the increase in our carbon footprint, and of course, the hardship of the town having to pay for this ridiculous and unneeded eye soar.

"I get it. Melissa's daughter was hurt, and she wants someone to blame. But we, the people of Chappy as represented by the CIA, don't think a sidewalk, which isn't needed, will solve anything." The man sits down, proud of himself. He is validated in his efforts with clapping by the same people that were rude during Melissa's presentation. I want to retaliate and boo and hiss just like they did. Our side is, no doubt, all thinking this, and I feel proud of our collective restraint.

Then one woman shouts out, "Why are we even having this discussion when we're only here two months out of the year? The rest of the year, it's so quiet."

The chairman of the selectmen smirks and bangs his gavel once again. He has a comment for this particular woman, but he doesn't dare speak it. She's a customer of his very lucrative landscaping business.

Melissa has no such reason to hold back and loses her control. "This is what I'm talking about! We, the people Chappy, the people that drive the ferry, serve your dinners at the yacht club, even mow your lawn, and are here year-round... our lives matter. Our issues and concerns matter. My daughters, Sasha and Ilana, ride the streets of Chappy all year round. Do we not count?"

Melissa sits down as the woman stammers that that's not what she means. "I meant that the roads are not busy the rest of the year." But she is drowned out by an eruption on both sides of the argument. Everyone starts speaking at once. The gavel is once again banged for what seems like an eternity to get everyone's attention. I slump down a little in my seat as I again calculate how many customers I'm going to lose by taking this stand.

"It seems reasonable as Chappy gets more congested with houses over time to re-visit the discussion of a bike path," one of the selectmen declares in an effort to come off as an elder statesman.

More hisses from the audience from an undetermined place. The chairman once again bangs his gavel. "We'll form a committee to investigate this project's pros and cons to be presented to this body in three months' time."

Melissa starts to rise, but I hold her back. She knew they were going to kick this down the road, but three months? I whisper that it's a start.

The chairman goes on to say, "The selectmen will take a five-minute recess so the people of Chappy can get to their ferry."

Peter blurts out in the friendliest and disarming manner, "Aaaah... excuse me, it's the summer schedule on the ferry, and we are in no rush, but I thank the selectmen all the same for their sensitivity to the people of Chappy's traveling restraints." Everyone laughs, as once again, Peter is able to humanize our life on Chappy and bring everyone back together with the simple fact that we all live on that rock together.

The people of Chappy depart. There's very little talking between the different camps, even though we are all walking en masse toward our only means of transportation home. No one seems victorious at this point in the game, and everyone seems to be grumbling. Melissa and I definitely feel more threatened by the current situation than we did before tonight—economically, socially, and spiritually. I think it was the hissing by our neighbor that did me in.

The divide is brought into tighter contrast as we all load onto the ferry. Each person hands over their passenger ticket. Like us, year-round residents hand over a green ticket while the summer people are relegated to using a pink ticket. The original idea for the green tickets was to give a financial break to the working people who're the backbone of this little island. Imagine paying a toll every time you leave your driveway. The thinking goes that summer people, with five and ten million dollar houses, can afford a little more and are forced to buy the more expensive pink tickets. The larger issue is that this policy divides the Chappy people by a class system—in reverse. Everyone wants to be known as a local, that they belong, and are special. And the summer residents believe the green tickets would give them that status.

It's ridiculous, but at the same time, it's also telling. Most of our group wanting to investigate a safer Chappaquiddick have green tickets tonight. The other group all have pink tickets. This fact doesn't surprise me on the surface. But I'm dismayed that more customers of mine that are newer to the island, have kids, and adamantly told me they were excited about the prospect of a bike path didn't show up tonight. Why didn't they?

Melissa turns to me as we sit on the ferry, looking at the big full moon and its reflection on the small rippling waves. We hug, and as if reading my mind, she sums up the evening, saying, "I just don't get it."

You Just Gotta Shake Your Head and Laugh

Having seen Jim, the painter, at the selectmen's meeting the night before reminds me I'm currently playing with fire. I need to make sure this fire is contained. I need to hope against hope that my ill-conceived faith in Jim and giving him a job this year hasn't backfired on me. It always backfires on me. He's so sweet, so earnest, and at times very talented. But life gets in the way. His fuzzy logic gets in the way. And I'm left holding the bag—a bag of shit. Damn, I wouldn't have even hired him, but then my customer dumped this job on me at the last moment. It appears Jim isn't the only one with issues.

Before dealing with Jim, my morning ritual goes as usual, except there's no walk with the girls. School's over. Our morning walks are over. I think about a new ritual. Maybe we can take the dog for a morning swim before I have to go off to work. The girls are still young enough that they might be up for this adventure, this ritual, this bonding. I hear stories of moody teenagers. Teenagers that wake at noon. Teenagers that don't look up from their phones. I want to hold on even tighter to my current role as a cool dad. Maybe not cool dad, but definitely a guy I can stand doing things with kind of dad. I need to thread the needle and think this through. Come up with a plan. All this occupies my brain as I drive toward the jobsite where Jim is hopefully finishing up the window painting job I gave him.

My inner conversation about my girls has distracted me from thinking about Jim and what I might find at this job site. I should have been checking on him and not distracted by his rosy pronouncements about the project. "Things are going great, Rob. You could have charged them more. I'm almost done." Jim is always saying things like this. It gets me nervous. Is he painting too fast? Is he not doing prep? Is he not sanding between coats? But the questions fade as other more pressing problems erupt. I never seem to be nervous enough to check on him. Out of sight, out of mind. Or maybe, out of sight, deal with the problem tomorrow. Either way, I have not been thinking about Jim.

The house being painted, like every other house on Chappy, is down a long dirt road. Every house is down a long dirt road. It's an unremarkable cottage that has welcomed three generations of family members over the years. The structure is simple, functional as a summer retreat, but without the modern luxuries of a dishwasher, TV, or sheetrock walls. It's a place to reconnect with family and enjoy the simplicity and beauty of Chappy. It works. I have seen this house in action. The family arrives, drops their bags, and... drops their baggage. Time is spent playing Parcheesi, touch football on the field to the right of the house, and swimming in the ocean mere steps from their front yard. This ramshackle cottage happens to sit on a bluff over Edgartown Harbor. This simple house is probably worth $3,000,000 with views that are to die for. A developer would love to buy this house, tear it down, and build a mega-mansion on it. But for now, the homeowners are affording the hefty property taxes. For now, that is.

As I pull up to the house, I notice Jim's bike lying against a tree with a paint can on its side next to it. The paint is dripping out of the lid that is obviously not on tight enough. I run over and turn the can upright. I go back to my truck, grab a shovel out of the back, scoop up the paint-stained soil, and put it in the corner of my truck bed. The truck is full of stains and dirt. One more patch of paint won't hurt it.

The front door is ajar, and I walk in.

"Crap."

The scene in front of me tells me all I need to know. Cigarette butts are stamped out on the old, wide planked, wooden flooring; food wrappers litter every table and the kitchen counter. Half-filled coffee cups seem to be on every windowsill. Jim is obviously not expecting me. Laborers get lulled into a sense of sloppiness, knowing that the home-owner is many miles away. They will get it all cleaned up before the job is done and an inspection is in order. But this scene sinks to a lower level. Jim is definitely living in this house. I'm momentarily paralyzed—should I start cleaning up or confront Jim. I hear him on the phone in the backroom and decide on the latter. Breathe, Breathe. I can't blow up at Jim. This will get me nowhere. I need to get him to help me rectify this situation and get this job done.

Jim's voice grows louder and clearer as I move through the house to the back bedroom. The one-sided conversation I hear makes my heart sink a little more. "Yeah, baby, what are you doing now? A huh? Oh, yeah. You know I like it when you spank yourself," Jim bellows out in a cheesy, sultry voice.

Crap.

I enter the bedroom Jim is clearly living in and stop cold. It's not the trash or clothes thrown about that freezes me. It's Jim. He's on the phone, but not his cell phone. He has made this call from the homeowner's landline.

Shit. Shit. Shit.

"Jim, hang up the phone!"

He turns to me and registers my displeasure with a sheepish grin. Jim tells the person on the other end he has to go and hangs up like it's no big deal. "Hey, Rob. I wasn't expecting you. Job's almost done. How much time do I have?"

All I can get out at this instant is, "Arrrrrrgggghhhh."

Jim begins to clean up the room and casually talks as I regain my composure. I stare blankly at him and really don't know what to say. Finally, I ask, "What are you doing?"

"What do you mean?" He shoots back with a calm and innocent demeanor that makes me realize what a great criminal he would be. What a great criminal he is. He really knows how to play a part.

"Jim, you're living here, making a mess and obviously racking up 1-900 sex calls on the homeowner's phone. What do *you* mean... what do I mean?"

"Oh that, yeah, well, my wife threw me out again. I don't know why. She's crazy. So I crashed here. No big deal. The people aren't coming today, are they?"

I cut him off as he obviously doesn't see the bigger picture. "And the phone?"

"Oh," he says. "These rich people never check their phone bills, and if they do, I'll pay them back."

Jim's logic is beyond reasoning with. Why try?

"Jim, here's what's going to happen. I'm going to help you clean up this place, move your stuff outside, and we're going to figure out how to end this job. I'll call the homeowner, tell them the truth, and take double the phone charges off your bill. This is ridiculous."

Jim doesn't respond and just continues cleaning up. I wonder if I'll see him again for a while after today or if he'll bail. I can't decide which option I'd prefer.

The clean-up goes fine, and I call my cleaners to come over to do a real cleaning, which I inform Jim will come out of his pay. I'm almost calmed down, feeling back in control, when I discover a new problem—a bigger problem. A problem that makes me call my lead, in-house painter, to rescue me. It turns out Jim slopped the paint on so thick in an attempt to apply fewer coats that he painted all the windows shut. Jim is always trying to cut corners. He's always going too fast.

"Rob, honestly, this is no big deal," Jim tries to explain. "This always happens, and then I go back with a putty knife to open the windows."

"Jim, just leave." Is all I can muster to say.

I love Jim. The ability to double down when you have messed up is an art form that he has perfected. The amusement I get from seeing this train wreck in action, slightly takes the sting out of this situation. Slightly.

I hope next time I have the will to avoid this situation. I wonder whether saying "no" to a customer, seeing the disappointment in their face and having one less paycheck would be worse than dealing with Jim and this mess? I want to find out.

Within no time, it's the end of the day. Lots of sweat rolling down everyone's body. Lots of dirt on clothes. It doesn't matter what division of Chappy Unlimited a person is involved in—everyone has that same tired, drained, and unclean look. I imagine my workers are like me. Strip off all clothes outside and towel off before even thinking of walking in the house. Decontamination is the first step in the process of becoming whole again.

I grab Santiago and Kyle before they bolt from unloading the tools at my house and ask for a word. I do this a lot about various subjects. They're used to it. They don't squirm much. I begin with accolades from customers and ask about their day. It's a preamble. But Santiago gives me a knowing smile as if to say thank you. Then I get to my ask.

"So, how is Rich working out?" I'm a little nervous because he has thrown me a curveball. Rich, in his exuberance, quit his janitorial job and is now full-on tethered to Chappy Unlimited. I didn't sign up for this, at least not yet. I cross my fingers.

Kyle takes the lead in answering as Santiago is quieter and always stumbles with his English. "He's OK. Loves to talk. He really has no skills or common sense. But he seems eager to please, and so he's trying hard to impress us."

"Yeah, I get that. If he works at it, the skills will come. The fact that he wants to please you is a good start."

Santiago grunts. "More bodies, less work for me. You don't cut my hours. Right boss?"

"No, you guys are my number one priority. You know that. Just keep pushing Rich to learn more and more. So if one of you is sick or something—he could step in."

"We're never sick. When have we been sick?" Kyle says with a little anger.

I make up some excuse about just trying to think ahead and help them out. I have plans. Still in my head. Not sure if I'm going to implement them. But I need to start thinking, and plans are a good place to start.

The 4th of July

Interactions like the one with Jim, the painter, arrogant summer people, dysfunctional employees, and demanding customers fade away as the bright shiny penny that is Martha's Vineyard makes me turn my head and smile. The beauty of the Vineyard and its rituals cleanse my soul whenever they get my attention.

Cue the 4th of July. Cue the parade. It's time for small-town America to shine. It's time for traditions. It's time to look at a green grass moment that washes away any doubt about this rock I live on. This holiday is as big as Christmas on Martha's Vineyard. The real world stops in its tracks on this weekend. Customers feel this holiness as much as I do. And thankfully, the idea of calling me for help with anything less than a total catastrophe seems sacrilegious. I love it.

No one is working. The chickens have been given the compost scraps from breakfast. I begin to gather my supplies, and the countdown to the 4th of July festivities is on. It's now 10:00 a.m., and the parade isn't until 5:00 p.m., dinner at 7:00, and the fireworks at 9:00. What to do? What to do? Let's see...

Cooler with Mexican Coke, a sandwich, and Fritos. Check. Sunglasses. Check. Tevas, foul weather gear (this is the Vineyard—fog and rain can roll in on a dime). Check. A good book from my nightstand—maybe *Impossible Vacation*? Too dark? OK, let's go with *Spartina*. Check. And I'm on my way.

Whoa, whoa, whoa, you say. It's 10:00 a.m. Where are you going?

Well, Melissa and the girls will be making food all day. They have their chores. My job is to move the sailboat from our mooring in the inner harbor to an anchorage in the outer harbor, where a barge is set up for the fireworks display. Boaters come from all over to anchor their boats in prime locations to be right under the fireworks. We're no different. You can almost walk from boat to boat at showtime. It's a congested site to see. It's a little unnerving. I actually hate anchoring. I'm a great sailor but lousy at setting an anchor. But it's the 4th of July, and I can suck it up and make a good show of it. Hell, I have plenty of time to get it right before the parade.

It takes a total of four tries to get the anchoring just right. I feel like all eyes from the other boaters are on me as I pick up the anchor each time and try again. Stop looking at me! Their look might really be one of wonderment as my first attempt was probably good enough. But the anxiety of making sure our boat has enough space pushes me to perfection. The job is finally done, and it's now 11:30 a.m. I'm on a boat, by myself—with no responsibilities. What, pray tell, is there to do? I feel a little guilty as Melissa and the girls cook and prepare food nonstop until parade time, but it's a ritual Melissa loves. So, I know I shouldn't feel bad. And so, I don't. Instead, I grab my lunch out of the cooler, eat, sip my Coke, read a book, and snooze until showtime.

I wake up at one point and call my dad. "Hey Dad, guess where I am?"

"Are you sailing? It seems like a perfect day for it."

I smile and take a long exhale. Part of me wishes he was out here with me. But this is one of the only times all summer when I have a stretch of time with nothing to do. The solitude is welcome. The sound of the rippling waves is calming. The nap was lazy and indulgent... it was awesome. Any visitor, even my dad, especially my dad, would load layers onto my psyche and ruin this moment. Yet, I did call him.

I break away from my thoughts and get to the reason I called. He's alone. He's probably at his desk, piled high with useless papers, watching Fox News. It can't be healthy. "What's on your agenda?"

"I've been pouring over the documents I got from the law library at the courthouse yesterday. I'm always working for you. I believe I've figured out how to legally pay your illegal aliens—if you insist on hiring them.

"Great, but I think my biggest problem will be getting them to do the paperwork I know this will entail. Most don't even trust the banks and use Western Union to move their money around."

"Well, you're going to have to demand it. Find an accounting firm and make it easy for them. Hold their hand. You're good at that. Hey, I'd have you just fire them. But you don't want to do that."

I sigh. I shouldn't have called. "I can't do that. Santiago has been with me for years. Many of them have."

"We'll work it out. I'll help you. I always do. I can't have you getting in trouble. I need you. Now I've got to go. I'm going to go down to my kayak and paddle around the harbor. I'm starting a new diet and want to lose some pounds."

"That's great. Call me if you make it to Edgartown for the parade."

"Will do, kid," he says and hangs up.

I wish I could believe my dad's plan. He's been on so many diets. Tried to get healthy so many times. But the rusted lock on his kayak tells a different story. I raise a Chips Ahoy! in his honor and scoff it down. The choice of cookies goes back to the days of sailing with him when I was a kid. They were always mushy and stale because we left them on the boat all summer. I smile as I bite into the soggy treat as I still do the same thing. I think this current pack is from last summer—at least. I rearrange the cushions on the benches. Then read a few pages of my book before putting it back down to look around my baby bobbing in the water while other boats pass by. I want to stay in this moment forever, even though I know that sitting in any moment forever would be my hell.

Melissa calls me every so often with questions about what we have and don't have on the boat. It wakes me up from my stupor, and I try not to sound drowsy—it pisses her off to no end if she's busting her butt and I'm lounging. I finally notice that it's 4:00 p.m., and we make a plan to meet on the beach directly across from the anchored boat. Did I mention that I drag our small motorboat behind the sailboat when I go to anchor in the outer harbor? The motorboat is great for ferrying all our guests and the food to the sailboat. Many people rely on the harbor launches, but I'm too impatient for that. And too cheap. I feel like the world is divided into two groups of sailors—cheap ones and really cheap ones. Again, thanks, Dad.

I grab the many bags and coolers from Melissa and the girls on the beach and safely stow them aboard the boat. I take one last look around at my placement within the maze of boats and check the GPS, which shows my location and how I have swung in line with all the other boats throughout the day. No movement out of the ordinary. Great! I see the girls rushing up the beach toward the Chappy ferry while I'm checking and double-checking all the lines. We'll soon rendezvous at the Chappy parade viewing spot at the old library. The entire parade route is filled with people, but for some reason, all of Chappy stands on the library lawn to view the parade. We all mingle and talk like we didn't just see each other at the ferry landing or the last potluck. I mostly show off my girls that I'm rarely with and try to avoid shop talk.

I arrive at the top of the street across from the library and spot Melissa talking so effortlessly about the sun or our girls' beautiful French braids or whatever, and I want nothing more than to be a part of that conversation and to be with her on that lawn.

But Sally Kane stops me before I can cross the street to join Melissa and the girls. She's always so sweet and starts our conversation with a nod to our past. "Ready to cater another clambake for us? Your dad is such a hoot." Then she notices me looking across at my family and adds, "Your family is so beautiful. You all are so lucky to live in this paradise all the time. I envy you."

I smile and flippantly say, "The grass is always greener."

The truth is I struggle with this notion of nirvana. I love being on this island, but the logistics of actually living here are complicated. I've tried telling people who profess their envy about the real world we live in. Tell them stories about the hardships surrounding them in this paradise, describe how their quaint island turns into a cold and desolate ghost town when they're not here, and the bad choices people they bump into every day make. That's when they start rolling their eyes. They want to push away from me. They have a bucolic idea of what this island is about, who I am, and how their summer life all fits together in this utopia. And they certainly are not interested in having the fantasy broken. And I don't blame them. It's the 4th of July. The grass is very green today.

Just looking at my family chilling on the library lawn helps put the darker side of the 'grass is greener' quote out of my mind. And it doesn't hurt that one of my childhood crushes, Meg Ryan, is standing next to Melissa. Yes, she lives on Chappy. She's one of two celebrities living on our little rock. The other is Susan St. James. Another childhood crush of mine. How lucky can one boy be?

Today Meg Ryan is just another summer resident on the library lawn, chatting up some neighbors. All very innocent. All very picturesque, in a 4th of July sort of way. But then the parade starts up, and everyone's eyes are on the approaching floats. I want to scurry over to my family while there's still time. I see an opening and am about to dash across the street when a float stops in front of me.

It's the Jensons' float. They pick a movie each year and act out a scene from it. This year they picked the movie Top Gun. All of a sudden, the Jensons start singing, "You lost that lovin' feelin'." This is all happening in front of Ms. Ryan. The Tom Cruise character looks like he's singing directly to Meg. We all feel like time stops. All eyes are on Meg Ryan. I know she's not in that scene, but it's still her movie. Her eyes revert to the downward position as she slips on her patented sunglasses. Do the Jensons know who they are standing in front of? It doesn't look like it—just dumb luck. I want to take a picture, but at the same time feel bad for Meg and don't want to add fuel to the fire. I'm glad everyone around me feels the same way and keeps their phones at their sides. Soon enough, the float passes by. Soon enough, everyone goes back to their small talk. Soon enough, kids are jumping for the next float's candy. No harm, no foul. I hope Meg can enjoy the rest of the parade. I know my kids do as they gleefully show me their sugar haul, and the last of the fire engines go by with their blaring sirens killing the serene mood.

The fire engines are our cue to run for the Chappy ferry. As I said, there are 400 homes on Chappy. Each with five to ten guests. You do the math. Lots of people want to get back to Chappy all at the same time. There are so many walk-on passengers that they close the ferry to car traffic. They place fancy chairs down the middle, which gives the ferry an air of sophistication on this special day. It definitely feels different.

We say goodbye to all who happen to be on the same ferry as us and swing down to the beach where our little motorboat is anchored in the shallows. I run Melissa and the girls out to the sailboat so they can relax, take a swim, and enjoy the scenery before dinner needs to be put out. I go back to town in the boat and pick up our guests on the Edgartown side, so they don't have to wait in the line to get over to Chappy.

Everyone is on the sailboat now. Kids are running around, through hatches, out onto the skiff tied to the back of the sailboat, and back again. It's a constant loop of activity with plenty of screeching and yelling. Aaaaahhhhh, 4th of July—that's the good stuff. Melissa and some of our guests put the food out. I sit back and take it all in— watchful. Things tend to happen on a boat, and it's my job to be alert. I'm always looking out for those emergency situations. My job is boat cop. But tonight, all goes well, and everyone has a magical evening.

The food begins to disappear. The kids lose steam and head to the V berth to play cards, and the adults hang out on the cushions at the stern of the boat to watch the sunset. Edgartown in the summer. It's always a crapshoot what type of sunset you'll get. You hope for the yellow, orange, and burning red kind. Sometimes you get a lot of fog added in, and it's more of a watercolor scene. But it doesn't really matter because we're with friends, taking a beat, and feeling lucky we live on this rock. Look around. It's easy to feel there's no bad in the world. Nature is so good. Scenery is so good. This beer is so good. My happy smiling friends are so good. It doesn't get much better than this.

The first sounds of the fireworks abruptly shatter the lull of the quiet night air. The barge is so close we can see the people onboard scurrying around. Everyone on Noah's Rejects re-groups back on the benches at the aft of the boat as the show begins. Tonight is a clear, dark night with not a cloud in the sky. The bright lights of the fireworks pop and expand one after another with such vibrance. The grin on each of our faces suggests we have never seen fireworks before. But isn't that the magic of fireworks? The kids can't keep quiet and scream with delight at each new burst of light and sound.

I look at Sasha as she's deep in conversation on top of the hatch with her friend, Emma. They have been experiencing this same scene for years. I can remember a time when they both wore earplugs and stayed down below during the excitement. Occasionally, they would peer their heads out of the hatch long enough to see one or two explosions before escaping back to the safety and calm of the cabin below. I want to yell, "Remember this! Remember this!"—to Sasha, to Ilana, to the world, to myself. Instead, I hug Melissa a little tighter. Her red hair looks so wonderful backlit by the colorful night sky. I'll remember.

By the time the fireworks have ended, we're all out of discussions about island life, politics, and our families, and I'm ready to reverse the procedure and bring everyone to shore. Melissa and the kids stay onboard, and after everyone is gone, I pull up anchor and motor back to our mooring in the harbor, where we'll spend the night. We're silent, exhausted... and happy. What a long day. We all look forward to a long sleep with the hope of waking up to calm seas and nothing but a few cormorants to disturb the water around our boat. The 4th of July was a good day. It always is.

Bat-Shit Crazy Customers

July 5th. Back to the insanity. Back to my customers. Back to putting out fires. Back to a new list of work for my different crews. How did the mower get broken? What? It's been breaking for two weeks now, and no one told me? Why not clue me in so I could have the parts on hand to fix it?

Arrrgggghhhhh. Well, I'll have to overnight parts and figure out how to mow twenty lawns with our backup mowers that are really not up to the job. Life. Never a dull moment.

No time to dwell on equipment for long as the noise of customers in my ears becomes overwhelming. Most mean well. But some are just narcissistic, batshit, and plain old crazy. I used to always be amused by their peculiarities and demands, but lately, I have been feeling like an unappreciated nursemaid. These people, these clients, these dependents of mine are wealthy and seem to have their act together to the outside world, but in reality, they are barely holding it together, just like everyone else.

The Khalils are a funny example. I don't know what to expect in most situations, but with the Khalils, I know. Oh,

ROB KAGAN

I know. Armin Khalil, a retired Lebanese physician of some type, and his wife spend every summer at their house on Chappy. I always wonder what kind of physician Armin is but never ask. I think I'm too scared to. His wife won't let him cut his own bread. How could he be a doctor? It's always the same scene when I arrive at their house. Armin, in his tighty-whitey underwear, answers the door while simultaneously yelling up the stairs to his wife about the coffee on the stove. Lila, his wife, yells back, unrelated, about the birdhouse hanging from a tree outside their kitchen window. Their conversations never line up. It's just constant yelling. One agenda never meshing with the other. Chaos. It's my job to guide the conversation to a point where they stop yelling nonsense and get on the same page. Namely, why I have been summoned to their home. I want to fix what's broken and move on. Sometimes I'm too blunt. I tell them to focus. They laugh and continue to yell at one another, but at least it's now about why I'm at their house—progress. Soon I learn the outhouse their son built from an online drawing has a loose hinge. I run out to the truck, fetch my screw gun and tighten the hinge in no time. I point out they will yell at me when they get the bill for thirty seconds worth of work. Maybe they want to group their jobs for me instead of calling me over every couple of days. I ask for too much. They're already back to yelling random thoughts at each other. I dash to my truck, barely saying goodbye. I'll see them in a couple of days—no need to fret.

I look back at the house as I'm leaving. I take a long look at all 'my' houses when I'm on the scene. There're many layers to my look. Obviously, I think about what's wrong with the house or what could go wrong in the near future. But I also love thinking about its history. Who built

182

the house, and why the architect decided to shape a certain section of the exterior edifice a certain way? The Khalils' house is a simple affair. Not that pretty, in my opinion, but functional. It kind of looks like a woodsy Brady Bunch '70s style house but with raw exterior boards to make it fit in the woods rather than suburbia. It works. It's merely the occupants that don't make sense.

I have just backed out of the Khalils' driveway when I get an urgent text from Savannah Holmstead. I call her and get an earful about a rogue skunk ruining her life. She needs me to drop everything and come over now so she can get to her tennis lesson at the yacht club in town. I arrive to find Savannah eloquently talking on the phone about a recent charity event as she paints her nails. I quietly wait on the front deck and shuffle a potted plant from side to side, so she knows I'm outside. The Holmstead's own two houses on a completely stripped piece of barren lawn with slight views over the neighbor's roofline to the ocean below. The houses are old conventional Cape Cod style structures. The interior walls and ceilings are all wood, painted white and off-white to make it feel clean and breezy. It's calming. They're simple houses meant to convey a simple lifestyle—read a book, walk to the beach, have a lobster dinner—rinse and repeat.

My phone rings as I wait. It's Melissa. She wants to tell me she saw Jerry today. He was riding his moped in the middle of the lane with a cigarette dangling from his mouth. I guess he has un-quit smoking again. Melissa debates with me about the optics of driving in the middle of the lane instead of on the side of the road where most moped traffic is relegated. I tell her Jerry's side. He read in the law library that mopeds have the right to drive with the flow of traffic, so that is what he will do. This erupts into a heated discussion about convention over the law, which I'm not going to win. I tell her I have to go. I'm dealing with a customer crisis.

Savannah finishes her call and her nails and comes outside with an entirely new demeanor of desperation, exasperation, and impatience. I always marvel at how people can change their persona on a dime, depending on who they're talking to. I see it mostly in certain types of women. It's a skill. One I don't have or like in others. I get the feeling I'm not seeing the real person. Do they realize they're showing me their different personas? Do they care that I see the switch? The weight of these encounters is sticking with me a little more each time. The stories I tell the girls at night of crazy customers doing silly things are morphing into darker tales. I worry my 'dad' stories will linger with them and not in a good way.

Savannah, oblivious to my inner conflict in response to her Jekyll and Hyde routine, scrunches up her nose and proclaims that she needs my help. Or, more accurately, she thinks she needs my help.

Here's the deal. A skunk was in the yard—big surprise. And it had the audacity to spray at something or someone in the vicinity of her homes. So what we need to do... What Savannah needs me to do is wash the house, the entire house, inside and out—every surface. It smells of skunk. We need to get rid of the smell. This is where I try not to laugh. I love it when people use the term we like they'll help or have any part of the process other than writing a check. It's like when people say, "Do you like our house? We just renovated it last fall." Like they even know what a hammer is.

Anyway, Savannah informs me she would love to stay and help, but she has a tennis date with blah, blah, blah, and then has to blah, blah, blah in town, and she will touch base with me later. I stop listening and wait for the goodbye hug. It comes fast and insincere. Instantly, she is back on the phone and in her bedroom, making lunch plans. I change gears and call customers whose homes were to be cleaned today. All except one can have their cleaning put off until tomorrow. Hell, it's mid-week, and the onslaught of new guests won't arrive until Friday. Next, I inform the cleaning crew employees to put off their current jobs, put one employee at the house that needs cleaning today, grab a particular list of supplies and ladders, and head over to the Holmsteads'. Of course, I'm simplifying this process and leaving out the thirty minutes it actually takes me to get everyone on the phone or informed by text because this is Chappy—and cell reception is nonexistent on this little rock. I sometimes find myself climbing trees or going on roof decks to get a signal.

I take another stab at subtly telling Savannah that fans will do the job as she stacks her tennis rackets in her bag and ties her sneakers. This job is so unnecessary. It's going to cost her upwards of $2000. Wind and nature will do the same job if we just give it a little time. For God's sake, the spraying happened outside in the first place. But then again, everyone is smarter than me.

Savannah gives me a dismissive smile. "The Hawthorne's had a similar situation and recommended an organic citrus cleaner that you can get in Vineyard Haven. Oh, and feel free to grab some beach plumb cupcakes for you and your crew while you work."

"Great. No problem," is my reply. Inside I am seething at the suggestion of going off Chappy and driving an hour each way through summer traffic to get some random nondescript product. And why do they think their absurd demands can always be made palatable with tasty treats?

The Grass Begins to Wilt in Late July

The craziness of summer people, traffic, and work create a warped sense of reality. The off-season routines of school, doctor's appointments, yoga classes, and trips to the mainland are long gone. We're lucky if we get to the supermarket on a regular basis. The winter seems so far away—we're almost nostalgic for it. Good thing we can concentrate on a cause that is tethered to our community and the long-term happiness of our family—the bike path.

The Chappy Community Center is the site for the first bike path committee meeting. It has been a month since the selectmen's meeting. Melissa, Peter, and a slew of other concerned parents have been busy. But so has the other side. We know who is who, as there was a sign-up sheet for both camps at the Chappy ferry. Some of the same participants here today were on the last bike path committee formed in 2000. We had just moved on-island full time at that point and knew very little of town politics. Frankly, as a newly married person with no kids, I didn't feel passionate about the project. But I'm sure I wouldn't have cared if sidewalks were installed.

Who has time for such frivolous passions? Well, the

summer people of Chappy do, and they squashed the effort then and are confident they can do it again. But Melissa is still hopeful. I tell her she needs to be forceful and bold at this meeting to be heard, but Melissa plans to talk from the heart. She plans to connect with them as neighbors. I nod my head in agreement but have been the son of a lawyer for too long. Jerry has taken on banks, the government, and small flower shops with the same ferociousness. Many times for petty and vindictive motives. My dad's words ring in my ears. "You don't have to be right to sue someone. Just have time and money."

The meeting starts amicably, and Melissa talks once again about Sasha's accident and the many curves on the road. She paints a picture and describes the difficulty small children have keeping their bikes from sliding with the ever-present sand on the road. It all sounds so logical to us. It doesn't sound unreasonable or like it's a big ask to make our roads safer.

Then Melissa unveils the big news she thinks everyone will be happy about. "So, I understand that many of us are seeing two sides to this coin. Emotions are certainly running hot. This is why I'm excited to announce that graduate students from Northeastern University are here today and have agreed to study our situation and make impartial recommendations about making the roads of Chappy safer. Can you guys please stand up?"

Five young, bright-eyed students get to their feet and wave their hands. No doubt they think they will be viewed as saviors. "Hi. Hello," each of the kids chimes in. Then the lead student wraps it all up by saying, "Nice to meet everyone. My name is Brian Janson. Our team is excited to roll up our sleeves and get to work. We'll put together a traffic study, create questionnaires, look at accident data, and wrap our heads around this problem. Your island is so beautiful, and we want to help you create the best solution for your community."

An older gentleman dressed in a madras button-down shirt and long khakis appears to be taken aback by this development. He doesn't see it as an olive branch or impartial in any way. He attempts to blow these kids out of the water before they even get started.

"Excuse me, Melissa," he says with an air of superiority. "How is this going to be paid for. This all sounds very expensive, and the town has not given us any funds for a study."

"Yes, thank you, Tony." Melissa beams with a smile as she's been ready for this all week. "The team you see before you are using this study as their senior thesis. They have been studying problems like this their entire time in grad school. The only money needed will be the actual costs—their out-of-pocket expenses. We have an estimate of $15,000, which has already been pledged by our family and others on Chappy that really wants to see what they come up with."

Thomas Hawthorne, my neighbor and a constant thorn in my side, pipes in, "How are we to accept the word of these neophytes? They're students. We need a real city planning firm. I move that we set up another committee to look into who to hire and then apply for the town to pay for it in their next fiscal year."

There's a bunch of approving mumbling as the summer people have mastered the stall tactic. The students in the back who moments ago had grins now look like their best friend just died and start whispering to one another.

Peter pipes in, "Well, Thomas, I'm happy for you to do that if you want. Seems like a waste of time and money, but go ahead. In the meantime, these kids can get going on their project. I'm very excited to see what they come up with."

Thomas is not amused. "So, this is bought and paid for by the people who want a bike path. That's convenient. I'm sure the study will be impartial."

Melissa jumps to her feet before I can grab her. "Are you serious, Thomas? These are students coming down from Boston for their graduate thesis work. This isn't a covert nicotine study done by a cigarette lobbyist."

Peter calms everyone down and makes a joke about the students being paid in scallops. The students nervously laugh along with everyone else. But it's clear they don't know what they got themselves into. Peter steers the conversation away from the students and over to Melissa's and his big map of the Chappy road.

Everyone crowds around the map, and the reactions are very consistent based on party lines. In the end, the meeting goes nowhere. Compromise doesn't seem to be an option with this crowd. And then Melissa, with tear-stained eyes, stands up and says, "We're all very passionate about our positions and concerns. I get that. But we're not Chappy. There's about fifty of us here today out of the maybe two thousand people who consider themselves Chappy residents. Let's let the students of Northeastern do their work. They proposed doing a questionnaire. Feel free to contact them with verbiage, so everyone feels like they have contributed to it."

There's a smattering of applause. The CIA representative jumps in, as he doesn't want to lose his seat at the table and offers to coordinate the questionnaire since he has everyone's email through their organization. Melissa, Peter, and a few others agree to also meet with the

Northeastern students, and a new meeting is set for the following week where this group can discuss the proposed questionnaire.

Everyone helps put the chairs back against the wall and sweep up after the meeting ends.

One of my customers comes up to me and pulls me aside. "Boy, that was fun."

"Yeah, I'd rather be out cutting trees at your house, but this is important to us. Melissa is trying to make a safe place for everyone's viewpoint to be heard, but it's hard."

My customer gives me a, "Hmmmmmmmm. Yeah, I get it. We don't agree. But I respect you, Rob, and you do what you gotta do. By the way, you have been doing a great job with the lawns of our houses. What has it been, seven years? But Martha wants to switch to Ramono's Landscaping and Nursery. Change is good. She likes the flowers they plant."

"Oh sure," I blurt out, not knowing what else to say. I could have said that it's convenient he's picking Ramono's, whose owner is the chairman of the selectman who will ultimately have a prominent voice in how this process is settled. But I don't. And I don't yell at the two other customers who also approach me and give me a similar story of no longer needing my services.

"Of course, it has nothing to do with this situation," they say. "Please keep sending us those lovely pictures of your girls."

I thank them for the heads up and tell them it's been a pleasure serving their family for so many years. I'm still trying to play the long game. It's hard, but I'm trying.

Fair to the Rescue

It's now August, and I'm officially hitting a wall. The yearly novelty of good weather, beautiful scenery and the bright shiny faces of the summer people has been replaced with a feeling by islanders of 'get these self-serving, self-indulgent summer people out of here, I want to take time to think, and more importantly, sleep'.

I definitely need a nap. It's a good thing the Ag Fair is this week. Just in time to save my soul and give me some more enjoyable family time. The fair comes at a great time of the summer. The lawns are all hay, so the guys aren't mowing and are happy for the break. The painting and construction crews are lying low as no one wants work done on their house while they're 'summering' on the Vineyard. This just leaves the cleaning crew, who, by now, is on autopilot. So, bring on the fair.

The Martha's Vineyard Agricultural Society and its yearly fair is a staple of Vineyard life. We look forward to it all year round. It takes place yearly during the third week of August. Let me just say I know it's a rinky-dink fair that happens in countless counties across small-town America, but I don't live in those counties. I live in Dukes County on Martha's Vineyard. So the prize pig is my neighbor's. The first place quilt in the hand-stitched division is sometimes my wife's. The blue Araucana eggs with an honorable mention are usually awarded to June, my girls' friend. And speaking of Ilana and Sasha, they always have a ribbon or two for their artwork. It's all very predictable in a Norman Rockwell kind of way. Simple life. A life where these artistic endeavors mean something to the community. And let's puff up our chest as if to say, "Hey, I created this because I love something—just because."

Our lifetime membership to the Agricultural Society includes free passes to the fair. We go for three of the four days. On Thursday, we arrive at 4:00 p.m. after the judges have done their due diligence, looking at all the artwork and tasting every piece of cake, jam, and bread entered. There's always a race to the kids' section. Melissa and I stand back, praying that each child gets the same number of awards and that none of their entries got lost or, God forbid, put in a younger age group section. Knock on wood; we've done pretty well. It all evens out, and I think the girls take the disappointment like champs when they don't get the prize they'd expected. I'm another story. My close-up photograph of the lighthouse at sunset was magical—but no ribbon. Hmmph. Life goes on. But really?

We exit the exhibit hall and take a quick cursory look at the craft tents, food area, farm animals, and take stock of which rides are set up this year, but only a cursory look. We need to pace ourselves. We have three more days of fair fun ahead.

On the way home, my dad calls. This happens daily. The conversations are varied but always challenging. He has so much trouble with technology. I try to stay calm.

"Dad, tell me what you see on your computer screen."

"I don't know. Word is gone. A big 'W' used to be at the bottom of the screen, and now it's gone."

"OK, Dad, just open your Finder and click on Applications."

"The Finder, what's that?"

My voice rises. "The happy face icon on the bottom left corner." I think by talking louder, he will understand me more. It's like I'm in a foreign country speaking English. He doesn't get it. Melissa and the girls are annoyed. Ilana is yelling instructions from the back seat, Sasha has put on her headphones, and Melissa is doing her best to ignore the situation.

"Happy face? I'm looking for the Word program where I write letters. Did you see what the Gazette said about the Steamship Authority reservations policy in the paper today?"

"No, Dad. We're coming from the fair. You don't see an icon with a happy face on it?"

My dad answers like a little child after being scolded. "No, sorry, Robbie. I don't."

"OK, hold tight. We're still in West Tisbury. I'll swing by and fix it. It'll take two seconds." Everyone gives me a look, but Melissa touches my hand and nods her head, giving me the sign—I made the right decision. I remind everyone to stay in the car when we get to Grandpa's. His place is not for the faint of heart.

I feel bad about losing my temper with my dad. I especially hate doing it in front of the girls. But it's hard. It's endless. One day it's the presence of a computer porn virus, which he has no idea how it got there, and another, it's because the cleaners have called me over to his place. It appears the house is littered with smoldering cigarettes and food everywhere.

I lose my temper a lot with him, but oftentimes it has nothing to do with him—I'm just tired. He always brushes off my apologies when I come around to how gruff I've been. He tells me, "No apologies necessary. You and your brother are the only good thing that ever happened to me." This makes me feel worse. I wish he had more. I hope to help him with that. Tomorrow. Next week. But for right now, sleep.

Our next trip to the fair is Friday night. Starting at 6:00 p.m., the kids can ride on all of the rides they want until 10:00 p.m. for the one low price of $30.00. It's the bargain of the century. Basically, it's a way to offset the draw of the impressive display of fireworks going on in Oak Bluffs. The ploy works on money-conscious locals. We get the fairgrounds to ourselves, and it feels for a brief moment like the off-season again as everyone takes a minute to reconnect.

Picture it, Friday night at the fair. We arrive around 5:00 p.m. to get our ride bracelets early, so we don't have to stand in a huge line when 6:00 p.m. rolls around. Then go to the picnic area to have dinner. I grab a pulled chicken sandwich with corn on the cob from the Morning Glory Farm van while Melissa gets a burrito from the charter school stand. The girls bring their food as they are picky, picky eaters. We sit, and a parade of people we know flows by our table, stop and talk. It's like a holiday party where I get to mingle with friends, have a quick chat, and then they move on. Quick snippets—enough to get caught up. Love the fair.

Juanita runs up to me with her daughter Christiana in tow. "Good evening, my boss." She gives me a big hug, and I can smell the alcohol on her breath. "Isn't this wonderful?

Christiana, say hello to Mr. Kagan." Christiana hides behind her mother and grabs her leg.

"Wow, she's getting so big. Christiana, have a great time tonight. Maybe you can go on a ride with Ilana and Sasha at some point."

Ilana and Sasha look over in unison to see who and what I have just promised. Sasha shrugs her shoulders, but Ilana pipes in, "Sure. We can go on the sack slide. Would you like that?"

Christiana peers around her mom's leg and smiles. Juanita mouths the words, thank you, waves, and runs off.

It's like a school class reunion. Lots of talk about the last time we've seen each other. Lots of talk about who is showing up with whom on their arm. And lots of laughter. So good times are being had by all.

The kids wolf down their food so they can make a quick escape for the rides—even though there are still fifteen minutes until the ride bracelets are active. Never once, even when the kids were younger, did I ever freak out when they disappeared at the fair. They probably know most of the roughly one thousand people here. These people know them, too. No one is going to walk off with my child without me knowing about it. It's just like the old days when I was a kid, and we would leave our home on a Saturday morning, tramp around all days with our pals, and not come home until suppertime. Dirty but happy and safe.

Gabe and Neal bump into our table—speaking of kids. They're Rich's kids. He and his wife, Missy, rush up to our table and catch my water bottle right before it topples over.

"Hi, Rich. Hi Missy. Seems like these two have all the energy in the world."

"Hey, boss. Sorry about that. Kids."

"No worries. Missy, I don't get to see you much. I hope I'm not working Rich too hard?"

"Best thing that ever happened. We are finally on the right track, thanks to you. Now, all we need is year-round housing." Missy is beaming and confident.

It's good to see a healthy family unit every once in a while. I mentally pat myself on the back. I did good.

"Rich is great. He's learning skills, and customers love to talk to him. It's a win, win. Well, have fun." And just like that, they're off to their next social encounter.

Boom, it's now 6:00 p.m. The girls check back in at our table for whatever reason, and then they're off again. I excuse myself from a group of friends and say I want to shadow the girls. But what I really want is some fried dough, and they only sell that in the carnival area. It really is my crack. Let's be honest; all sugar is my crack. But chocolate goop on fried dough makes my eyes flutter like I'm having a seizure, and I never pass up an opportunity to inhale one. You're probably now thinking I'm pushing 250 pounds with a big belly. Nope. Dripping wet, I weigh 135 pounds—same weight for the last thirty years (I'm 5′ 4″). I think it's because I'm always running—running to the house from the car—running down the street to a store. I have two speeds. Stop (which means sleeping) and running.

So, I'm walking around with a big smile, chocolate around my lips, and more chocolate on my jeans. Like the roadrunner stopping for some birdseed—Sasha runs up. "I'll take that, please." And a big chunk of my fried dough is gone.

"Do you want a napkin?"

She waves and runs away with no answer. I laugh as big arms wrap around me and lift me off the ground. I turn. "Hey, Ron. Wow. Great to see you. Are the kids around?"

"Ahhhhh, yeah, the kids are around, and Karen is here too," he says with a look in his eyes I can't just place. Ron is a tall, wiry guy with a long blond mane that seems to go on forever. He's much more athletic than he looks and pretty adventurous too. He'd just as soon jump off a cliff with his hang glider as carve up a mountain with his tele skis. I swear he displaces half the mountain on each turn. We met when our kids were toddlers and now see each other socially as well as on job sites. He's an HVAC guy. I always laugh, and at the same time, feel bad when I have to coerce him to descend into a crawlspace that's only eighteen inches high to fix one heating issue or another. He's always so good-natured and never complains during these encounters. But today, something's off.

"Yeah, I would assume Karen's here." Where else would she be on Friday night of the fair? "I'll text Melissa. And we can all sit down and catch up."

"Hold off on that, Rob. Stuff's happening. I don't want to get into it now."

"Oh, OK. No worries. I'm here if you need me." Weird. Yeah, I don't know what's up. Something with Karen, no doubt. They always fight when we're together. Not a good match. But a good family. Does that make sense? I try to put it out of my mind as the sugar kicks in and the lights of the Round-Up spin in my head. I'm sure it's just a fight. They've been together as long as Melissa and me. We fight. Everyone fights.

The sun is setting. Puffy clouds are all around. Dust kicks up as kids run by. The carnival barkers try to yell over the sound of the kids screaming to get our attention. Good times. I have my camera out and try to document it all. Every once in a while, I'll get a magical shot. The lights on the Twister look so otherworldly when I catch them swirling and blurry with the static dusk sky behind them. That's a keeper.

None of us want the evening to end. The kids are dirty and dragging by 10:00 p.m. They've gone on every ride at least ten times. The only reason they finally agree to leave is the notion that they'll be back in this very spot the next day. We have not even seen the barn with all the animals or taken in any of the competitions. Did I mention the women's skillet toss? We leave the fair with chocolate on our faces and clothes, happy with the fact the fat lady has not sung.

Shit Show

We sleep in. Well, everyone else sleeps in. I see the crews meeting at my tool shed. I quickly dress in work clothes and run out to see them off. There's a long list of added 'emergency' situations that got relayed to me by text during our night at the fair. We need to pivot.

I wear work clothes to meet the crews even when I'm not going to join them in the field. I feel guilty enjoying life when I know others in my employ are sweating for my benefit. I even try to time my sailing excursions, so I'll be passing the Chappy ferry when I know my crews won't be there.

But this morning, I'll just be lounging around the house. Maybe I'll keep my work clothes on to clean the chicken coop. I need to put some new hay down. It's been a while. I can smell the chicken poop from the tool shed. I say my goodbyes, knowing full well every one of these employees has my back, and head back to the house, only slightly giving the chicken coop a sideways glance and a pinch of the nose. Woooooo—that smells.

I walk back into the house to the aroma of pancakes

cooking. Everyone is sliding their feet across the floor as it takes too much energy to pick their feet up as they walk. It was a long day yesterday. I smile and sit down just as the phone rings. I grab it and slink out to the porch. I can't stop myself from panicking each time I pick it up. I need to change my attitude. I need to not believe every phone call is the end of the world. But the problem is each phone call pretty much is a shit show. I let the family crunchy granola mantra seep into my head in most instances but thinking positively will not stop some city-dwelling family on vacation from shoving sanitary napkins and baby wipes down the toilet—which, in turn, clogs up the septic system—which, in turn, makes the shit back up into the house and on the lawn—which is why I'm getting this phone call at this point in time. Fuck.

My customer is so apologetic on the phone. She assumes, as the homeowner, it's her fault. I know differently. I saw the renters when they moved into the house at the beginning of last week. Two families, two nannies, and five kids under the age of six all packed into one house. Chaos enveloped the arrival scene like a swarm of bees around your head that just got pissed off for some reason. And no sooner had this carnival arrived than the dads were already out the door for a golf outing. The moms weren't much better as they gave clipped instructions in Spanish to the nannies and rushed out for a quick bite at a fashionable brunch place only serving meals for another hour. I knew I was going to get a call to this house—this week. And here we go.

I call Kyle, Rich, and Santiago. I call the 'Plumber of Last Resort'. Then inform the tenant we'll be right over. It's no problem for my guys and the plumber. They know the drill, and the plumber is getting bookoo bucks for an emergency call. The customer is relieved. The tenant is another story. She's been coming to Chappy for years and has never dealt with such a situation. She's outraged.

We all arrive roughly at the same time, and everyone gives the other a knowing look. Here we go again. There's chaos swirling around the house as I enter. Excrement has backed up into the tubs and on the floors next to the toilets. The fathers avert their eyes as if to say, "Sorry, I know this must be our fault somehow."

The moms are a different story. Instead of letting us triage the situation and get it fixed, they want to inform us this situation is unacceptable, and they want money back from their rent. I'm calm. I tell them I'm here to fix the situation and allow them to get back to their vacation as quickly as possible. This isn't good enough. They want their pound of flesh. They berate me and my guys on and on. Good thing the plumber is still outside. I want to keep them away from him because I know he'll lash back and, worse, probably leave and never come back. So I take one for the team and continue to listen. As if I'm the one keeping these people from getting a rebate on their rental.

Jeff, the actual 'Plumber of Last Resort', doesn't get out of his van right away. He probably senses the preamble going on inside. But eventually, he moves the pile of old New York Times stacked on his passenger seat and searches for the tools he'll need for this job. His van looks more like a homeless shelter than a workspace. And the man doesn't look dissimilar to his vehicle. He has the long beard of a Harry Potter character. Earrings, a ponytail with many elastics, and hand-rolled cigarettes round out his costume.

Eventually, he slams the sliding van door. Looks at me with a sincere smile as he enters the house and says matter-of-factly, "Hey Rob, what do we got?" I believe this place could be on fire, and Jeff would have the same opening line. In his world, something's always on fire.

Jeff moves toys off the hatch to the crawl space and shimmies down into the dark, damp underbelly of this old house. My guys stand ready as they know they're merely present as a show of force until the situation is fixed. The clean-up to this shit show will come later—literally.

It takes about thirty minutes for Jeff to reemerge with a bucket full of sanitary napkins and baby wipes that were clogging the septic line. All this time, the women of the house have been yelling at me nonstop. But this ends immediately when they see Jeff with the bucket. A hand-rolled cigarette is dangling from his mouth, and the women want to yell at him about second-hand smoke and the ash falling to the floor. But at this moment, they know better. One look in the bucket, and they know all their yelling and posturing was a mistake. A big mistake. They attempt to backtrack as Jeff ignores them, flushes all the toilets, and checks the newly cleared septic line. "We didn't know you couldn't put that stuff in the toilet. Who would know that?"

I'm ready for this moment and pull out a copy of the lease they signed before starting their vacation at this quaint farmhouse oasis on Chappy.

More yelling occurs as the women turn on their husbands. "Why didn't you tell us about this? I feel so embarrassed. This is all your fault." The husbands somehow knew they were going to get blamed. It was only a matter of time. They stammer with their reply, and I come to their rescue because I'm done with this situation.

"Excuse me, but I recall when we first talked on the phone that you said you've been coming to Chappy for ten years. Well, every house on Chappy has a septic system with the same restrictions. So since you're such a seasoned Chappy person, you should be well aware of the etiquette for using the toilets."

The fair had me in such a good mood last night. This summer morning is beautiful and had so many possibilities. But these people have ruined it for me. Why do they have to be such assholes? I've clearly hit my summer wall. I'm done with tourists.

The tenants stand still for a second. Quiet. I'm ready for more of a fight. But instead, they turn without another word to me and start yelling at their nannies while simultaneously attempting to get their kids ready for day camp.

We get to work with the clean-up. Jeff leaves. I give the guys an abridged schedule for the day. I apologize to them. Remind them there will be a bonus in their pay for this shit duty... as always. I tell them to just smile at the tenants and convey to me any crazy thoughts and comments they utter. I don't think there will be much trouble. The guys agree and smirk a little at the recollection of me telling off the tenants.

I'm bummed they saw me lose my cool. I don't want them making that judgment call and telling off some tenant in the future. Damn, I should've controlled myself better.

Now, back to my home where life is peaceful and happy, and everyone knows what doesn't go down the toilet.

A Shit Show of Another Nature

My family doesn't even look up as I walk in the door. There's lots of grumbling about the time. Lots of running around. Oh, yeah. One more day of the fair! I drag myself upstairs to change for more fun in the sun. Or, more accurately, more fun in the dust bowl that is the fair on a hot August day. And it's hot. We drive with the windows down and the tunes blaring. Ilana wants to hear Hozier. Sasha wants to listen to the Avett Brothers, and Mom and Dad are hooked on XM's Road Trip Radio. We fit it all in as we make our way up-island.

We arrive at noontime. It's our third day at the fair. We've already spent about $200 so far on food, trinkets, and rides. So, bringing food feels like a good move. We wolf down our lunches, and half run/half walk to the barn. Everyone has their phones out. We need a picture of the bunnies. We need a picture of the prize chickens.

Wait. Our chicken, Bunny Love, is prettier than this chicken with a blue medal. "Why didn't we enter Bunny Love?" Sasha asks. I try to use logic in my explanation, which gets a blank stare.

Melissa merely listens, says a few "hmmmms," and tells her it's worth considering for next year. "We'll look at our options and make a plan. Does that sound good?"

How does she do that? How does Melissa know how to listen, not try to fix things instantly, and get through to Sasha on a level that doesn't instantly piss her off? I'm bad at this whole parenting thing. I try, but I'm hard-wired wrong.

We make two loops through the barn to make sure we haven't missed any of the animals and their cuteness and head out to the field to watch an ox pull, a chainsaw contest, or, if we're lucky, the women's skillet toss. We settle in on the bleachers, and I eye Karen sitting with their friend Billy. I turn to Melissa. "That's weird. I didn't know Billy was out of jail." I'm up and sliding over to where Karen is sitting before Melissa can grab my hand and stop me.

"Hi, Karen. Fancy meeting you here. Ron said you were around last night with the girls, but I must have missed you." I keep it light and breezy. Still remembering Ron's words last night. The fact that Karen is here with Billy shouldn't be a big deal. They are old friends. But the jail thing...

"No, Ron was wrong. I didn't come last night," she says flatly. Karen is looking from me to Billy and then over to Melissa. They wave, but Melissa doesn't come over.

I get the impression I've stepped into something I shouldn't be a part of and make my exit as fast as I can. "Well, enjoy the show. Big hugs all around." I hug them both, even though Billy isn't someone I would usually hug, but I'm nervous for some reason and just do it.

I move back over to Melissa and the girls. Melissa gives me a look and whispers, "There's stuff going on. Wait," and then turns to the girls. "Hey, why don't you see who else is here. I want to talk to Daddy."

Melissa doesn't have to tell them twice, and they're gone. She takes a minute, asks me to accompany her to the camping area, and then just lets it fly. "You know Billy was in jail, right?"

"Yes. He was caught embezzling funds from the non-profit he works for. What was it?"

"The Children Outdoors Fund," Melissa says flatly.

"Right. It was the seventy-year-old secretary that confronted him about it. And he hit her or something."

Melissa shakes her head. "He was sent to jail for assaulting her to the point of unconsciousness and then tried to cover up the embezzlement. They caught him shredding the evidence."

"What? He was only in jail for a year. How does that happen?" I guess I don't want to know. They have two kids. What a mess.

"Well, it gets worse. You know that Ron and Karen are good friends with Billy and kind of gave him a pass for his actions."

"Yes, Ron told me they were visiting Billy in jail. They chalked it up to a bad decision as a result of gambling debts and a heated discussion that got out of hand. But I didn't know he beat the woman unconscious. Crazy."

Melissa pulls me behind a tree, sits down, and motions me to do the same. "The problem is Karen started visiting Billy alone and more often. They now have feelings for each other."

This isn't registering in my head. Embezzlement—two marriages ripped apart—kids! It takes me a moment before I catch up. "Wait. Karen and Billy are together now? That's ridiculous. He beat an old woman! How's he able to be around kids—Karen's kids? Oh shit. That's why Ron was being so weird last night."

Melissa tries to tell me more, debate the situation, but I cut her off. This is the fair. This is supposed to be my time to recharge my batteries and connect with my friends—not hear this crap. What am I supposed to do with this information? I want to cry, but tears don't come. They never come. Wish they would now. Instead, I get up, pull Melissa up, hug her as tight as I can, and tell her, "I love you." I can't think of anything else to say other than, "Let's find the kids. I'm done."

On the way out, the girls run to the information shed to get this years' poster with the big hand-drawn sheep looking out through a split rail fence. I'm thinking about posters from years past as the girls wait their turn to make their purchase. All of a sudden, Ken's in my face. Ken is an acquaintance from the fire department. He needs to tell me something. I listen as EMT stories are usually good and uplifting. And I need a good story after what I just heard.

Ken smiles, "You know Hank from the West Tisbury Fire Department?"

"Yeah, what's up with Hank? I haven't seen him since that educational class on frostbite I took last winter." Hank's the nicest guy—a teacher, I think. Always around to help out in a pinch. I don't know him well but have always gotten a good feeling about him.

"Well, ahhhhh," Ken stammers, but at the same time, it's evident he wants to pass on this gossip. "It turns out Hank has been letting some of the kids with family problems he sees at school hang out at his house. You know, to get a break from the chaos of their life at home."

"There are enough of them on this island to go around. It's good Hank doesn't stop caring when his kids leave the classroom."

Ken puts his hand up in a halting fashion. "I'm not done. Kids are starting to live at his house."

"Oh, crap. Can you stop there? I like this guy. No, go on. I'm going to hear it eventually, anyway," I reluctantly say.

"So, on top of that, it turns out Hank is supplying kids with porn and booze. The parents are in an uproar."

"Jesus Christ. OK. Wow. I don't know what to say. He seems so normal. He's always so helpful on an EMT scene." I'm beside myself and sit down as my girls are running back, poster in hand. I give Ken a nervous smile, a nod of the head, and basically, run away with my family. Get to our car and race back to Chappy. What the fuck?

I'm in deep. I know way too much about this rock and its inhabitants. I want to be anonymous. I see Ross dropping Amy off at the ferry, still wearing the wrinkled dress from the night before. Boom—I don't want to know. Mike isn't at the fire meeting on Sunday morning, and everyone must tell me it's because of a domestic abuse call that came over the police scanner the night before. Boom—I don't want to know. David has schizophrenia and wants to end it all by driving his car off the Chappy ferry at warp speed. My beeper goes off to save his ass. Boom—I don't want to know. And now the situations with Ron, Karen, Billy, and Hank—I don't want to know.

What's it like to be anonymous? To not know your neighbors, to not know your town's politics, to not know the problems at every corner of your universe. I want to experience that feeling. I'm tired, and it's wearing me down seeing so much dysfunction in the people I know, the friends I love, the community I live in. I like to fix things, and these people can't be fixed. This is all going on in my head as we drive back to Chappy. The kids are screaming about who's on whose side of the car. Melissa is texting a friend, who's at the fair and wondering where we are, and I'm screaming inside my head. That's about right. Breathe. Breathe. I can get through this.

Summer Ends

This summer took a lot out of me—more than usual. The balance of good times, good weather, and family fun didn't seem to offset the drama of the world around me. But happily, the last week of summer is upon us. The offseason is so close I can taste it. It always goes by so fast. It's like a car crash. In the moment, everything goes so slowly, but in a flash, you're on a stretcher and asking yourself, "What just happened?"

We still need to make it through Labor Day weekend. I say this, but on the Vineyard, it's a non-event. I always have to remind myself of this fact. Growing up in the real world, one remembers the last hurrah of this weekend, the traffic and the back-to-school shopping. On the Vineyard, it's like crickets in a field—silence. Summer families with kids are already back home playing pre-season sports or getting ready for school. The remaining lot are quietly packing up their homes for the long winter's sleep. My chore, if I choose to accept it, is to visit this bunch in order to drum up business for the winter. So, I jump in my old yellow Jeep, outfitted in some torn and weathered

Patagonia shorts, a collared yet faded polo shirt, and a pair of docksiders circa 1987, and I pound the pavement—or more aptly—the sand.

I arrive at my customers' houses all light and smiling with notebook in hand. These meetings will dictate my winter work schedule. Lately, I have been peppering my conversations with the subject of the bike path. It's time to remind these people of how integrated our lives are. Dierdra Lacombe is a good example. We caretake her house year-round, clean her house once a week, mow the lawn, and our kids know her kids from the community center sailing program.

"Hi, Dierdra. Is this an OK time to switch out the porch screens for winter panels?"

"Sure, Rob, whatever you think. I don't believe we'll use the porch again this season."

"Sorry, I'm a little late. I had to walk next to Sasha as she rode her bike to a friend's."

"Oh, that must be fun, spending time with Sasha. She's getting so big."

Dierdra doesn't take the bait, and I have to keep moving the conversation toward the bike path issue. "I love spending time with Sasha. But it's sad to see her still a little gun shy on her bike. She used to be more of a free spirit."

"Oh yes, the accident. That must have been hard on you guys. But she's young. She'll bounce back in no time."

Still not biting. I have to go at this head-on. "Have you gotten the questionnaire about the bike path initiative we're working on?"

It's been weeks since they were sent out, and we filled ours out and sent it in within hours of getting it. All the people at the 'meetings' did the same. The rest of Chappy has been slow to check off boxes. Both sides have been trying to nudge the stragglers along as I'm doing today.

"Yes, of course. It's on the top of the pile of mail on my desk. We're eager to help out the community in whatever way we can. I'm so appreciative of everyone who has gotten involved with this issue."

Not the response I'm hoping for, and so I go for broke and push on.

"It seems like a no-brainer to me. It comes down to safety. We even came up with an eco-friendly design with recycled materials and a way to pay for it."

"Great, Rob. We have had similar issues in our hometown. I understand your perspective and am mostly in favor of the bike path. However, I do understand some of the arguments against it. The CIA board members and your neighbor, Tom Hawthorne, have been very persuasive. It's all so tiring. We live so much of this drama at home—so many issues. We come to Chappy to get away from all of that. We just want to be anonymous. Sit by the pool, read a book, and escape the complicated world. You're so lucky you live in such a simple and beautiful place."

The simple and beautiful comment takes me aback. My inclination is to debate each point. I want to lay out my case more. I know pushing will alienate Dierdra. My customers love me and depend on me. But I have begun to see that my political views are putting a wedge in our relationship. Their need for peace and quiet trumps their need to keep me, their caretaker, happy. It's weird. In the beginning, I didn't see my customers filling out the questionnaire as a favor to me. I thought families would jump to get involved. Now it's their ambivalence getting me mad. No, not getting—I'm actually mad. First, the facts are not pushing these people to do the right thing. And after talking to them, I find they're not even willing to get on board to help out their trusted caretaker with a pet project. Sometimes the way my customers and I hug and interact makes me feel like family. But I'm not—I'm just a hired hand.

In the end, I wrap the conversation up in a nonthreatening way. "I get it. I believe the committee just wants to hear from the people of Chappy so they can make an informed decision. This is why the questionnaire is so important. I'm confident it will work itself out."

"You're so right, Rob. It will work itself out. You're doing the right thing. I have to run. Grab a piece of banana bread on your way out."

I smile. Make notes in my scheduling book. Rinse and repeat. No problem. As she said, "It will all work itself out." But this isn't why I'm smiling. I'm smiling because September will soon be here, and with it comes the best weather of the year, late-season baseball, walks with my girls to the bus stop, and the hope for a quieter phone.

FALL

"Slow Down, You Move Too Fast, You've Got to Make the Morning Last..."*

Drop the kids off at school, meet with my crews, check-in with Melissa, respond to customer emails, and breathe. Breathing and recuperating is what September is all about for me. Shangri La takes a lot out of a soul. Running nonstop physically as well as in my head leaves me worn out in September. I recuperate, and at the same time, stress out about recuperating. Getting my customers out of my head takes time. But I take great solace in the fact I'm in full charge of their homes until May, and the control makes me breathe easier... eventually.

Still, I fill my days, some with work, some with puttering, and some with reconnecting with friends. Keep your head down. Get through it. And before you know it, the season is over, and you're seeing Ron again at the Dock Street Diner like no time has passed.

I talk about the pace of work and life slowing down, but that doesn't stop me from running wherever I go. I still can't walk, even in September. The anxiety of leaving the littlest chores undone makes my mind pile up on itself. The

---

* "59th Street Bridge Song" by Paul Simon

self-imposed anxiety is overwhelming—control. Order. I think of Ilana and her struggles. We both need to get ahead of our anxiety. So, I run. Even though it's September, quiet and no deadlines looming, I run. And as I'm running, I see Jonah out of the corner of my eye putting away tools from the day's jobs.

I pause, mid-step, looking at him as I make my way to the chicken coop, grab some eggs, categorize the level of the smell emanating from the coop, and move on. I make the snap decision the coop clean-up can wait, and I turn my attention back to Jonah as I hear clanging in the shed. Jonah is a big boy of twenty-two with muscles and a farmer's tan that prove he has known hard labor. It's his last day working for me, and I can see in the way he's unloading the tools not so gingerly that he just wants to get out of Dodge. He's worked for me for four months, and in that time, I feel I have a pretty good read on him.

Jonah has lived his entire life on Martha's Vineyard. He's a local with all the bravado or baggage that comes with that moniker. His dad works for a plumbing company, and his mom weaves rugs to sell at an artisan's fair when she can find the time. Jonah, like most island kids, has an independent streak that comes from a life of physical safety—or at least perceived safety. He learned to drive at thirteen in the backwoods of some friend's farm. He knows his way around a boat, any boat, and can land a fish with his eyes closed. And the pot his father harvests on the conservation land next to his family's house is there for the taking. The local police are not going to bother him. They did the same thing before joining the force and probably play pool with Jonah's dad down at the Lampost Bar.

I think the independent streak in Vineyarders comes from knowing their surroundings and its inhabitants intimately. Hell, it's a pile of sand in the middle of the ocean. The players in the game tend to be more stagnant than most places. Everyone is somehow related to each other, had an interaction in school, the volunteer fire department, or knows the brother of a girlfriend of their dad. It's less scary if the person coming out of the shadows on a dark night on the beach is someone you know. There are many whacked-out, bat-crazy people on the Vineyard. But you tend to know them. Know how to act around them. Or fuck it—as many people do... just marry them and roll the dice.

Yet, we know in the end, the house always wins. My mind starts to categorize all the married couples who have gambled and are on their second or third spouse. The graph of family connections becomes too complicated for me to keep straight. My thoughts are brought back to Jonah and his last day of work when I hear him throw something onto a shelf. I run over to catch him before he does any real damage to my tools. He's already planning his escape. He has a lot to do before he leaves this rock for good.

"Hey, Jonah," I say a little too loudly in an effort to get him to stop throwing my stuff. "So, you're off to Boston next week. Have you landed a job yet?"

"Right now, I'm concentrating on housing. I met a few folks at the Farm Institute this summer who have a research grant to study the monarch butterfly's changing migration patterns. They said I could crash at their place. It's in Braintree. You know, near the mall."

"Yeah, I know Braintree. Should be fun. Don't spend all your money at once and forget to look for a job. Maybe the kids you're living with will have an opening."

"No, you're right. And Tonya, one of the girls, is hot.

We're friends, but she's bound to know some other girls. Boston is packed with women. The odds are in my favor for an easy hook-up. If you know what I mean?"

I laugh uneasily and change the subject. "Won't you miss the small town living of Martha's Vineyard?"

"Hell no. I'm going to get on that ferry and never look back. If my folks want to see me, they're going to have to visit me at my apartment in the real world."

I try to give him some words of wisdom. Talk to him about who he might meet in that real world. How different it might actually be from what he thinks. But Jonah doesn't hear me. No one hears what they don't want to hear. At twenty-two, Jonah has it all figured out. Why should this kid be any different? But that's the point; he is different. He's an islander. In the end, we shake hands, and I wish him well. That's it. That's all.

Sadly, I predict Jonah will be back on-island before next spring. I have seen this time and time again. Vineyard kids are ill-equipped to deal with life off-island. They have a fantasy of what the real world is all about. Wealthy people invade their space each summer with an air of entitlement and confidence. And the off-season is spent inhaling social media that glamorizes a fake narrative about life in general. No wonder these kids have a warped view of how everyone else lives. Trips off-island to the mall for clothes or field trips to Old Sturbridge Village to experience this country's origins are a poor substitute for understanding the complexities of modern life or a useful roadmap to successfully prepare oneself for life off-island.

These kids can't help but get disenchanted when they go off to college or move to another locale to just get away. They find the reality of life in the real world isn't the reality they'd perceived. People in the real world aren't all rich.

They don't all act like the characters on reality TV shows. It's different for sure. It's complicated but in a different way than they hoped and anticipated. It's certainly not what most of them are looking for.

It's easy to give up when the reality of the mainland doesn't live up to expectations—easy to retreat back to the Vineyard. The safety, the comfortable, and the known are easier to take when you find life off-island is also challenging.

I stand by my assertion that the odds are stacked against Jonah. I wonder if the odds would be stacked against me at this point if I left. I think maybe I'm a little envious sometimes of him even trying. I walk around the yard in a daze after Jonah goes, shooing chickens off the porch. Thoughts of living in suburbia with normal people and a regular job as a cog in some corporate wheel swirl in my head. It sounds mind-numbingly serene. I could do that. River runs by me toward one of the chickens, just for fun, and in an instant, I'm out of my head and back on my island.

Martha's Vineyard is this great little ecosystem, almost closed off, but not quite. People are quick to accept others for their bad behavior as it becomes normalized. It creeps up on you. Acquaintances' actions become friends' actions. Questionable lifestyles become tolerated in your day-to-day life as we have no choice but to interact with these people as we move about the island. I know old Timothy Ledbettle stole from the town coffers to take his seventeen-year-old girlfriend to Aruba. At first, I wouldn't look at him when we bumped into each other. But then I couldn't get a sprinkler guy to service a client. Timothy owns a sprinkler business. So I reluctantly called him. I reluctantly talked to him. Soon, I'm saying hello to him and his nineteen-year-old wife at the Lampost. I'm like a frog being brought to a boil slowly and inevitably. The outrage is pushed to the back of my brain. I rationalize. I compartmentalize. I become numb and move on. I guess we all do that.

I have lived on Chappy for better than twenty-eight years. I think of my own baggage and how it's shaped my worldview and decisions. I'm fine. The dysfunction that defines others is so clear to me. I feel like we've sidestepped it so far. We've done our best. But can our kids continue to live here, see all that's in front of them, and not be impacted? What makes them more special than Jonah? Is our parenting so strong we can mitigate society's influences? Should we leave now while the kids are young and adaptable? What's the answer? Can I conduct a controlled experiment and then go back in time and make the right decision? I want to know how much power I really have. I have always believed in free will. But now I'm thinking I have free will as long as it conforms to a finite list of options picked out by my personal history.

I walk inside after my interaction with Jonah and see Melissa sitting in the playroom's window seat. She's starting a new quilt from the samples of materials she got from fabric stores over the years. It's going to be a rainbow pattern of sorts and sure to win a prize in next year's Ag Fair. She sees me staring at the material in her lap for way too long and somehow knowingly jumps up and says, "Let's go for a walk and find River."

"Yeah, she's in the yard under the hammock. But yeah, I need a walk."

"So, how did it go with Jonah? Same old thoughts running through your head?"

"Wow, is it that obvious," I say a little too abruptly, shocked at how well she reads me.

"Rob, you take it personally each time one of your employees doesn't make it off-island. When you pick up the phone and Jim's on the other end of the line, it seems you forget his history. You forget everyone's history until it hits you in the face, and you feel you have to fix them." Melissa, the mother hen, sees the Vineyard more clearly than I do.

"I love our community, but I'm coming around to the fact that we're not immune to our surroundings. People continually make wrong decisions, and at a certain point, our kids are going to become aware of the world around them. We need to do a better job of insulating our kids from this dysfunction." I can't believe I'm saying this out loud. I've been the defender of our lifestyle for so long.

At this point, we are outside, and on cue, River comes running up to us. Melissa takes my hand as we make our way down the road twenty paces behind River. Our guide dog is good at setting the pace and pointing us in the right direction.

Melissa stops and looks at me. "I want them to accept people for who they are, but you hit the nail on the head. The patterns are adding up. Just the other day, Ilana told me about the guy who used the town dredge for his own property, remember? Well, he built his boys a clubhouse in their backyard so they could get away from their parental units... and smoke pot. These kids are fourteen years old!"

River stops and looks back at us in quizzical alarm. I sense her alarm. It's time for me to walk back a little of my worries. We are starting to go down a road that I'm not comfortable with. I try to calm Melissa down as she describes the kids, their parents, and the situation. I try to talk about, how above it all, we are. "You are so incredible, honey. The girls see you as their example—not these kids. We bring them all around 'the real world' to see how life is outside our sandy pile of land. They get it. Give them credit. The more they know, the more they will be able to sidestep what others can't."

But Melissa can't calm down. "Ilana asked if she could go check it out, all the time telling me she wouldn't smoke. Ilana actually said the words, 'It's no big deal.' She said, 'It's not like their parents aren't smoking nonstop, also.'"

The girls believe island life is no big deal.

Our conversation isn't as serene as the country road we're on, but it still feels good to be outside. Getting out in nature is always helpful. I just wish the conversation was different. I just wish life around us was different. I'm still hoping for the relaxing pace of September and the fall, in general, to kick into gear and put our life back into a healthy perspective. I instinctively push back against Melissa out of hope rather than facts. But sadly, deep down, I know her concerns ring true.

Semi-Local Barbecue

The mantra of locals is that God gave Vineyarders the magic of September as our payment for making it through yet another summer. It's a beautiful Saturday night, and our angst-ridden discussion about our place in the world feels a million miles away. The air is crisp and dry. The views surrounding us are unobstructed by the clutter of the tourist season.

We're on our way to our friends' house—off Chappy. We're excited to drive our old Jeep as it won't be long before the top and doors must be put back on. What a shame. The girls stand on the back seat, arms wrapped around the roll bar screaming, "In the jungle, the quiet jungle, the lion sleeps tonight..." Melissa and I look back and smile as we bounce along the dirt road toward the Chappy ferry and our excursion to Oak Bluffs.

It only takes us forty-five minutes to go the twelve miles to our friend's house. So we count ourselves lucky. They live on the water. Not the ocean with crashing waves and a beach, but more of a bayou feel to it with trails of waterways surrounded by seagrass. Melissa has made a playlist for our friends that will waft gently out over the back lawn as guests drink and kids run about. We are thrilled to get off Chappy—so many friends to catch up with.

Ilana taps me on the shoulder. "Will Ron and Karen and the girls be there?"

Before I can answer, she cuts me off. "And what about Annie and the twins? I haven't seen them since June when we got out of school!"

"Yes, yes. They should all be there." I try to keep my voice calm to settle Ilana down, but I'm just as excited as she is. I don't even notice when Melissa gives me a look and tries to get my attention.

We arrive, and the girls open the car door and dash off before the car stops in the driveway. We laugh and marvel at their ability to jump and run. Wish I could do the same. Melissa and I grab our contributions to the party and walking—not running—head to the backyard. Melissa takes hold of my arm and pulls me aside just before I'm about to drop my beer in the tub and make a beeline for my friends. She has a look on her face that tells me she has some words of caution or probably marching orders while at the party.

"What?" I say a little too abruptly. "Sorry, what, honey?"

"So, Ron will be here tonight with the girls, but Karen will not. Try to talk to him about laying off Karen, OK?"

I roll my eyes. Melissa hates when I do that. I wish I could stop myself. It's just that their story is so bizarre, even for Martha's Vineyard standards. I'm shaking my head as I'm thinking about this whole ordeal. Ron's wife has chosen to be with an embezzling assaulter of old women over her husband. "I just don't get it. I assume Ron is lashing out because, he too, can't wrap his head around it all and is searching for answers."

"But that's all he's talking about. He's bad-mouthing

Karen all over town. He's the one who said it was OK for Karen to explore her feelings for Billy."

"I think he said that in the haze of the situation coming to light. Do you think Ron should've been thinking clearly when he found all this shit out?"

Melissa gives me a look that says, "That's not fair."

"Come on, Rob. It's not that black and white. Karen and Ron's marriage hasn't been good for a long time. I get it. I have a hard time understanding it all, too. But it is what it is, and they have their three kids to think of."

"Yes, exactly," I jump in, almost talking over Melissa's words. "I get why Ron doesn't want his kids around that guy. So it took him a minute to understand the ramifications of the whole situation. He's awake now. I agree; maybe a little too awake. He reminds me of my dad. Boy, Jerry doesn't miss an opportunity to bad mouth my mom. And what has it been, forty-five years?"

"Rob, you're making my point. Your parents' divorce really damaged you and your brother."

"We are not."

It's Melissa's turn to roll her eyes. "Ron has a lot to process, but somehow he has to compartmentalize his problems. The kids are going to start getting dragged into this mess."

That's all she had to say. I don't want to, but I think of my mother. I think of my past. "You're right. He needs to hold it together for the kids. Poisoning them on their mother will be worse in the long run. I'll talk to him." And with that, we make our way to the party—all the while noticing the stares from our friends who probably heard our heated discussion.

The barbecue in full swing looks pretty run-of-the-mill. Lots of catching up. Lots of conversations about nothing in particular. Most of the guys here have their own businesses and look like they just got a weekend pass from the front lines. A few of us huddle near the ten-foot industrial grill and drink a beer, mostly in silence. Every once in a while, someone will bring up a story about their businesses. Lewis has the best ones as he deals with the wedding industry on the island. Some billionaire wanted to put a shark in a saltwater pool and cover it with plexiglass so the guests could dance on top of the circling shark. Seriously?

Stories like that are interesting. But we're just as interested to hear Ron's description of the building projects he's working on. Someone has designed a house with secret staircases, an escape room, and a tunnel to a man cave. Never a dull moment on this rock. But mostly, we stand in silence, watching and listening to the kids scream in the night air. This is what we're working for. Our servitude is all worth it when we see our kids free and happy.

Occasionally, I look up to make sure I see the kids weaving in and out of the seagrass-lined waterways on their stand-up paddleboards. All seems good, and I go back to my beer. But I know it isn't all good as I look a little closer at the scene in front of me. A good-looking, eighteen-year-old boy is giving my daughter a hand back onto her board. He also happens to be knee-deep in a court case to determine if he should be incarcerated for giving another child a gun that ended up being used for a crime. Another teen we see at dance recitals regularly is deep in conversation with my other daughter. She can't go home. It's not good at home. There's more. These kids need help. How much do you dive into this as a friend or just a community member? Life. It should be simple. Create a family, a community, work hard, play hard, and enjoy.

Martha's Vineyard should be a place to live a simple

life. Customers are constantly telling me they perceive it this way. But I have learned that perception is a slippery slope. The mask of a pretty picture clouds the reality. It's more like a messed-up jigsaw puzzle where all the pieces don't fit.

My friends snap me out of my daze with a nudge and a beer. They're also taking in the swirling activity of the kids. I wonder if they notice what I notice? I take a sip of my Magic Hat no. 9 beer and key in on their conversation. It turns out that both fathers are sending their seventh-grade kids to private school off-island close to the ferry terminal. I thought I was getting nudged out of my doldrums, but I'm right back in it. I'm not alone in my worries. This doesn't make it any better for me as I don't have their options. My friends live on an island. I live on an island, off an island. They can get their kids to the first ferry off Martha's Vineyard each day that will take them to this private school and a bigger worldview. My little ferry doesn't start up early enough for us to have that option. And anyway, is homogeneous privilege any better than homogeneous dysfunction?

Rather than dwell on this question and my own dilemmas, I take a break from the conversation for an opportunity to pull Ron aside and see how he's doing, as well as seeing if I can make good on my promise to Melissa.

"So Ron, the kids are having a good time."

"Yeah, I'm just glad Karen didn't show up with that asshole, Billy."

"Are you doing OK with all that?" I say with as neutral a tone as possible.

"Billy wrecked his own family. His wife doesn't want him anywhere near their kids. Fuck if I'm going to let him near my kids."

"No. I get it. Just remember, no matter what's going on, you need to make sure your kids aren't pulled into the middle of it."

"Oh, I don't talk to them about their mother. I wait until they're at school before I call that bitch. We've already started talking to lawyers. She's living with that jerk and is going to want alimony from me."

I don't know what to say, and this conversation is more heated than the one I'd had with Melissa. No doubt, everyone can hear us and knows exactly what we're talking about. "Ron, take it one step at a time. Are you seeing someone to talk to?"

"Yeah, I'm seeing someone. I'm fine."

"It's definitely healthy to talk about the situation, and I'm here for you. But maybe distance yourself from Karen while you work through this with your therapist. Listen, I don't know shit, and neither does anyone else. This is a fucked-up situation. But I do know personally that you have to work through this stuff, and the anger isn't going to help you."

"As long as that bitch stays away from me, I'll be fine."

I'm not getting anywhere. Hell, I don't think I would be reachable mentally if this situation happened to me. I know Ron and Karen will eventually come to terms with it, and things will settle down—normalize. But right now, I don't think there's a road map for either one. I end by saying, "Just call me anytime to vent. I'll listen. It's better than saying stuff to Karen you can't take back, or worse, having your kids overhear."

Instinctively, we both look up at the same time to look for our kids. The waterways are silent. The jubilant screaming of the night has given way to dirty kids slumped in chairs and hammocks around the yard with little or no more energy. All the parents, in unison, realize that a good thing is coming to an end and begin to collect their kids.

Melissa and I compare notes on the barbecue as we make our way back to Chappy. The girls are fast asleep in the back seat.

"They definitely got their exercise tonight," I say with a half-smile.

"I'm still feeling a little raw from our walk with River. So many kids tonight, playing like nothing is wrong in their lives. Playing with our kids. I don't want this for them." The barbecue has obviously not changed her assessment that island life normalizes bad behavior. If anything, it has intensified how close to home the problems are.

I try to change the subject to something more positive. It's just too late for a serious conversation. "Our friends, for the most part, are different. They're positive role models..." I pause to think up a good story. "Susan Henderson told me about the yurt they erected in their yard so another couple, also at the barbecue, I can't remember their names, could have a place to 'live'."

Melissa reminds me, "Uh huh, that 'couple' living in the yurt are the Harlowes." She gives me a look, and it jars my memory, and I remember the Harlowes lost their house to the feds for a Ponzi scheme that went awry.

Melissa changes the subject once again, brings up Ron, and asks me about our talk.

"Oh, you saw that?"

"Yes, everyone basically got the gist of what you guys were talking about."

I tell her about our conversation, my insightful or bullshit words of understanding, and that he can always call me to talk. "I didn't really know what to say. It's fucked up. My main goal was to tell him to keep the girls out of it.

And, he said he is. I tried to tell him not to talk trash so much to Karen, but he's angry. I think there's going to be some trash talk for a while."

We talk it out and don't come to any constructive conclusions about our friends' situation. We get back to Chappy by 9:30 p.m., exhausted, and collapse on the couch to watch the last innings of the Red Sox game after pouring our sleeping kids into their beds. We can wash them and their sheets tomorrow. Melissa makes popcorn and is by my side just as the eighth inning is heating up with JBJ at the plate and one man on third. I relax for a moment—just a moment. Then the phone rings.

As I'm picking it up, my brain screams at me not to do it. Just let it go to voicemail. But I answer it. It's Jim, the painter, and he has a story. He has a problem that needs fixing. It all sounds rational, and matter of fact, as Jim tells it. But it's still a problem to fix, and it's 10:00 on a Saturday night, and he's out fishing.

Jim's calling from his cell in a 'borrowed' skiff in the middle of Cape Pogue Bay. He's been trying to get someone for hours, but the reception on Chappy... yeah, yeah, I know.

He's been fishing. I get that. He lost track of time. I get that too. But then he tells me the engine on the skiff quit, and he has been paddling to shore. Ah crap, now I know where I fit into this.

"Rob, I'd be home right now, but the current has been a problem. Can you help?"

So many questions start filling my head. I know not to ask any of them as I really don't want to know. The one my wife mouths to me is the most telling, "Why did you answer the phone?" The bottom line is Jim's in trouble. I'm the only idiot stupid enough to actually pick up a call from him on a Saturday night. God knows his wife is smarter than that.

Within minutes I'm out the door as my wife looks on and shakes her head. She doesn't bother asking what I'm doing. Melissa is tired of trying to get me to see the futility of saving these people from themselves. More popcorn for her.

I grab a spotlight I keep charged near the mudroom door, my EMT jump kit out of my truck, and fire up my trusty Jeep Wrangler. I blare the Stones through the empty night air as I prep the Jeep's tires at the Dyke Bridge for my sandy drive out to Cape Pogue. The London Tabernacle Choir sings the intro to "You Can't Always Get What You Want," and gives the still night an eerie tone.

I drive twenty feet on the beach, stop, shine my light and yell, "Jim!" No answer, and so I move on. It takes me about forty-five minutes to find him. He's draped over the bow of a metal skiff with both his hands in the water, paddling toward shore. It's a small, light skiff, so the back end of the boat is lifted out of the water as he paddles. He slowly and calmly paddles toward me as I half-heartedly berate him from shore. He has to be cold. I dip my hand in the water as the small waves lap onto the rocky shore and dry it off quickly on my jeans. Yup, it's cold. I jump back into the car to wait. Stupid Jim. Why am I here? Why am I the one to save him? I know. I know. I answered the phone.

Jim gets in the car after pulling the skiff up onto the shore and into the seagrass area. He tells me he intends to come back tomorrow, fix the engine, and return the skiff to the Dyke Bridge area where he procured it. He starts to ask where to put his catch (he is so proud), but I cut him off. "Just get in, put the fish on your lap, and let me get you home."

I'm pissed—more at myself than at Jim. He gives me a hurt look. I pull back my tirade and tell myself the smell in the car will be a reminder to my future self. I'm coming to terms with the real reason not everyone got on Noah's boat. They weren't meant to be saved.

Late September
Bike Path Saga Comes to a Head

Obviously, we feel our family is worth saving. Chickens, employees, EMT patients, friends, loved ones—I fight for them all. I will protect our brood. The fight for the bike path is a good example of this. And unfortunately, the saga continues to consume our lives. It's a significant conversation theme at the dinner table. At this point, a balanced questionnaire has been sent out to the people of Chappy. Some questions skewed toward the pro-bike path argument, and some decidedly written by the opposition. It's not a perfect document. But we all agree the responses will show us where most of the people of Chappy lie on the issue.

I have lost about fifteen percent of my NIMBY customers to the issue. About half of the rest haven't even filled out the questionnaire. These summer people have kids, summer guests, and shiny new bicycles. This should not be an us versus them debate.

I should be more upset. I should be more confrontational and call out the hypocrisy. But I knew all along how this would play out—even if I didn't admit it to myself or

Melissa at the time. I know these people—how they tick and what motivates them. I'm more sad than mad. I feel like giving up more than fighting on.

Each side has been lobbying for their point of view since the committee meeting this summer. The deadline to turn in the questionnaire has come and gone. The tallies are in. And the winner is? Mediocrity, lethargy, and laziness. The number of Chappy respondents is pitiful. Most of my customers didn't participate. The opposition could care less. The lack of responses goes to their side. The loud minority wins. Melissa is so sad. She's so hurt. She can't understand this world we live in where safety is a debatable topic.

The town meeting to vote on the viability of a bike path for the Chappy roads finally arrives. We hang our hopes on the graduate students from Northeastern who have put together a flashy presentation. It highlights a need for a new and safer solution to the status quo. It describes many options that seem reasonable and a place to start negotiations between the two sides of the issue. There are lots of nice graphs—lots of quotes and statistics. But the NIMBY folk successfully frame it as a piece of partisan propaganda created by a misguided and sympathetic group.

The town seems to key in on the lackluster response to the questionnaire and decides the will to create a bike path is just not present—even if it's needed. Why waste the taxpayer's money? Why heap something onto people who don't care about the issue? We'd lost before we even started. We just didn't know it.

Mrs. Lacombe runs into me at the ferry the next week. She's back on-island for a quick trip to meet with an architect. I haven't talked to her since Memorial Day weekend when I tried to talk to her about the bike path.

She never sent in the questionnaire. I want to tell her that their patronage is no longer appreciated. I want to hurt her. Tell Mrs. Lacombe the marijuana I found on the washing machine was not one of my employee's but her teenage son's. He has been dealing for over a year. Why should their world be so perfect and mine feel like shit?

Dierdra smiles as she approaches me. "Hi, Rob. How's the family?"

Everyone always asks me about my family. Easy question. Easy answers. Dierdra gushes as she hugs me. I smile and lamely mutter, "They're fine as usual. Melissa is lying low and not feeling well."

"Right, I read about the bike path situation in the paper yesterday. I'm sorry. In the end, we just wanted to leave it to the locals to decide. It's your island. John and I get so wrapped up in these things at home that we thought the year-rounders should decide this question."

Her husband standing next to her doesn't say a word. He just smiles. I don't even think John knows what Dierdra is talking about. He comes down on weekends, late after work on Friday, and only on-island until Sunday midday. John barely has time to read a chapter in his book and take in a round of golf while he's here. His summer home is a vacation retreat. My agenda isn't his agenda. I believe the last full conversation I had with him was almost a year ago. He talked to me about putting chocolates on the pillows of the spare bedrooms for when guests arrive. I'm a servant. I get paid well, but I'm still just a servant.

I struggle to say, "I understand," without yelling my real feelings at these interlopers. And this conversation is again repeated with most of my customers who call, or I randomly see as autumn marches on. They come here to escape reality—their reality. Summer people don't want to get involved. They don't want to care about one more thing. They just want to detox. They want to enjoy their oasis.

It's so antithetical to their butting their heads into every other aspect of Vineyard life. It seems so effortless the way they trample norms, customs, and rhythms of island life to suit their needs and wants. I ultimately view their inaction as just another way of getting what they want—solitude from tourists (aka non-summer home-owners) and islanders alike.

The Russians

My dejection over the bike path throws me deeper into work even though it's the off-season. Something I can control, fix, and feel good about. But there's a catch. I have to deal with my past on this one—Lyle Hollander. Yes, I see him at the fire station, the ferry, all over Chappy, really. But he hasn't been in my life for the last five years since I walked away from the construction company we co-founded. It's another example of an island marriage of sorts that was dysfunctional from the start and didn't work out. But you know Chappy at this point. He's there in my face, day after day, whether we're in business together or not.

And even though Lyle and I don't work together anymore, there's still the small fact that we co-own some major machinery we never liquidated. A big-ass wood chipper and dump truck are all that's left of our old relationship. And they bring in a lot of money for us each year. Lyle hasn't used the equipment more than a few days a year since we parted ways, but I still give him fifty percent of the profits from their service like clockwork. In the end, I rationalize the no-show profit sharing as penance for me getting in bed with Lyle in the first place.

The reason I bring Lyle up is because I have a big job this week where we need to clear five acres of trees. Big trees that are seventeen inches in diameter. Oh, our chipper can handle them. It's a beast, and it's so much fun to feed that thing. But it needs guys to run it, and I'm short for such a big job. Enter Lyle. He has two kids working for him doing odd jobs for the one or two clients he still has on the island.

I see Lyle while he's going down the road on his big excavator. I never know if he's driving it as a vehicle or actually going to a job to dig a foundation. I give the cut signal with my hand for him to shut off the excavator, and we exchange pleasantries. "Hey, Lyle. I see you got your rig working again. Looking good."

"I do what I can," he says with a grin and then launches into the newest island gossip, which involves me, and ultimately him. "I see you got the Corona land clearing job. Can't wait to get my dividend check."

"Yeah, really excited. It's going to be fun. Do you want to help us with it?"

"Oh, I would love to, Rob, but I'm busy every day."

Busy? I scream in my head while the smile is still plastered on my face. He spends two hours a day reading the paper at the Dock Street Diner, and then the rest of the day is puttering around on his house that he built too tall. The building inspector is making him cut it down to code. And Lyle is a contractor! I don't want him at the job anyway and get to my real ask. "Can I borrow your employees for the job? Are they capable? They're from Russia, right?"

"Oh yeah, you can use the Russians. I'm not using them right now. They're great workers and strong."

I tell him great, we wave, he starts his excavator, and

we are both on our way with no fighting.

Lyle's words are still ringing in my head as we head to the clearing job the following week. The guys tell me their names, Vladimir and Dimitry, as we travel over a bumpy dirt road to the Corona's house. Overgrown brush scrapes at the sides of the truck and chipper on the narrow road, but it barely registers as aesthetics have never been important to me. Functionality is what I care about, and the chipper we are hauling is an impressive working machine—with or without the blemishes on its paint job.

I look over at Vladimir and Dimitry as we bump along and gauge that they're probably in their late teens, but they could easily be in their twenties. They are so nondescript in their appearance. Their faces are drawn and haggard-looking, as if they could use a good meal. My first impression isn't encouraging. But I still say their names over and over in my head. I want to connect with these guys and get off on a good footing. But it doesn't stick. There's no time for my memory to take hold of who they are because as soon as we start the job, I find out they're worthless.

"Hey, don't stick your head in the mouth of the chipper after you put a log in there. You're going to get killed!" I yell for the umpteenth time.

After about thirty minutes of them being unable to lift anything more than twigs and their inability to fathom the most basic safety precautions, I call Lyle. "Hey, you need to come to get these guys. They're worthless. What the hell do you use them for."

"Oh, they help me move stuff at my house or paint the picket fence at the Nealy house."

I can hardly hear him over the chipper and walk farther away. "Can you come get them? They're going to get hurt. They're idiots."

I don't know if Lyle is insulted by my quip or just happy to get these guys off his hands for a day, but he doesn't want to help. "No, Rob. You asked for them, and you need to pay them for the day. Send them home if you want, but you need to pay them, and it can't come out of my part of the profits." And with that, he hangs up.

Why did I kid myself that Lyle would tell me the truth about these guys? You would think that since he had a financial stake in this endeavor, he would have been helpful. When am I going to learn? I head back to the crew, shaking my head and waving frick and frack to come to me. "Here are two rakes. You guys just clean up the debris after the other guys pull the trees to the chipper." They nod, but it still takes Kyle two more instructional talks, so they don't get in the way and are productive. Arrrrgggghhh.

I wish this particular story ended here. Lesson learned once again. And move on. But not even close. The next day I see Lyle at the ferry as I pick up supplies for a job, and he's going off for breakfast at 10:30 a.m. It must be good to be a trust fund reject.

I tell him as kindly as possible, "Listen, Lyle. Thanks for loaning me those guys, but they are dumb as rocks. I took them off any real work and just had them rake twigs. That's all they're good for. You should fire them. They're going to hurt themselves, and you are going to be liable."

"You paid them, right?" Is all Lyle says and walks onto the ferry.

What a dick. I'm so glad he is, for the most part, out of my life. But Michael Corleone's haunting words come back to me. "Just when I thought I was out, they pull me back in." I just need to stay away from Lyle. Period.

The next week I find the chipper and dump truck not in

my yard. OK, Lyle took it. He does that once or twice a year. He owns it too. It's his prerogative. Then I get a call. "Hey, Rob. I need your help. Vladimir had a chip fly out of the chipper and hit him in the head. We're at the hospital. What should I do?"

Did I say, "Aaarrrrrggghhhh" before? It would be prudent, compassionate, and strategic to be helpful and not poke the bear, but I'm pissed. "I told you to fire those two knuckleheads. They should be nowhere near the chipper."

"I don't want to hear it. It happened. You own the chipper with me, and it's your problem too."

"OK, call your worker's comp insurance company and start the claim. Have you filled out the paperwork at the hospital yet?"

"Rob, I don't have workers comp insurance. You always dealt with that stuff."

"Whoa, whoa, whoa. Those guys are your employees. I have nothing to do with them. What happened when I gave you my insurance agent's name to set up workers comp insurance for your company last January? I know he sent you the paperwork because he asked me for your address."

"Listen, Rob. Vladimir was using our chipper, so you're involved. Don't bother me about insurance."

The situation gets worse. I talk with Vladimir a week later back on Chappy, and he has a severe concussion. It's bad enough he barely speaks any English. Now he's also slurring the few words he does know. At this point, he's staying at Lyle's house and just wants to go home. Lyle pulls me aside to say, "Vladimir is talking about money. He wants some."

I cut him off. "I'm not involved. This is your doing."

"You are involved. It's your name on the title of the chipper with mine."

"You're right. I own the chipper with you. I thought when we dissolved the construction company, I was done with this bullshit. But I let the chipper's easy money blind me to the fact that I'm still in bed with you. So yes, I'm going to deal with this problem—your problem." The gloves are off. I usually don't burn bridges, but I'm done.

The next morning happens to be Sunday, and I see Lyle at the fire station meeting, and he throws me a curveball. Actually, I would characterize it as a knuckleball. "Hey, Rob. Vladimir wants $34,000 and is leaving next week for Russia. So we need to come up with the money by Monday."

"Are you shitting me? Lyle, if this is some get-rich-quick ploy with these assholes, then..."

"Fuck you, Rob. I need you to come up with a check for $17,000, and I'll do the same. We'll present it to Vladimir, and he'll be on his way. We learned our lesson."

"What? What? Learned a lesson? I told you to fire these guys. I told you to get insurance. The lesson I'm learning is to stay away from you."

And with that, Lyle walks away to look in one of the pumper trucks' engines as if nothing earth-shattering has happened.

I'm fuming and scared and unsure what to do next when Rich runs over to me the minute he parks his Jeep. I'm not listening, but after a while, I get the word "housing" repeated over and over again. It eventually gets through my foggy brain what Rich is complaining about. He's worried about his housing. He's pissed at his landlord for selling his house. Now Rich has to move out with no place to live. I knew this was going to happen. I know his landlord, and he's a nice guy. It's just that he has four siblings stretched across the country, and no one wants to help pay for the house's expenses that they just inherited from their dad last spring. So, life, it happens. I've actually been thinking hard about Rich and his situation for a while. I've started to come up with a plan—but not now. One fire at a time. Besides, the sale of the house doesn't go through until next summer due to the probate on his father's will. My plan is still half-baked, and I don't even know if I want to execute on it, but that doesn't stop me from pushing the chess pieces around without thinking everything through. This isn't like me. But this plan isn't like me.

"Rich, don't worry. I might have a place for you to live when your family has to move."

"What? Where? How big is it?" Rich peppers me with questions that just don't stop.

"Shut up, Rich. I have a lot going on. Just do your work, trust me, and I'll take care of you."

He hugs me. Like I could've stopped him. Still makes me uncomfortable, but at least this time, it's justified. If all goes well, I have just thrown Rich a major lifeline. This might be a big plan with lots of moving pieces—kings and queens as well as pawns. I hope this all works out. I'm playing without a net.

But I can't think about Rich anymore at the moment. I need to save my own ass right now.

I get home and tell Melissa about the new wrinkle Lyle has thrown me. I forget to tell her about Rich. Maybe I did that on purpose—one crisis at a time. She's confident and stern and lays it out. "You've got to deal with Lyle, protect us, and separate yourself from him later. He's not going to be able to deal with this on his own. You know this about him. That's why you stopped working with him in the first place. He's obviously scared, more scared than you, and definitely embarrassed. He's lashing out at you because he knows he messed up. Do what you do and fix it."

"Lyle just wants us to get the money and pay Vladimir—in cash! Ridiculous!" This is all I can muster in response.

The next morning I'm thinking more clearly, and I call my dad. The documentation I have that shows I told Lyle to get insurance for his own employees helps. But it's not enough. Vladimir was using a piece of machinery that I partly own. It's messy. Throwing money at this problem with some backup assurances looks like my best way out of this mess.

I get an agreement written up. I get an interpreter to translate it into Russian for good measure. I set a time for us to go to the courthouse to get the agreement notarized and deliver the checks. It takes all the persuasion in the world to keep Lyle from going off the deep end. He's certainly scared. Worried this kid he was responsible for is permanently hurt. I need to keep him in line for this fiasco to be resolved. I don't have the option to lose it. Someone needs to be the adult in the room and get this done.

In the end, Vladimir gets paid $34,000! It's a big payday. But unless he's the best actor in the world, he deserves it. That boy will be hurting for a long time. I think about the quality of care he'll get back home. Could I have done any more for him? Would it have pulled me further into this mess? Regardless, he leaves the Vineyard the very next day. His friend goes with him. I comfort myself by believing I did my best and tried to do the right thing.

I learned this very same stupid lesson ten years earlier with Juanita, my lead cleaner, when she fell off a ladder. Maybe that's why I'm so angry. I honestly tried to save Lyle from making the same mistake. This is what hurts the most. I was stupid, learned from my mistake, got insurance for my employees, even the illegal ones, and preached to Lyle to do the same. And in the end, nothing changes. Disillusionment is creeping in. And I need an antidote!

Sailing to the Rescue

The evidence is piling up. The anecdotes are piling up. Ron and Karen, the bike path saga, Jim, the painter, and now Lyle are crowding out my autumn in New England vibe. The expression Noah's rejects is no longer a moniker I proudly wear as a badge of honor.

Melissa and I decide we need to seize the slower pace of fall while the weather is still good and get 'back to nature'. The plan is to recharge our batteries with one last sailing adventure for the season. It's the first week of October, and the weather is rock steady. Bright sunny days, so clear you feel like you can almost make out the houses on the mainland. And the nights, well, the nights are crisp and cool. The sky is continuously alive with a light show of stars and planets. The crisp air feels magical—fall in New England.

Hopefully, the memories of one last sailing voyage for the season will hold us through the winter. The girls can stay with friends. The dog can stay with the neighbors. We can do this. We can sail out of Dodge and think about the beauty without the dysfunctional complications that seem to surround us.

It's the day of our big sail. Bags are packed, provisions

are bought and put on ice, the kids and dog are all set. And so, we're off. It takes two trips from shore out to the boat to get everything on board. Melissa puts supplies away as I tie off our trusty Avon dinghy and ready the sails for our trip to Cuttyhunk. It's one of the Elizabethan Islands to the north of Martha's Vineyard and south of the mainland. It's home to eighty-six year-round residents. Hey, I thought Chappy's year-round population of 179 was small. I can't wait to see it. I can't wait to talk to Cuttyhunk's residents and compare notes. This will be exciting. It's time to trade one paradise address for another. And we're on our way.

We leave the harbor on a slow north-easterly wind with big, gentle, rolling swells. This allows us to make a straight shot for Vineyard Haven, where we'll have to turn directly into the wind and tack most of the rest of the way. As we turn the corner at the East Chop Lighthouse, the wind kicks up, and our leisurely sail becomes a bit of a haul. It takes a lot out of us. We tack first to port and then to starboard as efficiently as possible to crawl our way up Vineyard Sound. This isn't the relaxing and recharging excursion Melissa signed up for.

The wind finally shifts, and we can let our sails out and go at a more leisurely pace downwind. Exhausted, Melissa decides to go below to change into a bathing suit now that the sun is warming up. She doesn't want to stay in the cabin long, as the musty smell sticks to anything and everything within minutes. I catch a glimpse of her bare bottom as she writhes around on the cot and have to smile. I'm sailing off of Martha's Vineyard with a beautiful woman and nothing but time on my hands—for now.

The warmth of the steady wind coming from behind us wipes away all our dark thoughts. It feels like heaven as we slowly and rhythmically make our way toward another nirvana. Life is so straightforward out here. The sea is so freeing. The wind, the currents, the landmasses in front of us are all so concrete. Skill, beauty, companionship, and time all weave together to make a perfect scene. A natural noise machine, the ebb and flow of the waves against the boat is dancing around in my head. I'm present now.

The wind is still mainly out of the south as we cross from Martha's Vineyard to the channel between Cuttyhunk and its eastern neighbor, Nashawena Island. Straight shot across Vineyard Sound. No tacking. Easy peasy, lemon squeezy.

Melissa comes up on deck with some apples, nuts, and hummus. We just ate lunch, but rituals are rituals. I give a nodding approval as I know I'll want a slice of apple or two before the day is done. Melissa lays out the food and settles in on the cushion to soak up the rays and take a nap. Nothing for her to do right now. Just relax and enjoy.

Soon enough, we approach the channel that separates the two islands. Rolling hills and rocky beaches with waves crashing on them fill our view. I nudge Melissa awake so she can see the scene. She smiles as she stretches.

Suddenly, bam. The wind from the passage hits us. Somehow it has looped around and is now coming from the west. The wind smashes the mainsail across the boat to the starboard side and rips out the traveler holding the sail in place. Ball bearings fly through the air like buckshot. The line from the traveler whips across the boat.

I yell, "Duck," and Melissa hits the deck as the line grazes her cheek. The boom catches some of her hair as it whips over her head. She's lucky to be alive as I start my mantra of yelling, "Fuck, fuck, fuck" over and over. I instinctually maneuver the boat into irons where it can stay still as the wind whips past either side of the flapping sails. The sounds of the unfilled sails are deafening.

I quickly take stock of the situation. Something else is wrong, and I'm far from out of the woods. At this point, the boat should be standing still or slowly being pushed backward by the head-on winds. But this isn't the case. Instead, our boat is being dragged toward the shores of Nashawena Island like a fish being reeled in by a fisherman. In the chaos, I didn't realize that our rubber Avon dinghy had flipped over when the westerly wind came upon us. The Avon immediately started nosediving into the ocean and is now acting like a sea anchor pulling us toward the shore with the incoming tide.

My mantra begins again. "Fuck, fuck, fuck." This is not a test. This is real, and if I don't want to be a colorful story my Vineyard friends tell as a cautionary tale, then I need to act. I find the knife Melissa used to cut up the apple sloshing back and forth on the cockpit floor and cut the line to the dinghy. I can't believe I'm saying goodbye to my trusted Avon dinghy that has transported me to more shores than I can think of. But I don't have the luxury of rethinking my actions. It bobs to the surface, upside down, and floats off toward shore. The sailboat begins to behave predictably—slowly moving backward with the rolling waves pushing it up and down as it goes.

I turn my attention to Melissa, who is still face down on the deck. How long has she been motionless like that? I take Melissa in my arms and tell her she's OK. She's shaking and maybe not so fine. But I'm trying to will her to be OK as I don't have time for her not to be. I prop her up against the cabin wall and go about repairing the boat.

My mind is racing, and at the same time, a calm comes over me. I know what I have to do. Panicking isn't an option. Panicking does little more than shorten the time I have to fix this situation now. First, Melissa is physically safe. Check. I see her eyes darting around the boat as she sits motionless where I placed her. But I can't concentrate on that right now. I need to get us to shore. So, I jerry-rig a new traveler out of some extra line from down below in the cabin, kick start the engine, and take stock of the wind and the journey before us. Check.

No longer am I lazily sailing on a port tack. Now the wind is coming directly at us again, but this time in huge gusts of thirty knots. Where the hell did this wind come from? The tacking this morning was manageable and fun. Sure, it was tiring, but nothing like this. And now, I have a broken boat, and the winds are kicking up even more—how the afternoon has changed. Why didn't I see this coming? I should've noticed the conditions in front of me—damn beauty.

The wind is now overpowering our boat. I need more momentum to overcome the waves pushing us back as we tack inefficiently from side to side. Our engine is helping but is being offset by the powerful current underneath the boat.

I'm working it. Back and forth, back and forth, slowly making headway. This goes on for two hours as the Cutty-hunk's port comes into focus. The winds begin to subside as the island's landmass cuts off some of its strength. Eventually, a sense of normality kicks in, and the end of today's journey is within reach.

Soon the buildings of Cuttyhunk take shape. I can make out people walking around oblivious to our drama. And then I notice Melissa staring wide-eyed at me. We haven't spoken. What is she thinking? I can't tell from her blank stare. She has let me control the chaos, which I'm eternally grateful for, but at a cost. She saw the chaos of the moment, knew she almost died, and then was relegated to sit mute while I fixed the situation. She didn't know what I knew. We were in trouble. I knew that, but I also knew what we had to do to get out of trouble, and it was always doable. Melissa never got the memo from my brain—we were always going to be OK. I didn't have time or the skills to calmly tell her what I was doing. So, there she sat, thinking her thoughts, and watching the chaos around her. Fight or flight takes over during emergency situations, and Melissa looks to be purely in the flight camp at this point.

We're OK now. We're out of physical danger. The boat is semi repaired for the time being. It's time to try to repair Melissa. We start to talk as I maneuver the boat and pull up to a mooring in the harbor. There are a lot of questions.

Melissa fires them at me as she gets her voice. "Why did that happen?"

I shake my head. The words are hard to say. "I was taken off guard. I wasn't prepared. I don't know. The change of wind direction just kind of happened. The wind overpowered the traveler and broke it. But we're OK. I can fix the boat—better—later. It will get us home tomorrow. I promise."

I don't know if any of this is registering with Melissa. She stares at me for a long time. Then her gaze moves to the broken traveler, and finally, her eyes rest on the back of the boat. I think it's all starting to sink in. She's taking it all in. Maybe just a little delayed.

The next question comes softer with a hinge of sadness. The same feeling I felt in the heat of the moment. "Did we really lose our dinghy?"

"I had no choice. It would have made us crash into the rocks off Nashawena Island if I didn't cut it loose. It killed me to let her go. That boat has been with us forever."

It's now Melissa's turn to shake her head. She looks down. Takes stock of her body for the first time since this situation arose. She rubs her arms back and forth as she listens to my explanations. She gingerly pulls her knees up to her chest. And then she gently raises her left hand to touch the brow of her head where dried, salty blood marks how close she came to real harm.

"Did that line hit me? Am I hurt?" She's distraught. Like so many patients I see as an EMT, she doesn't even know if she's hurt.

"Oh, honey," I say as I drop the line I'm coiling and hug her as she sits curled up in a ball. I think this is the first time I have touched her since the initial accident. Melissa stiffens at my touch but then melts into my shoulder and sighs. "The line just grazed you. But you're fine. We're both fine."

The image of my locked knuckles gripping the wheel of the sailboat for hours fills my mind even as I hold and comfort Melissa. I need to put it out of my head. Normalcy and calm are what's required. We need something to occupy our minds—in a good way. I encourage Melissa to help me clean up the mess of food and debris around us in the cockpit. We get to work, but in a reticent and robotic kind of way. It's a start.

A smiling launch attendant approaches our boat as if nothing in the world is out of place. He guides me through the registration process for staying the night, all the while not knowing there's a voice screaming in my head. What the fuck just happened?

My internal dialog, thankfully, doesn't come to the surface, and I quietly pay the kid and slump back down onto my butt, leaning against the wheel. I kiss it and say thank you as this old boat had as much to do with our survival as my skills did. She held it and us together.

Melissa sits down next to me, and we embrace once again. We sit there for what seems an eternity before we hear the approaching guttural sound of a diesel engine. An old, weathered fisherman in rain coveralls steers his boat straight for us. We jump to our feet and hold off his boat as he expertly comes up alongside us. He has our beloved Avon dinghy. What?

It seems the fisherman witnessed the entire saga as he was pulling up lobster pots in the outer harbor. There wasn't much he could do to help us, and besides, he says it looked like I had everything under control. But he was able to rescue our dinghy off the rocks. I try to give him some money but know it's fruitless, even before the words come out of my mouth. I settle for promising to look for him in town and buy him a beer or three. This he agrees to and waves as he leaves as quickly as he came.

It's late in the day. We need to stand on dry land and feel safe, feel steady, feel dry. And to that end, Melissa and I change into walking around clothes and take the launch into town. I know we could take our newly returned Avon, but it has been through a lot, and we have been through a lot. I hate to spend the money, but I'm done for the day. I'm hardy. I can take a lot. But, yeah, I just hit my breaking point.

The ride in is a non-event. All I can think of is standing on dry land. I want to be steady. I want to feel safe. And right now, even though land is only 100 yards away, I don't feel like this escapade is over yet.

Stepping off the launch and making it to dry land in the middle of this small town centers me. Instantly, I feel OK. It feels familiar. The weathered cedar-shingled buildings with white trim stand side-by-side like a picturesque postcard.

The shingles are grayed by the sea, wind, and time. Bicycles, lazily on their sides, dot the streets as locals and tourists discard them to go in this shop or that. The town is so small and compact. All the essentials with no overlap. One ice cream store, one hardware store, one real estate agency. Very economical. They have so few inhabitants.

Our sea adventure already feels a million miles away. My shoulders relax, and I'm happy. I look over to Melissa, who looks less OK but is smiling just the same. We're both famished and know there will be plenty of time to explore tomorrow.

Melissa suddenly stops on the street, turns to me, exhales, and says with a sheepish grin, "I feel like the world has stopped spinning."

"Yeah, I know." Stepping off the launch onto dry land is like getting off a carnival ride. It never changes. It never gets old. I love the sea, but the steadiness of concrete earth, for some reason, makes me feel whole again. We took on Mother Nature and endured. And today, we can say that in spades.

We go to the only open restaurant on the island and are guided to a table. Melissa and I don't say much when we sit down. Then, I start apologizing—a lot. "I just want to say sorry again for today. Sailing is my life. It's our life. But I got sloppy today—in the moment." I don't know why I'm blubbering. Melissa is my wife of twenty years. I think at this point, she knows what she signed up for. But it still seems like the right thing to do. "I'm truly sorry that our trip isn't the perfect getaway we both needed so desperately. We count on these moments to recharge our batteries."

Chappy takes so much from us. My customers demand so much from me. Melissa and the girls are always second fiddles. This was to be a first fiddle moment for Melissa and me. Maybe it still can be.

Melissa takes my hand across the table and says, "You did awesome today. I'm still processing it all. I'm just sorry I didn't have the wherewithal to help you."

I shake my head. "Really, honey? You did what I needed you to do. And you almost got hit with the boom. I would've lost you forever."

We slump back into silence as we concentrate on our meal and recharging our batteries now that the adrenaline has seeped from our bodies.

Our desserts have just been placed in front of us, and Melissa mentions she doesn't have a knife or a spoon or whatever. The nice waiter happens to hear her as he's walking by and grabs one from a nearby table not being used and places it near her plate. No big deal, right? Wrong. All Melissa sees is a flash of metal at the periphery of her eyesight coming from high up down to her level. Suddenly she's back on the boat, and the traveler line that had broken loose and came whipping at her head comes roaring back to her. She starts crying. Sobbing. It takes me a beat to figure out what's going on, but I do eventually and just start rubbing her back.

"You're safe," I say. "You're OK." I try to sound reassuring. The waiter is obviously freaked out and starts apologizing. He doesn't know what he's apologizing for, but that doesn't stop him. I motion with my eyes to just... leave, and he's happy to oblige. I continue my mantra, "It's OK."

"But it's not OK!" It's as if Melissa has just woken up, and everything is suddenly clear to her. "I never wanted to sail. I'm not a sailor. But I love you. I wanted to be a part of your life, your world. So now I'm pretending to be a sailor."

I look around at everyone staring at us and want to tell Melissa to lower her voice, but I know that's futile and will just set her off in another direction. All I can think to say is, "I'm sorry."

"I know this isn't your fault. You fixed it. You got us through it. That's what you always do. You're the fixer. But that's not what I want. That's not what I ever wanted. This journey we're on is just too broken for you to fix."

I'm trying to keep up with the conversation and not be embarrassed by the scene we're making. What is she saying? "What are you saying, honey?"

"I don't know. I don't know. This sailing trip changes nothing. It fixes nothing. It was supposed to be so beautiful, so tranquil. Well, Mother Nature had other plans for us. It's not in our control. The crap around us. Life on Chappy. None of it's in our control."

Later that night, in my sleeping bag on the sailboat, I think about Melissa's and my differing reactions to the day's events. And what comes to mind is the fact that Melissa didn't grow up with Jerry as a dad. She didn't have to deal with one emergency after another on a boat or in life.

Melissa didn't have a dad who thought nothing of sending a kid up the mast of a boat at twelve years old during a gale storm to fix a ripped and flapping sail. Or be the go-between for alimony payments to his ex-wife, my mom. This is normal to me. Batshit crazy situations are normal to me. Nerve-racking at the moment, but normal. This is what I grew up with. But Melissa isn't built for this shit. The incident with the waiter makes me realize my normal is not Melissa's normal. Nor should it be.

I know the next twenty-four hours are crucial. I'm a heartless bastard, and I'm sorry I'm thinking these thoughts, but if I don't turn this trip around, if I don't erase the stigma of sailing from my wife's brain, then I'm going to be a solo sailor for the rest of my life. I don't think about the bigger picture. I don't even understand the bigger picture. I'm just trying to fix the current situation—one thing at a time.

I work hard. Keep it light. Be present and attentive. And it works. The next day we see all the sights. We marvel at this little island that is similar to Chappy but in the same instant, not at all. I make all the fixes on the boat while Melissa takes a nap after an afternoon bike ride. And then Monday, our departure day, brings with it calm seas, clear skies, and a stiff wind from the west.

We have a great sail. The wind is steady and brisk the entire way. Smooth sailing with no need to tack. And the sun is just warm enough for Melissa to have a good doze on deck without wrapping a blanket around her. We arrive back to Chappy with another sailing adventure under our belt.

The girls love the story. I tell our treacherous tale over and over again. They can't get enough of it. Melissa goes to bed, wasted from the weekend's events, while I do laundry and deal with planning work for the next day. It turns out I got a total of twenty calls from customers on my mini-vacation, which they knew I was on, asking where I was and if I could come over. None of them were crucial. Do they call as part of a power trip—"You work for me! I summon you now!" Or just as bad, do they not consider me as a person at all? They have a thought, a need, an emergency, and it needs to be voiced, attended to, made a priority right then and there. Is it too much to ask for a moment for myself and my family? Don't they get that?

The story I told you about Ilana's birth being interrupted by a customer in the delivery room invades my thoughts more and more. The customer worked in the hospital and thought nothing of stopping in and asking me to come over to his house when I got home to look at a loose trellis. I should've seen the interaction as a cautionary tale. I should've drawn the lines earlier in my life. But I didn't, and this accessibility issue has festered and become all-consuming. Melissa saw it for what it was from the beginning.

She had daggers in her eyes as I replied, "Sure."

Melissa was quiet for a while after the customer left, then said, "We are on this journey together, right?"

And all I could think to say was, "Sure."

I'm only now understanding what she meant. What an idiot.

Cranky, Tired, and Sad

My failure to fix Melissa and my mood with our sailing adventure clouds the rest of the month. It does more than that. The balance of reveling in our island's beauty versus the price we pay to live here is shifting. Behavior that I used to slough off as quirky and laugh at now gnaws at me.

Tonight's drama doesn't help my mood. It's another EMT call—which is fine. But I get to the scene of a car crash, and the victim is nowhere to be seen. He must have been thrown from the crash. I yell the hack lawyer's name over and over again—no answer. This guy is in the bars more than he's ever in his office processing real estate deals. His beat up F-150 is on its side in the woods. Looks like it rolled a few times. The sight of broken glass and the smell of whisky ten feet away from the truck tells me all I need to know.

Others arrive and help with the search. There's no moon in the sky, so we point our vehicles at the woods to help with the search. An hour later, in the dead of night, Peter gets the idea that maybe this idiot actually walked away from the crash, as improbable as that seems. The truck is mangled.

I head over to his house, where his wife is surprisingly

awake at one in the morning. Her husband is also home and sleeping. No, She doesn't know where his truck is. Yes, he's been in all night. No, I can't come in... whatever. I report to the others and go home. Someone else can clean up this mess tomorrow.

Nothing comes of the truck accident. Stories fly, but it's nothing new. The hack lawyer knew enough to lay low until his blood alcohol level was normal again. The talk at the ferry of the accident persists a few more days but then dies away.

There's always something new to talk about. The weather, which tends to rule our world, is a good one. It's getting to be mid-November, and although the leaves have not started to fall off the trees, it definitely feels like winter is coming. Most of the talk at the ferry centers on the severity of the weather and its potential for disruption. I walk away as I have no appetite to think about winter. Instead, I need to concentrate on a job I don't relish. Yes, there are jobs like emergency septic tank cleanings that are disgusting. But I can wash that stuff off. Filth has never bothered me. Fish guts, poop, dirt, etc., it's all just stuff to wash off.

Today is a different kind of unpleasant job. The Kanes have died. Husband and wife within months of each other. First Tom in August, and then Sally in October. It's been sixteen years since my dad and I prepared that lobster dinner for them, but it cemented our relationship, and they have been a part of my life and business ever since.

Sally came out one last time in September. She had all her family around her for the visit. Lots of joy. Lots of laughter—just not for her. You could see it in her eyes. At least, I could see it in her eyes. I'm sure her kids could too. But they ignored it or kidded themselves that their mother was enjoying herself so they could get one more vacation out of 'it'. Sally was a good sport and smiled.

She confided in me one morning when I stopped over to help her with some gardening. "Being here is just all too much for me." Putting the garden to bed was a job she usually relished doing with her husband. I was no substitute.

Her husband was a decorated Second World War veteran—lots of medals, lots of pictures on the walls from all over the world. But that isn't the man I knew. Back in the States, back in their charming house down a sandy road on Chappy, he was just a soft-spoken, kind man.

So, both of the Kanes are no longer part of the Chappy community. The story is a common one. The kids live all over the country. One wants to keep the house as he lives in Boston and will make use of it. But he doesn't have the money to buy out his siblings. The others just want the cash. So, the house goes up for sale. But not like it currently looks. We have been called in to clean out and stage the house so potential buyers can visualize their own family making memories within these walls. Crazy. Sally has only been gone a month.

I'm being asked to wipe away the Kanes' existence from their beloved home on our island. People I have known and cared about. Their house tells a story. I know why there's a chip in the countertop. Tommy tried to open a watch with a screwdriver and missed the mark. I know why there's a dark spot on the hardwood floors near the fireplace. Tie-dying shirts indoors isn't a good plan. It's just a mark on an inanimate object. Easy to explain. Easy to fix. But these blemishes are a part of something deeper. A detailed, colorful story that stopped the Kanes from wiping away the imperfections that made their house a home. Now I'm tasked with erasing that history. It's sad. Washing away these memories feels as if I'm cleaning out my own parents' home.

The Kanes' children don't want to do it. It's just too painful. Sometimes a family will give me a list of possessions to put aside, but rarely do they show up. Most times, I send more items than they ask for. They often forget things I know will jog a memory. My job is to look out for the Kanes—not just their property. Preserving their memory is part of that job. I wonder if the Kanes know they had this effect on me? I wonder if my customers who are still alive know what effect they have on me?

I feel my sentimentality getting the better of me, and I need to focus. I put aside a clam rake to save. The one Mr. Kane taught his son to use when he was old enough to wade into the shallows of Caleb's Pond. Not working. Still thinking too much about the stories and not the task at hand. I leave the Kanes' house to my employees. But not without giving strict instructions not to throw anything out. Just put it all on the lawn. I'll go through it with them later. The Kanes have a lot of stuff, a lot of memories. An entire life, gone. Two people spending a lifetime together, and in the end, who they were is reduced to just so many boxes.

I leave the Kanes' house on yet another mission. I need to meet my dad down by the boat landing in Edgartown (off Chappy). I need to cut the lock off the chain that protects his kayak. I do this about once a month. No worries. He buys these locks in bulk. He either loses the key, forgets the combination or sand has gotten in the lock mechanism, and it's toast. I used to try to help keep track of the keys and combos, but it never helped, so I gave up. It's better just to help him when the crisis occurs, say hello, and then go about the rest of my day. I don't know why he has a kayak anymore. Each year he uses it less and less, just like the skiff with the 9hp engine in Katama Bay. I know he loves his boats. And he loves the idea of his boats, even if they don't get used much. Maybe next week, when he catches up with 'his work', he'll get to use the boats more. Funny, he always has so much work to do. I wonder what it is? He hasn't had a real job, one that pays him money, since 1982 when he gave up his law practice. Today he tells anyone who'll listen that he works for his boys.

"My boys are so good to me," he'll say. "They are going to double my salary next year." Everyone smiles. "They currently pay me one dollar a year." Everyone laughs. He's a good dad.

I think about my dad and all his toys, his stuff. I think of the Kanes with much of the same stuff, but different.

Dad pats me on the back after I cut the lock. "Thanks, Robbie."

"Isn't it time to take the kayak out of the water for the season?"

"No, there are still some good days left. I might still get out there. Maybe do some fishing off of it."

I know this is a pipe dream. Dad can barely get in the kayak and stay balanced. The idea of an eighty-year-old man pulling in a Bonita or, God forbid, a striper would be the end of him. But I'm hopeful for him. "Why don't you go out right now? It's nice out. You have the paddle in your car."

"No, I have papers on my desk. And Land's End refuses to refund the money on my khaki pants. I'm in the midst of filing papers with the SEC and the Better Business Bureau for deceptive practices."

I know when to walk away and keep my mouth shut,

and this is one of those times. "OK, well, call me when you want me to take it out." We part, and another five-minute interaction is concluded.

My interactions with my dad fill me with glimpses of warmth but ultimately leave me empty. I look back at how fleeting they are. How much he is railing at something... anything. He says he's happy and loves us boys. But the anger never leaves him.

My dad rattles around my head as I head back to Chappy. I barely acknowledge my surroundings. The ferry is quick, with no conversations. I sit alone and think about my dad, the Kanes, myself, and all the things we don't need but can't live without.

The bumpy dirt road under my truck's wheels is rhythmic and mind-numbing. I have every intention of stopping at the Kanes' home but drive right by it. My own memories have been stirred. The 'things' from my past call to me. I need to touch them and remember.

No one's home when I arrive. Not even River with her wagging tail to greet me. The basement and my storage boxes draw me down to make sure my own memories are intact. Visually and physically, I'm transported. The metal clank the *Happy Days* lunch box makes as I open it brings me back to grade school. I set it aside and find a pile of my old camp yearbooks. I cry as I leaf through them. I miss every moment of this past. I want to be back there and relive them all over again.

I look around at all of this discardable stuff and wonder what it amounts to—for others. Will these moments in time be of worth to anyone else—my kids? Does it matter?

I hear thudding above my head, and all of a sudden, Beyonce is telling me "to the left, to the left." The girls are home. One last look at the fresh young faces in the pages in front of me as I head for the stairs, and I take solace in the fact Ilana and Sasha have their own stack of camp yearbooks upstairs.

I head back to the Kanes' after looking in on the girls, who are deep in choreographing their next great dance number. Tom and Sally's history is laid out on the lawn in front of me. It's a treasure. It's scrap. It's a memory. Whatever it is, these items served a purpose. Whatever meaning will be attached to them by their new owners is anyone's guess.

Storms a Coming

I get melancholy like this a lot in the fall. Now that there's time to sit with my thoughts. November is so raw. Something about the colorful leaves falling. All that's left is the flatness of the tan sand of the roads blending with the grey trunks of the gnarly scrubby oaks in the woods. The sea feels so far away as I drive the interior of Chappy.

Melissa sometimes tries to tease out of me what I'm thinking. It angers me when she pushes. And then she senses her misstep and stops. But I'm already angry. Sometimes the anger is better than the melancholy feeling before it.

But most times, Melissa has no time to decipher my mood as she needs to get the girls to one appointment or another off Chappy. Today one of the girls has a big science presentation, so she's driving them to school. Sasha made a weather machine that can create snowstorms. She's running late as school starts in an hour and needs to run. Wait, an hour, you say? That seems like a long time. But you forget, we live on Chappy. We never forget.

The Chappy ferry, the stepchild to the Steamship Authority, rules our world, as I've mentioned. The off-season is no different. The destinations just change. Dance classes, doctor's appointments, and school plays take center stage. We are needed at these locales at a specific time. And even at this time of year, with Thanksgiving only a few short days away, the ferry line can stretch into a forty-five-minute wait since Peter has cut down to using one boat to save money.

Can you imagine sitting with screaming kids in an idled car most days while life slips by? Missing appointments, stressing out, always rushing to make up lost time. Or consider you prepared for a line, and there's none. Well, then you're off Chappy with your kids with an hour to kill and nothing to do. You can only do the surprise pop in on your friends so many times. Melissa tries her best. She makes up games while waiting at the ferry. Reads kids' stories or lets them run around on the beach with the dog. But it gets old. We need to get off of Chappy to live our life. And we can't get there if the ferry or the line isn't cooperating with us. So there's no going around the ferry.

Melissa sits... and waits. And to top it off, we're scheduled to have a nor'easter today. It's like a hurricane but different. It has to do with the direction of the wind. I think nor'easters are worse because they get less advertised or hyped, and we never really know what the intensity will be beforehand. Anyway, we're having a nor'easter—a big fucking storm off the water. And to make matters worse, it's happening when there's a high tide. The storm is pushing water from the sea toward us at a time when the level of the sea is already high. Bring on the flooding!

Melissa isn't clued into the nor'easter. I forgot to tell her. No one at the ferry mentioned it either. They probably assumed she already knew.

I get the first angry call around 11:00 a.m. It seems

Melissa was having a perfect morning. "I dropped the girls off, was doing burpees at CrossFit by eight, and then made my loop of grocery stores where I efficiently got everything on my list."

Wins like having a successful shopping outing might not seem like much, but to islanders, it can make or break your day. The necessity to travel to all three grocery markets is a complicated formula based on prices, organics, locality of the food, and parking considerations.

I start to interject about the storm, but she doesn't give me a chance. "No one stopped me to gab. Everyone was in a hurry. Didn't even think anything of it until I got back to the Chappy ferry. You know, I'm sure you're seeing it. The waves are splashing over the ramp. The white caps in the inner harbor look like the open ocean. The sky is pitch black. I have no idea how I missed that."

"I know. I know. I'm sorry. I should've given you a heads up. It's just that..."

Melissa isn't even listening to me. "Charlie's the ferry driver this morning. And he's his normal cranky, stoic, non-verbal self. He sticks his head right in my window and blurts out as he's taking my ticket, and the rain is pelting me in the face, 'Better get your kids home. Storms gonna get bad. Might stop running 'til tomorrow.'

"That's it. He just walked off to the next car. I was having such a great day."

"OK, Melissa. You know the drill. He'll take it trip by trip until the surge of the current overpowers the ferry. It looks bad on the radar." I can hear the protective chain of the ferry being lowered and Melissa's car bounding down the metal ramp on the Chappy side. Squeals fill my earpiece as she is obviously turning around in the rain to get back in line to get off Chappy once again to get the kids.

She finally comes back on the phone. "You should've seen the looks on everyone's face as I got back in line. Screw 'em."

I say I'm sorry once again and that I will call the school to get the girls ready. I think I hear a grunt. I definitely hear the phone being thrown and hitting some part of the interior of the car. The phone goes dead.

That didn't go well. I beat myself up a little for being so preoccupied with work. But Melissa is now on track, and I still have more storm prep to do. Most houses are put to bed at this point. But some still have wicker chairs on the lawn, hammocks strung between trees, and screen doors that have not been fastened shut. People always think they're going to come back down for one more piece of paradise. So they want to keep everything just so, in its place. But they rarely come. And so their "stuff" just sits.

I think about the next house I must deal with. At the same time, I'm thinking about the image of Melissa fuming in her car. I decide to at least text, I'm sorry, before driving off. It makes me feel a little better. But I don't think it will help the situation. Maybe actually make it worse as I envision Melissa stomping on the phone when she eventually sees my useless apology.

The girls' school knows the drill and is ready for my call. There are many unique situations on our island that they need to be prepared for. It could be a baby calf coming early that a future farmer must-see, a ferry reservation to the mainland coming through at the last minute for a doctor's appointment, or a load of stripers coming in off of a family's commercial fishing boat that needs an extra hand. And of course, there's the weather.

The scene is worse by the time Melissa arrives back at the Chappy ferry with the kids and calls me. She is clearly overwhelmed by the ominous nature of the waterfront. I can hear it in her voice. "I know you've seen it before, Rob, but it's downright scary. I can hardly see the harbor in front of me as the rain is coming down in sheets—literal sheets. I know the fishing trawlers are banging up against the wharf. I can hear them. The banging is deafening. But all I see is gray."

"I get it. And you're right. It's nothing we haven't seen before. We'll get through this."

It's as if Melissa doesn't even hear me, and maybe she can't with the storm raging. She just talks on. "And if that's not enough... the storm surge has pushed the ocean up onto the streets. Our car has waves lapping against it."

I give an, "ahhmmmm," as I don't know what else to say.

"Wait. Charlie is coming out of the ferry office and motioning me on the ferry."

"OK. I'll stay on the line." A wave of relief falls over me as I now know they will get home.

I can hear the rain louder as Melissa undoubtedly opens the window. The girls are screaming questions and complaints in the background.

Charlie's gruff voice cuts through the noise of the wind and the girls. "I made it across about five minutes ago. It took some doing. I'll do my best."

I can hear Melissa trying to calm the girls as I listen to the ferry's engines being gunned—undoubtedly to overtake the current that is pinning the ferry against its docking station.

"The ferry cleared the slip, but it's standing still in the storm. Not making any headway." Melissa sounds deflated. I can hear the powerful diesel engines trying to match the storm's ferocity. But when I hear them rev down and then back up again. I know Charlie has given up. He is heading back into the slip.

Charlie returns to Melissa's window and yells to be heard, "Sorry, I tried. Need to come back later."

Melissa starts to yell question after question, "How much later? Can the harbor master help?" But I can already hear in the background the chain being lowered on the ramp. Charlie is done.

Melissa backs off the ferry, pulls into a parking space adjacent to the ferry building, puts the car in park, and cries. The girls sit mute behind her. I feel helpless listening in the background with no answers or ability to comfort my family. At this point, I'm already at home as there's nothing more I can do for my customers, and all that's left is to fill the bathtubs, pull out the candles, unplug the computers, and plug in the old rotary phone that doesn't need electricity to work. The home front is safe, but most of the occupants are missing in action.

Melissa and I talk after she takes a minute to compose herself. We come up with a plan. There's nothing more we can do other than react to what Mother Nature hands us. Right now, a way home isn't in the cards. The girls will go back to school. Melissa can go to a friend's house, eat lunch, and we can wait. Let's see how fast this storm moves and if low tide brings a respite that will allow the Chappy ferry to resume service. I promise to touch base with her on an ongoing basis.

Melissa is still pissed at me for not giving her more of a heads up, and I have no retort. Again, I say sorry. Melissa wipes her eyes and looks back at the girls sitting quietly during the entire phone conversation, but at the same time taking it all in. She puts the car in reverse and begins her journey once again up-island.

I putter around doing nothing in particular for a while until once again I'm needed. It's not Melissa this time or a customer. It's a rescue mission. A situation that only Chappy's finest can handle due to our isolation by the storm. And by finest, I mean that in relative terms. Sometimes I look around at the volunteer Chappy Fire personnel at a scene and wonder why anyone trusts us. Each character looks more disheveled and clueless than the one next to him. When I see pictures of us in a group, it reminds me of hikers after they've been rescued from a near-death survival experience.

Today's adventure includes one nor'easter, one secluded piece of beach with very little ability to access it by any means, and a lone—I repeat, lone kiteboarder. Don't these people ever go to Cub Scouts or camp or horror movie prep classes? You don't do shit alone—period. So this moron thinks it'll be fun to kiteboard during the storm—lots of waves, lots of wind. He's just lucky a neighbor could see that stretch of ocean from their big picture windows during the storm.

Normally, it's a beautiful view with shoals at low tide and a crashing surf when the tide comes in. But because of the presence of these shoals, boats have grounded themselves off Martha's Vineyard throughout history. From time to time, pieces of these vessels make it to shore—like the one we saw this past summer with bronze cleats on it.

Well, today, during this storm, the sea kicked up a massive piece of metal. Even though the sea level was way over the normal high tide, this thing jutted up ten feet out of the sea. And that's what's hanging up this kiteboarder. His strings somehow wrapped around the protruding object. The constant flow of the waves and current proceed to wrap this guy up and around the piece of metal. It looks like a villain from an old superhero cartoon has strung this kiteboarder up and is planning on feeding him to some mechanical sharks or drowning him slowly. Waves crash around him. The sail fills with water, the wind catches it, and off it goes pulling the strings around the surfer tighter. There's no camera close up on this guy to see the grimace on his face, but I'm sure it's there.

We're onshore by this point, five of us in our pick-up trucks and nothing we can do. A rescue boat would have to travel ten to twenty miles from Edgartown around the outer harbor to get to this guy. The harbormaster's boats are just not equipped for this type of rescue. The Coast Guard has also been notified, and it's unclear if they will respond. And they are easily forty-five minutes away. It's getting serious as the kiteboarder is becoming fatigued. I'm watching a man die with no way to help him.

Peter somehow recognizes the kiteboarder and makes a call to the guy's friend who has a fishing boat. Peter only gets the friend's wife on the phone and is informed that he's already on his way. And less than ten minutes later, we see the fisherman's trawler appear as a black smudge on the horizon, bouncing up and down in the waves.

Eventually, we can see his engine is tilted way up so as not to hit the shoals. As it gets closer, we see there are two other guys on the boat. They know they can't approach the metal projectile. The boat might crush the kiteboarder in the chop of the storm. They rig up a spear gun with a life jacket and an oyster knife. I know all this as a resident Chappy war nut has come on the scene with night vision goggles. But as a bystander, the binoculars make us feel all the more useless.

The projectile is shot over the kiteboarder and misses wide right. This is insane. The gunman's dealing with a pitching boat, waves crashing over him, the howling wind, and the sight of his friend hanging on for dear life twenty yards away. Luckily on the third try, he hits his mark, and the life jacket catches on a piece of protruding metal near the kiteboarder. This probably took mere minutes, but it felt like hours. It felt like even longer for the kiteboarder to cut enough of the line around him so he could slip down into the water.

We're all happy for a second but soon realize the next danger that lies ahead. This guy still has to get to shore. He could be swept out to sea by the crazy undertow. Luckily the kiteboarder had the presence of mind to cut the life jacket loose from the spear when he first got the knife. He's now using it to help him stay afloat and make his way toward shore. One minute I think he's OK and going to make it. Then the next, a wave breaks on him, and we hold our breath to see if he'll re-emerge. In and out. In and out. His friends stand helpless on their boat as they can't get any closer with the shoals and waves breaking all around.

The kiteboarder correctly swims diagonally to the current in order to make progress against the vicious waves. But the rhythm of coming in one minute toward shore and then losing ground the next is tiring and dangerous.

Finally, we break out of the daze of watching when Peter yells over the loud, whipping storm to make a chain. The largest of us is the anchor, then Peter, then Lyle, Rich, and a few other guys, and finally the small runt of the group, me, out on the end. We don't even think. We connect, look each other in the eye as if to say, we got this, and make our way out into the water.

I'm whipping around in the waves like the end of a snake, taking in more water than I would like. But it keeps me focused. Keeps me pumped. Someone's strong arm steadies me as it grips my elbow, and we're able to get out about fifteen feet in the surf. Far enough to grab this guy and pull him in. The guys on the boat cheer. The others on the beach cheer. I can't help but smile as the adrenaline courses through my body, and I momentarily forget how cold it is in the ocean.

Onshore we wrap the guy in blankets and give him oxygen and a good rubdown. He's OK. Stupid, but OK. Peter and another firefighter package him into Peter's truck, and they head to town. The harbormaster will meet them at the Chappy ferry landing to get him across and to the hospital. Later, I found out the fishing boat that did much of the rescue made it back to port an hour later. I'm already out of the shower and in bed when I see that text. Glad not to have to deal with another rescue. Glad to rest. I feel good but then think of real firefighters that deal with this type of danger on a daily basis. Don't know how they do it. "You're a better man than I am, Gunga Din."

Melissa calls and wakes me from my nap. She's a little annoyed I'm sleeping when she's out dealing with our family. I don't immediately tell her about my day. There's no need to make her feel bad. Instead, I tell her I'll get some information on the ferry and call her back in a minute. Gives me time to wake up and compose myself.

A phone call to Peter lets me know the kiteboarder is OK. Probably going to be hit with some kind of charge from the town, but health-wise he's doing fine. I ask about the ferry, and he informs me he'll try to do some runs at low tide around 7:00 p.m. This is four hours from now. The storm isn't letting up, but the tide is going out, and the wind is shifting around to the west. This will give us a good chance to get our girls home. Peter will not try it if it's not safe. I trust him.

I relay all this information to Melissa, who's dealing with girls running around her in a frenzy, literally running with scissors. She landed hours ago up-island at a friend's house and hasn't left since. It's good to be connected.

Art projects started, abandoned, and restarted two times already. She's tired. We're all tired. I finally tell her about my day. She wants to know everything. I tell her as much as I can. I leave out the part about me being the end of the chain. She guesses anyway and yells at me. We hang up angry about being apart, the storm, stupid people, our crazy life—you name it.

Melissa gets home around 7:30 p.m. The winds die down for about an hour, so the crossing isn't that bad. It does intensify later on in the night, and we lose power, but by that time, we're snug as a bug in a rug back at home. Lots of talk about adventures. Lots of questions about the rescue. Lots of 'sharing' of the disruption in the girls' schedule and will there be makeup classes to their hip hop dance class. All too quickly, the uglier side of tired rears its head throughout our family as the good feelings of being home are replaced by cranky, short tempers from surviving a very long day. We have a quick brinner and crash with the winds and rain whipping against our solid home. Tomorrow is another day.

Baggage

Melissa walks into the kitchen to find me with my head in my hands. "How's your morning going?" She asks, but in a way that should tell me she's still tired from the 'adventure' the other day and doesn't want any more drama.

Per usual, I don't take the hint. I never get the clues. And so I tell her, "Jerry Jeffers just got hit by a car and died."

I've told you briefly about him—the school bus driver. But now he's all I can think about. He's Chappy. He is history. And now he's gone. But I choose to think of him as still here. Still present. Still time for me to learn something from him. He's one of those guys who makes you smile when you see the life he lives and has lived—native American, war veteran, mechanic, firefighter, ferry driver, and old retired guy. So many lives lived in one lifetime. Maybe that's why I've always felt so good talking to him. I hear history in every word he speaks.

Melissa goes through the motions of being sad, but it doesn't hit her as it does me. I call her on it. "Jerry was such a rock for this community. It's such a loss. It's such a tragedy. Just being around him made me feel centered in this place and connected to its past. And its goodness. Do you see that?"

"The man lived, what, eighty-five years? I wish my mom lived that long. He had a good life. He saw his children grow up, and he met his grandchildren. My mom never met Ilana and Sasha. I just miss her so much."

I close my eyes and emotionally hit myself on my head. I tend to miss the connection Melissa always makes with old people's deaths. Melissa's mom, Ilene, died from a brain tumor when Melissa was still in her twenties, and Melissa has never gotten over it. I think it's also why she never became close with my mother. The comparisons were too much. The void can never be filled.

Pivot! Pivot! I need to steer this conversation in a different direction to salvage the day. I go across the table and rub Melissa's back. I hug her and don't say anything for a long time. Silence gets me in less trouble. Then I start thinking about Jerry Jeffers again—about me and even about Ilene and her own sense of calm and wisdom as a social worker. Then I blurt out, "I think of Jerry Jeffers and want that calm in my life. I want that sense of presence and self-assuredness that what I'm doing is right and good, like your mom."

Melissa goes to the cupboard and grabs a mug. One of the mugs from my old retail business with funky sailboats on it and 'St. John USVI' written underneath it. She makes herself a Dandy Blend coffee-like concoction, out of dandelion roots, all the while not saying anything—not reacting to my angst. She puts the mug down between us when she sits across from me. Slowly she turns the image around, so it's facing me. "You've done so much. Look at this mug. You opened a store, one of thirteen stores on the East Coast, when you were twenty-one years old. You have this thriving business on Chappy you made out of nothing.

You should be happy. You should feel accomplished and secure in your choices. You should be able to coast a little and be present. I don't understand what you're chasing. It's all right here in front of you. We are right here in front of you. Why do you keep running, running right past your family? Try saving your family for once. God, you're constantly running around Chappy with your jump kit trying to save everyone, trying to please everyone. It's enough. You've done enough."

"I know. I know. I can't stop trying to please people and be a good person in their eyes."

We're interrupted by Ilana, who sheepishly slides into the kitchen after another long night. It's her second day home from school after the big storm. She's refusing to go on the Chappy ferry. The sight of how vulnerable the ferry could be to the elements has shaken her. "It's not safe. It's not safe," she yelled at Jerry just yesterday as he maneuvered the bus onto the ferry. He had to stop, let her out, and go on without her. Milly, who had been waving cars onto the ferry, sat with Ilana until Melissa could show up and retrieve her. This is the drama we should be talking about. Not Jerry Jeffers and his full and rich life.

"Hi, honey. How are we feeling today?" Melissa sings out when she sees Ilana.

"I'm good. I'm going to bring the food scraps out to the chickens."

"Why don't you eat some breakfast, and I'll bring you to school myself? We'll go to the ferry. Check the seas. Talk to Milly or Peter or whoever is driving to see how the ferry has been. We can make a whole plan."

"Sure, Mom. Let me feed the chickens, and then can I have pancakes?"

"Coming right up." Melissa gives me a look. It tells me

all I already know. Ilana is such a fighter. She really tries to overcome her obstacles. She plans and prepares to take them head-on. But it's never easy. The scene at the ferry will no doubt be challenging, emotional, and loud. She just doesn't have the tools in her toolkit to deal with her sensory integration issues. We don't have the resources. This island doesn't have the resources.

I look at Ilana and want to be her savior—find the solutions so she has the confidence to navigate her world. I know my mom did her best for me in that area—with my challenges. Dad was another story. He had a chip on his shoulder long before the divorce. His cold response to any hardship was to fight. We never talked of feelings or tried to understand a situation—just fight.

Visiting my grandmother, my dad's mom, in a nursing home years ago gave me a glimpse into where his philosophy on life was born. She was barely there. But then she would catch my eye and say, "Robbie!" Tears would flow on both sides. We would talk for a minute, and then she would start rambling again from dementia.

During one visit, she said, "I have sons. Well, really, I have one and a half sons." The meaning of the words didn't dawn on me until years later when I found my dad's correspondence with my grandfather during World War II—it appears my dad was thought less of because of his height—even by his mother. So much going on. So much baggage. So much to think about.

Prelude to the Long Sleep

Fall on Chappy. It's meant to be a time of reconnecting with the land as well as friends. But this year, the craziness of summer hasn't been washed away. The fall was not the palate cleanser that I needed. I haven't been reborn to the beauty of my surroundings like in years past. The emotional toll this place takes on my family has blended from one season to the next. I try to push down the hard stuff and concentrate on the wonder-like beauty that's Chappy in the fall. But then the drama of life on an island just erupts even worse when I least expect it.

The bombardment of life's messiness keeps me off-kilter even as I try to fix it all. Ilana and I are so similar. I have fought the comparisons, but now it stares me in the face each day. Each incident, I don't feel in control. The chaos of my childhood, the divorce, my dad, my Jerry, saw to that. Routines help. You forget how different your life is from the norm when you do it over and over again. It's normal to you.

Winter is almost upon us. A quiet descends over the island as more and more transient inhabitants of one kind or another move away for the winter. Thanksgiving has come and gone. Shops had their big sales as a way to raise cash to get through the winter months. Now they are mostly closed. There are fewer and fewer cultural distractions to entertain the locals. Soon only churches and bars will be open for business. A universal feeling that we are now in it for the long haul descends on us. The necessity to get things done and the drive to enjoy the beauty of the now quiet island takes a back seat to just surviving the winter. There's plenty of time before deadlines become a thing again. We all just want to get through the darkness and stillness so we can be reborn once again in spring.

Enter winter. Enter the monotony of horizontal rain against your body as you attempt to move about your day. Enter more frequent fierce windstorms that make our island a prison. And enter *The Shining*-like behavior of its inhabitants that tourists never see when they think about how great it would be to live on Martha's Vineyard year-round.

WINTER

Is This Normal?

In my opinion, it's living through the winters that make you an islander. All who gush over my lifestyle don't consider the cold, isolating, broken down days of winter when they state, "You're so lucky."

So, here we go. Let's live that life and see if we come out unscathed and cheery on the other end.

It's now November 30th. The last big group of Chappy summer residents is leaving after some big, raucous Thanksgiving get-togethers. I see the parade of cars in line at the ferry as I walk toward it. I'm going to the Dock Street Diner for pancakes with my dad. It's kind of exciting. They don't serve pancakes in the summer, only in the winter. Is it because they don't have time? Is it a special treat just for islanders? I really don't care. All I know is I'm getting pancakes today.

As I sit quietly on the ferry by myself, I see one of my new customers drive onto the ferry. Her family just bought their dream house at the end of the summer. The car is packed. People are brimming with smiles and what looks like new, matching clothing from Vineyard Vines. It seems like they must've had a good Thanksgiving. She rolls down her window to give Milly, the ferry captain, her ticket. And she can't help herself and blurts out, "The weather is glorious. You must kick yourself each day. Able to drive this ferry, look at this view, and live in this paradise."

Milly, who isn't one to bite her tongue, says, "Dear, come back in February when the cold rain is whipping across my face as I drag this one's sorry butt across the channel." She is, of course, motioning toward me as she lets rip on this astonished passenger.

Chappy's newest summer resident is just trying to make small talk. She's just living in the moment and loving the scenery. She wishes this could be her life. But Milly has no time for fairy tales. How often do you think she has heard that question before? Enough to piss her off, I would assume.

Really, the last thing my customer wants is to get on Milly's bad side. Her lifeline to her morning coffee in town. There's no need for her to worry. Milly won't remember her. She's just one of numerous cows in the herd Milly needs to move along, prod to take her seat, and be orderly as the trip commences.

My customer mumbles, "No, I get it. It's such an essential job. I just think it's beautiful and..."

Her words trail off as Milly is already moving on to the last car on the ferry to get their tickets. I know Milly didn't mean to come off as a cranky person. Milly is just Milly. I sigh. I feel the necessity to go up to the family's car window and lighten the mood. I only have a quick second to talk before the ferry docks, but I'm able to put a grin back on her face when I tell her Milly was actually my drama professor when I went to Vassar College. I was so scared of her freshman year. God only knows how I randomly ended up on an island with her. But she certainly has been entertaining.

Milly is one of those New Englanders with a stubborn and independent streak. Her lineage goes back a good deal on Chappy, so she gets some latitude with her personal demeanor and shenanigans. You can tell how long people have been on Chappy based on the stuff they get away with. Does a driver go to the police station or back to their bed when he's found slumped over the wheel of the car, on the side of the road, sleeping, and smelling of booze? Can you duck under the gate at the ferry after it's closed to get on the boat and back to Chappy for some 'urgent' matter instead of waiting five minutes for the next one? Do you really need an inspection sticker for your car from this decade? The list goes on and on. And for Milly, the first week of January is when she pushes the envelope on what she can and can't get away with.

Frozen Tundra

School is important to Milly. Hell, her family name is on buildings at Vassar and other colleges. So, it's no wonder she's perturbed when the harbor freezes over soon after new year's and her girls can't get to school. The ferry can't move. But if the harbor is frozen over, then it seems logical you can walk across it, right? And that's just what Milly does with her girls behind her like a mother duck. There are few people around at 7:00 a.m., but quickly, word spreads. Groups gather on either side of the harbor. She's halfway across at this point, standing next to a frozen red buoy angled sideways in the ice. Her girls are hanging onto it like a lifeline. Shouts of incarceration and DSS are the only things that get Milly to turn around and come back to Chappy.

Everyone has a smile under their scowl. What balls on this woman? We're all proud to call her a friend, but under the smiles is another layer of seriousness as we know what could have happened. People's lives were at stake. The girls' confidence in their mother and their sense of defiance is to be admired. But that would all have been gone in an instant if one of them slipped into the cold water. The ice looks secure. And yet, the current shifts, a solid-looking piece of ice splits and reveals the dark water below. It's a scary thought. Milly got lucky today. We all got lucky today. There's lots of finger-pointing and bruised egos on the shore when Milly sets foot on land again. The excitement of the moment leads to the realization that we all might be stuck on this rock for a while. It's now 8:00 a.m. Cars are lined up on either side of the harbor, wondering when it will run. Will the ice move out of the harbor so they can get to work? Peter is pressing the flesh with everyone on the Chappy side of the line, being diplomatic, and taking all the criticism and suggestions in stride. But then he starts thinking about the four or five elderly people who always have one foot in the grave and could need an ambulance at any moment. Peter needs to do something. He can't sit still, and the wheels start spinning.

The solution to a ferry stuck in its slip because the harbor is frozen? I hear the solution before I see it. Big metal roller wheels crunching over the asphalt pavement coming down the road. It looks small and moves slowly. But as it approaches, I see it's the mammoth excavator that's been on Chappy all week digging a new mega-mansion foundation. Peter motions it onto the ferry, all the way to the front. Then quickly loads the dump truck that's been following it at the ferry's rear to balance out the load. Now it's time to dig. Slowly. Let me say that again for effect, slowly, the excavator drops its bucket into the ice-covered water in front of it, pulls up a chunk of ice, and deposits it down current of the ferry... and repeat.

Mother Nature doesn't cooperate. As soon as the bucket brings out another slab of ice, the bay is kind enough to slide another into its recently vacated place. But eventually, the excavator is able to make a big open pond in front of the ferry. Peter fires up the engines and moves the ferry forward about ten feet. Peter's son-in-law, who's manning the excavator, is in no hurry as he deftly moves the ice out of the ferry's way. He sits there stone-faced in the excavator cabin's seat and works the levers with no emotion. There's no sense of tilting at windmills. It's a job. If he's not doing this job, he'd be rebuilding the engine on the other ferry in dry-dock or fixing a piling on the ferry landing. There's always a job to do, and this just happens to be the one that gets priority this morning—no big deal.

I'm sitting on land at this point, shaking my head. I want to get on with my day. I, too, want my kids to get to school. But this? This seems insane. This seems like one of those suggestions someone makes, and everyone just looks at them and begins yelling all at once how stupid it is. But they're doing it. It's slow going, but they're doing it. And boy, will it make a great story to tell at the fire station next Sunday when we're all sitting around not talking about procedures or the drills we should be practicing.

I call Melissa at some point during all this spectacle, and she's not amused. Her day has been planned out. Shopping for quilting fabric, picking the girls up early from school for dentist appointments, and food shopping were all on her agenda. But now, she needs to change gears, keep the girls occupied, and wait to see if the dentist's appointment needs to be rescheduled. I can visualize her eyes clamped shut. Try to will away the insanity of this life. But she can't. Suddenly, after a long pause on the other end, she blurts out, "You can't make this shit up!"

I nervously laugh. A laugh that telescopes my discomfort and unease with our predicament as a family and an island. Melissa tells me to keep her informed and abruptly hangs up. The quick finality of our conversations around the quirks of living on Chappy is happening more and more. I should call her back but don't know what I would say to change the outcome. Change the anger at the situation. It is what it is. At least the harbor ice is gone for the moment.

The ice trek by Peter and his crew started at 8:30 a.m., and by 10:00 a.m., the ferry has made it across the harbor once and is now ready to start moving people. There's a caveat. There always seems to be a caveat when one gets on the ferry. Peter stoically tells all on board there's no assurance they will get back to the other side once they've crossed. The tide will be slack for the next couple of hours, and then the ice will begin pushing back into the harbor. And there's not much space for it to move, so ice will climb on top of ice, which will climb on top of ice. Soon, Superman's fortress of solitude will be recreated in our very own Edgartown harbor.

The upshot is that everyone needs to go across the harbor on the Chappy ferry at their own peril. But people need to get to work, deliveries need to be made, and kids need to get to school. All agree we'll deal with the consequences of our actions later.

I beg my guys to come back to the ferry and come to work as we have some stud walls that need erecting at a renovation before the next day when a plumber is due to show up to do the rough-in. I'm only able to get one person on the phone, and he's already at a bar where he's soon to meet my other employees. "Not our fault, boss. We tried to get to work." And the line goes dead. It must be nice never to have to worry about getting fired.

If it's Not One Thing...

Hawthorne has been hanging around for the last few days. I don't usually see him during the off-season. I thoroughly enjoy the vacation from his harassment concerning my house, my business... my very presence. But he's closing on another property on our road so that he has fewer neighbors. At least he's getting a taste of what winter in January is like on Chappy. Maybe he will gain some compasssion for our existence on his island. But I ask too much.

I stop home during lunch today to find everyone camped out in the playroom—toys everywhere. It's a lockdown of sorts and not much else to do. But the girls are not playing with their toys. Sasha is glued to the window, and Ilana is pacing the floor. I try to hug Ilana, but she pulls away. She goes in a corner and starts smoothing her taggy on her lap that she still has from her baby years.

"OK, what's up, girls? You're freaking me out a little."

Ilana doesn't look up, but Sasha starts tapping the window and says a little too loudly, "You're freaked out? Well, we are too. Mr. Hawthorne has driven by the driveway about four times in the last hour. He's gone now, but he keeps coming back. He stops his car in front of our house and just stares. That big fat cigarette or whatever you call it sticking out of his pie hole. You can see the smoke all the way from here."

I try not to laugh, but at the same time, I'm pissed. I've mentioned the inappropriateness of this before to Hawthorne, but it obviously hasn't gotten through. I calm the girls down as best I can with excuses for our neighbor's creepiness, get Melissa to do a better job of it, and call Jason, our detective friend, at the police department.

My conversation is veiled and cryptic. I point out that Hawthorne is continually stopping his car and staring at my young daughters with his stogie dangling from his mouth. I imply a lot and say very little. Jason gets the message. He talks to Hawthorne. Hawthorne gets pissed at the implications. He hates me even more. But I believe the slow drive-by viewings will cease.

I wolf down my lunch and get back out to some small jobs I can do myself since no one else is around. I have my list. It's the only comfort to me right now. Check things off. Get them done. Order.

I see Rich on the road with Missy and the kids. He's taking the day off since the kids can't get to school. I don't mind. He's been such a big help. We stop—me going one way and him the other. No cars will be coming for a while. They never do in the winter, and now with the ferry out of commission, we could sit here all day.

"Hey, Rob. Going to show the boys the excavator action."

"Sweet. It's a site to see."

Missy leans over Rich, pushes him back so she can see me better, and says, "I want to thank you again. Taking Rich on. Giving him so many hours and responsibility. I'm doing our books, and we are finally turning a corner. We still need housing, but at least we are stable."

I have really come to admire Missy. She's competent, smooths out Rich's lack of bigger picture thinking, and all the while is the constant caregiver for Gabe with all his developmental problems. I beam. "I'm working on that, too. I'm here for you." And I am working on it or thinking about it. The solution, at least the one that keeps coming up in my brain, is insane, but it's been a dark day and a good one for crazy ideas.

I feel good and in control most of the afternoon as I scribble lines over my list as jobs get done. I'm back in a good mood as I drive the quiet roads of Chappy. I wave at the few locals going back and forth to the ferry to gawk at the ice excavation progress. A few wave for me to stop as they want to let me in on the details, but otherwise, I have the island to myself.

A call comes in from Jason, and I don't hesitate to pick it up. Probably an update on the Hawthorne conversation. But I'm wrong. "Hey, Rob. Have you seen Santiago?"

Arrrrggghhh. I shouldn't have picked up the phone. "No. I gave the guys the day off, or more accurately, they took the day off because they couldn't get to Chappy when they wanted to due to the ice."

"Yeah, I saw the show. Peter is a marvel. But back to Santiago. It turns out, from what I can piece together, Santiago was at the Lampost drinking most of the afternoon and tried to drive home. He got in an accident. No one's hurt. Don't worry. But he left the scene and ran into a field."

"I'm sorry, Jason. He's probably spooked because..."

"I know he's illegal. I assume he had too much to drink. But he can't just run away from an accident. Can you call him?"

"Yes, of course. I don't think it will help, but I will definitely call. And I'll touch base with his church and the others in the Brazilian community that I know."

"I appreciate it, Rob."

"No, I appreciate you calling and attempting to help the situation."

"OK. Let's keep in touch."

I hang up. My day officially shot—once again. I make some calls. Lots of calls to people speaking halting English. Everyone is concerned, but no one has seen him. My text messages to him go unanswered. I give up, put a happy face on, and go home.

It's Fucking Quiet

Santiago is found. The same lawyer that tried to help me with Lorna and kept Juanita out of trouble is on the case. It is what it is. At least the harbor ice is gone for the moment. Got to do what I can and stay positive.

I concentrate on the beauty and tranquility of Chappy this time of year—oftentimes escaping the warmth of our house to walk the desolate dirt roads of our island. The lack of movement on the land makes the scenery around me pop that much more. Little details like an owl on a branch or the mesmerizing rhythm of the waves stand out and catch my eye. I coax the family to join me to keep us active. We get our exercise and become voyeurs into the lives of our absent neighbors. Their houses, hundreds of them, sit quietly. Each one has a personality and a beauty all its own. Some of the houses we encounter on our walks are my customers', and I check them out as part of my caretaking duties—inside and out. But most are just lonely lifeless structures waiting for their masters to return and bring warmth and energy back to them. We peer in windows, sit on porches, and take in the views. Always careful not to disrupt anything, but making memories all the same.

Today's walk has brought us to a house on the water. It's not a customer's, so I don't 'inspect' it as we make our way to their waterside porch. The rocking chairs are stoically lined up as if waiting for someone to bring them to life on this cold day. We oblige them and sit. But the girls get restless and run off to keep warm.

I hear screaming. It's not a happy squeal from chasing each other around. It's a scream of terror. Melissa and I run to the other side of the house. I let out a sigh as I see the girls are OK. But what are they upset about? What are they pointing at?

It's a broken window. There's blood on the window frame. This is evident even from the bottom steps of the front porch. I also see the door is ajar as I approach. One look inside tells me all I need to know. I tell Melissa to call the police, take the girls, get in the car and lock the doors.

The house is a mess. Furniture is overturned, broken knick-knacks and empty beer cans are everywhere. Then I see a youngish woman sitting against a wall, knees to her chest and rubbing her head. It's like my raccoon adventure from the spring, but the reason this interloper can't leave is because she's probably still drunk from partying last night. I back away from the house, tell Melissa to take the girls home, and I call the coms center to give them a more detailed assessment of the scene.

My beeper goes off within a minute of hanging up. I sit and wait. Thinking about how I just wanted to have a nice walk with my family. I call my brother.

"Hey, Andy. What you doing?"

"We're at the mall. Just killing time as we're going to the theater tonight."

This is helping. It's distracting. I wish I could be there with them. Sounds so normal and undramatic. I want to know more. "Sounds fun. What are you going to see?

"It's a musical about Carole King's life. It's called, *Beautiful.*"

"What? I didn't hear about that." Then I let out a laugh—more of a hurrumph, and start singing, "When this old world starts a getting you down..."

Andy interrupts me. "Ah, don't quit your day job."

He's not picking up on my vibe at this moment. I want to vent. But no reason to ruin his day. I choose to end the conversation as I hear sirens in the distance and just say, "No, never quit my day job. Have fun—gotta go."

I hang up and ruminate on my words, "never quit my day job," as the first of the squad cars arrive.

Everyone does their job. I let other EMT's deal with the trespasser. I don't really care about her at this point. She ruined my day. And I don't want to hear about her no-good boyfriend that talked her into this mess and left her there to take the rap.

I don't stay on the scene long. I get someone to take me home. But the only one to greet me is River and a note— "went to Vineyard Haven to get some sushi and a birthday gift for one of Sasha's friends. Be back in a few hours."

I plop down on the carpet and click on the TV. River comes up to me for a good nuzzle. Ahhh, that's what I need. We curl up together, and the last words I hear as I am dozing off to sleep are, "I'm serious. And don't call me Shirley."

Minutes or hours pass by. Eventually, as always, River barks and runs to the door as the girls are home. I rub my eyes and use all my energy in the moment to drag myself up onto the couch.

I don't want to bring up our walk and keep it breezy. "Hey, how was your trip off Chappy?"

"Don't ask." Is all I get from Ilana as she runs past.

"Everything's closed." Says Sasha as she follows her sister.

Melissa is the last to come in with bundles in her hand and a scowl on her face. "Do you believe we couldn't find one restaurant open in Vineyard Haven except for that sandwich shop which has no gluten-free options? We had to get food from the grocery store and sit in the car."

"Sorry." Is all I can think to say.

She goes on without missing a beat. "Then we went to the toy store that was also closed. The sign merely said—Be back in April. They were open last week. What the hell?"

I take the bundles from her, and she takes my place slumped on the couch. I try and be funny. Try and be disarming, but it falls flat when I say, "The things we give up to live in paradise, huh."

Melissa gives me a look, and she too leaves the room.

Winter is kicking our butts—ferry disruptions, the weather, closed shops, people making bad choices all around us, and the harbor freezing—that was a new twist. Not even the distraction of a tranquil walk allows us to forget the dysfunction of our world.

I Hate This Place

During the winter, Chappy really accentuates the players and surroundings of this little play we call life. Each inhabitant is nuttier than the last. I'm not perfect. We all have our baggage. But it's so tiring, the wearing down of what we accept as normal. This Noah's rejects life we live. I'm sure you readers in your big cities and suburbia have people in your world with stories just as crazy. Probably even crazier and more disturbing. I watch the news.

But on Chappy and the Vineyard in general—life is in our face. I just saw a construction worker I see at various jobs in line at the ferry. I don't think I've seen him for two weeks, which is a lot in Chappy time. I say hi and ask how he's doing. He's supposed to say, "Fine, and you." But no. He tells me the truth. "Almost getting divorced. The wife thinks I drink too much. There are problems with our land's title. And my dipshit neighbor sent me some lawyer letter explaining how my land is really his. Oh, and I no longer work for Gable and Tweed Construction and am now the low man on the totem pole at Great Pond Builders. But I still got my truck."

I laugh—a nervous laugh. I hope he doesn't sense it. I start thinking about the laugh self-consciously and don't even notice the construction worker has run back to his truck to scoot onto the ferry as it's his turn to get off our rock.

Conversations like this happen every day. And if I don't happen to run into someone to let me in on their own personal tragedies, then I see the fiasco when my pager goes off. The calls and their memories invade my life. Real-life horror movies of hangings or self-inflicted gunshot wounds, girls throwing ceramic figurines at their father, drunks falling downstairs, marital disputes that get ugly, and people taking unhealthy chances with their lives just to keep from being bored during the winter all reel in my head. For others, it's vacationland. For me, it's complicated.

I have loved this place. But the dysfunction of it is tearing our family apart. The excuses we make for the sacrifices we have to endure to live amongst this beauty are getting to us. Melissa and I once again have that conversation. It's a nondescript Tuesday in January. The kids are at school. I have no pressing engagements, and we're sitting at the kitchen table, sipping our tea.

Melissa just comes out and says, "I hate this place," as I blow on my tea. Instantly, she's crying. "We're damaging our kids. We're going to get to a place of no return. We're damaging ourselves." The arguments come out fast and with heavy breathing. "I hate this place. I hate this place." The mantra spirals into a whimper.

I pull my chair close to hers and rub her shoulders. "Let it out. We've both been feeling this for a while, tiptoeing around the facts. Let's throw it all up. Maybe we just need to get it out of us."

Melissa's face relaxes a little. "You're right. Maybe we're just holding too much of this stuff inside."

We agree to get it all out. Tell each other all the

horrible stories eating at us. Purge ourselves of the negativity and see if we can emerge to then see the bright side we so desperately love.

"I'll start things off," I say—Bam, I hate this place. I have good news and bad news. "I told you about Santiago running away from the scene of an accident, but I haven't told you the updates. Seems the reason Santiago was drinking or celebrating was that his green card had come through. The US Immigration Agency's review of its interview with him and his American wife went well. He told me he thought as much months ago. But his lawyer called him the morning the ferry shut down. So, the good news is he won't be deported as an illegal alien, but he will have to answer for his car accident, not having a license yet, and leaving the scene. I had to send his lawyer more money. He thinks he will sit in jail for a little while. It won't be long, but it will be a while before Santiago can get square with his debts."

She wants to know more. How they caught up with him? How's his wife dealing with all this? I tell her as much as I know. It doesn't help. Then I nudge her. "It's your turn."

So she starts—Bam, I hate this place... "Remember when we were out on the town last week? Tony found out Sheila was cheating on him. He got good and drunk and confronted her at their home, waving a gun in the air. Lots of drama. Lots of danger."

"Oh, I remember."

"Well, I feel we were lucky nothing more came of it as Tony stormed out of the house and came to Alchemy where we were having dinner. It feels like yesterday. The image is so vivid to me. We were sitting at the bar at Alchemy, as it's one of the only restaurants still open at this time of year, and it was packed. Everyone had dressed up for their night out. Lots of happy talk."

I give a little smile. "I remember being very excited to wear a buttoned-downed shirt with no stains on it."

Melissa pats my shoulder, or maybe she's smoothing my wrinkled shirt. "But what did we get to witness? We got to see Tony's drama. The guy we know from dance recitals and friends' cookouts saddled up to the bar next to us. He was slurring his words, and his head was jerking unsteadily from side to side as if it wasn't secured well to his body. He plopped his handgun on the bar top and asked for a beer."

"Yeah, it sticks in my head that he inquired what brands they currently had and specifically asked for a Belgian white beer. Like we were supposed to ignore the Old West moment of him plopping down the gun. Was it just chafing at his side in its holster? What the hell?

Melissa gives me a look as I am jumping over her story-telling. "I recall staring at you with our forks in mid-air. The bartender just stood frozen, also. And the other patrons... they were completely oblivious. Then you did something incredibly stupid."

"I know," I say, shaking my head. "I have no idea what possessed me to slide my napkin over the gun. I know Tony. But I don't really know Tony. Why I was trying to protect him at that moment is beyond me. We should have been running. I should've taken the gun away from this drunk guy."

Melissa always with the insight postures, "Maybe you did it because you chose to see this moment and gesture as a cry for help. I don't know. I do know he's not alone. He's not the first to cry out. But in the same respect, because we've seen it before, I felt like we realized we couldn't fix him. Not at that moment. The best we could do was protect him from himself until someone showed up who could do more. I was glad when the restaurant manager stepped in and guided Tony to the back kitchen."

I shake my head. "I don't even remember tasting the rest of my salmon as we wolfed down our food. That was going to be a rare night out from the girls. I so wanted it to be a time for us to slow down and connect. Now it's just another story to tell."

Melissa begins to cry. "This crap is constantly in our face, day in and day out. The sheer volume is maddening."

"Yeah, I know. I was dialing old high school friends off-island last week. We got to talking about the craziness in our towns. They tell me about a person they heard who did this or that. But they never know them. They certainly don't know each and every one of them."

"Yes, exactly. And when we think, even with the volume of craziness on the Vineyard, well, it won't touch us personally or be close to home—but, we're wrong."

I shake my head and methodically, with no emotion, start back in—Bam, I hate this place... "Remember my EMT pager call last week?" The call was for a truck and driver in the Edgartown Harbor. "I thought it was a prank, some kids, maybe an accident."

Melissa puts her head in her hands on the table. "Yes, I remember. Poor guy." It comes out as a mumble, but I get the gist.

"All we knew was that a truck and driver went off the Chappy ferry ramp with no ferry in the slip, basically, *Dukes of Hazzard* style."

It turns out the troubled youth, based on the video footage, drove a couple of times around the Chappy parking lot. I'm going to say to get up his nerve and make sure no one would be in his path. He then drove, spitting up dust and rocks from his tires, straight at the semi-raised Chappy ferry ramp. The action was nowhere as impressive as *The Dukes of Hazzard*. The truck didn't go that far at all. The job was botched in all respects as the driver barely received a bump on the head. Was he wearing his seat belt? I kept thinking—maybe it was just a prank or a seemingly fun thing to do. It seems like a waste of a good truck to me.

One of the Edgartown Rescue guys on the scene grabbed his scuba equipment, hooked a cable onto the truck's front fender, and passed that up to a powerful lobster boat someone grabbed off of a mooring. It took some time, but the truck was dragged around the bend toward a sandy beach where the cable was then passed to the fire engine waiting in the Chappy ferry lot. The fire engine took no time pulling that truck out of the water. And just like in the movies, water, a crab, plenty of seaweed, and some fish spewed out of the cab when we opened one of the front doors. Never a dull moment.

"What a ridiculous answer to whatever question was in that young man's head. I don't get death as a chosen option. This guy had a child he brought into the world, end of story."

I don't want to keep going, as this last story really hit home. The guy in question lived his entire life on Chappy.

But Melissa is adamant. "No, we started this thing. We need to get all the hate out. I want to get through it. And the one I have next borders on the comical. It makes it all the more infuriating."

So she goes on. —Bam, I hate this place... "I hate our neighbors. I believe I dislike Keith Grommel, the one who accused us of scratching the tree on his property the most.

I can't believe he thinks we're encroaching on his land. It's a dirt road, for God's sake! It's empty forested land across from our house. Have we somehow made our little dirt road bigger and moved it onto his property?"

"He does seem like a dog with a bone. I hated when he roped other neighbors into the middle of our squabble."

"Right. Well, that's why I thought we needed a reset. You were going to have a heart attack if these heated discussions kept on cropping up," Melissa says with genuine concern. "I thought I was being kind and neighborly when I told Grommel we have such a big garden with so much produce. And suggested we bring some over to his house as a goodwill gesture?"

"Of course, he said yes. What else could he do in this situation?"

"Rob, you don't have to always be so pessimistic. The way his posture changed. His tone. I really thought we had turned a corner in our relationship."

"Yes. Thank you. That was a great way to connect with him—if he were human. I remember we walked over to his house the next day. No one was home, and we left the food on that shelf outside of his house and hoped for the best."

"I know it killed you, Rob, to just wait. But there was no word, no altercations for a while—all quiet on the Chappy front. I have to admit I thought there would be peace again on our street—until we got that letter last month from his lawyer. I didn't understand all the legalese. Your dad was good to translate it into English for us. I believe the gist of it was... 'Our client allowed you to come on his land to bring him some goods from your property as a one-time event. You don't have the right in the future to come on his land unless given written or oral permission from our client.' Was there a thank you somewhere in there? What a dick!"

"My only pleasure from that entire interaction, and I know you were against it, was I got to circulate that letter all around town. The people at town hall have had plenty of run-ins with that jerk. They all had a chuckle. I wish I had the opportunity to have a chuckle."

Melissa and I go on like this for hours. The stories add up. The carnage piles up. We're numb as it turns into early afternoon, and we need to make sure we're back to our cheery selves when the kids get home. Melissa and I look at each other. There are dried tears in her eyes and a blank stare looking back at me. All I can think to say is, "Did we do ourselves more damage than good by talking about these stories and getting them off our chest? We're in a dark place."

Melissa just nods her head and says, "Uh, hmmmm."

We clean off the kitchen table, and I look out the window into the glistening winter sun shining off our backyard-mounted solar panels. I notice one of our chickens pecking at the hard earth and then stops in mid-peck to stare at a doe that has wandered into the yard. I look away and mumble, "I don't think it's enough."

The next day doesn't get any better. Ilana's sensory issues sometimes make it hard for her to interact with the world. She knows this. She gets this. But it takes a toll on her. She's a trooper. She rarely complains, no matter how many tests we have her take, how many alternative remedies we push at her, or how many trips off-island to doctor appointments we bring her to. She's so special and strong and optimistic, and we just want her to have a happy childhood.

But the upshot is she's different, and in school that can be a problem. Turns out the craziness that permeates life on Chappy and the Vineyard follows my kids into the classroom.

Calls start coming in around fourth grade with reports of bullying. Ilana is getting ganged up on, verbally. The school gives us assurances they are on top of it. We try to be the parents who let the school do their job and not interfere. And then, yesterday, an anti-Semitic slur gets hurled at Ilana, and it's only because the Jewish teacher's assistant also hears it that a meeting with us is scheduled.

We walk up to the school office desk located smack in the middle of the hall. We greet the school's front office manager and talk about our families. She blurts out, "I love your girls to pieces. They are so sweet." Melissa says the same about hers. There's talk about going to a concert at Fenway Park the following summer, and then we are interrupted by Bob, the principal, waving us into his office.

We enter the office just as a child is scampering out with a donut in his hand and white sugar around his face. It's well known that kids being sent to the principal's office for discipline leave with sweets and nothing in the way of ramifications for their actions. We sit in silence as Bob runs out to wrangle the group of educators that will be sitting in on our meeting to discuss 'the issue'.

So, we're all assembled. We're told that the single-parent father of the girl who uttered the offending phrase doesn't believe his daughter said anything wrong. Kids will be kids and some nonsense like that. We sit calmly. We listen. And then Principal Dingbat tells us that the teachers have given a talk about bullying and they think all is good.

Whoa. Whoa. Whoa. I can't contain myself any longer. I point my finger at Bob. "What about the bullying that's been going on all year? How many times do you need to tell them it's not cool before you do something?" Melissa grabs my hand and squeezes. I look down at the pile of studies and results from tests done on Ilana in Melissa's lap. This meeting isn't going as planned. There are tears in her eyes. I know Melissa wanted this talk to be constructive. She wanted to have a dialog on how to help Ilana succeed socially within her peer group. The squeeze I get from Melissa is a recognition she is letting me go. I'm free to be the 'bull in the china shop'. I'm pissed.

Bob's face is calm, in a dopey kind of way. And he tries to explain. "You see, some of these kids come from broken homes. And it's a very fragile situation. We don't want to upset these kids and possibly disrupt the progress of getting them in school on a regular basis."

I almost fall off the chair. I don't exactly yell, but fire is coming out of my eyes. "You don't want to upset the bully? Is that what you're telling me? Do you see how absurd that sounds?"

One of the other educators in the room tries to rephrase their argument, but it comes out the same, nonetheless. "We're trying to be a place of inclusion. We need to understand the challenges these kids are bringing to the table and why. It's our job to show them how we can be one respectful community."

Melissa stands to talk. She looks tired, and her words come out like a whisper. "It has been four years. These kids have been together since kindergarten. Where is that sense of inclusion for our daughter? For her challenges? What are you saying to her when the rules of inclusion don't apply to her? What do we say to her when she comes home hurt and confused? I guess you think the policy of sugar treats for misconduct is a special or gentle stick. Well, you're wrong. But I see that no amount of yelling or reasoning will change that policy. A warped policy for a warped world."

And with that, Melissa turns, picks up her stack of papers, and leaves as quietly as her speech was. I want to yell some more but have nothing to add. What's the use, and I smile a sad smile and do the same.

On the one hand, we're outraged. On the other, we think, yeah, that's about right. And on our third hand, we think, we got to get out of here.

The Tough Talk

This is hard. We don't know how to do it. But it has to be done. Once again, we sit at our kitchen table, cups of tea in hand, and talk.

Melissa stirs some honey into hers, looks not at me but blankly out of the back window at the dormant and brown wildflower garden, and just blurts out, "I can't take it. I feel so worn down. I feel like I can't breathe."

"I get it."

Melissa turns back to me, and I can see so much sorrow in her eyes. "I don't think you do. You are consumed with your work—your customers. You're constantly in motion. Never really thinking about this stuff. You hear it and are taken aback, but then it flies out of your head, and you move on. I can't do that. I'm so lonely out here on Chappy. It's so isolating. There's nothing and no one to pull me back from this depression."

I put my head on the table. Maybe so I don't have to look directly at her. "You're wrong. It all stays in there for me too. But yes, I have to keep myself going for some reason. And that's what's killing me. I have no off button. My customers ask, and I want to perform. EMT calls come in, and I want to jump. Maybe you're right. I keep running to keep from thinking about my problems—our problems."

Melissa nudges my head up with her elbow. "So, we're agreed. We need to do this. We need to move." She stops for a moment, and then a flicker of a smile crosses her lips as she's pleased that she had the will to say this out loud. "Living in the city will be good for us—more interaction with healthy people, more continuity, no more ups and downs of the seasons, a bigger Jewish community, more resources for Ilana, more, more, more."

I smile back at her because I can see how happy this thought makes her. I'm right there with her, but the sadness is overwhelming—giving up on this life—giving up on the idea of paradise. It means a lot. But I'll adapt. I always do. It can't be harder than starting two businesses from scratch.

"It will be good," I say as assuredly as I can. "What I'm going to do at fifty-two after a life of being my own boss—it scares me. In the past, I was always working without a net—no kids, no mortgage, no retirement to think about. We have all this baggage now. What if I can't get a job?"

"You'll figure something out. You always do. And I already reached out to the guys I worked with when we first got married. Their web development business has come a long way in the past fourteen years, but they know me and say they have a place for me whenever we make the move."

"That's awesome. OK. You'll be the breadwinner, and I'll go to the movies and take care of the kids. We have a plan." We both laugh, which makes River perk up her ears and bound over to the table. I rub her behind the ears like she loves and say, "Anyone up for a walk?" River can't contain herself, and Melissa looks equally pleased.

Melissa and I convinced ourselves the move is good for

us for our own reasons, but the girls will be a different story. How will we make them understand this island that we have championed and revered for their entire lives is toxic to our family?

The Tougher Talk

It's taken a month for Melissa and me to come up with a concrete plan. It's a late February afternoon, the heavy sleet whipping against the windows has been coming down for hours, and the girls are in the playroom dancing as usual. Each has on a colorful outfit from one past recital or another. I know they are ten and twelve, but in those outfits, they may as well be five and six. They're putting together a dance routine to the song 'Hotline Bling'. I love it when they come together like this and don't want to stop them. We stand in the corner and watch as they unabashedly work through their moves and sisterly interactions. They fall to the ground laughing as the song ends, and Melissa goes over and turns off the stereo.

"That looked awesome. You really have those moves down. Can you come over here? Daddy and I want to talk to you about something."

Ilana and Sasha run over to the couch where we're sitting. There's some jostling to see who will sit where but no indication they understand their world is about to be turned upside down. "What's up?" Ilana gasps, still a little out of breath from the dance-off.

I don't know how to start. Looking in their eyes, all I

can see is joy and innocence, and trust. They are so happy in their current life. It's all they've ever known. Maybe we're wrong. Perhaps we should stay. But then Melissa starts, and the Band-Aid is ripped off. "Daddy and I have decided we need a change. After next summer, we are all going to move to Boston."

Melissa pauses to let it sink in and to gauge the girls' reaction. As we thought, Ilana is the first. "No, no, no. Where will we live? What about my friends? I don't want to move." It's so hard for Ilana to deal with a change to her set routines. This is upending her world.

"Honey, we go off-island so often to get you help. The occupational therapists, the vision therapist, all the tests. This way, we'll be closer to them and not have to deal with the ferry. It's tiring dealing with the traveling off-island." Melissa tries to take each counterargument for staying as it comes, but it's challenging. It's heartbreaking.

Sasha is younger. She's quiet. She's letting her sister say all the things she's thinking. But then she speaks up and tries to use logic, which has not, to this point, been Ilana's tack. "Wait, Daddy has his business here. We can't leave. What's Daddy going to do with all his customers?"

I take a big breath. "You know I'm not getting any younger, and I ache for hours after work each day—my back is always hurting me?"

Sasha nods her head and says, "Yeah, yeah," as tears roll down her face.

I refrain from saying, "You mean, yes, yes," as my father would say to me, and push on. "Well, it's getting harder for me to do the jobs I once did. I know I could have Santiago, Kyle, and the others do more. But you know I have control issues."

The girls both reluctantly smile at this but are nowhere

near convinced. "What about money? And my friends and the house. You are not selling the house!"

"No, no, no," Melissa reassures the girls. "We're still figuring it all out, but we're not selling this house that your dad built. Daddy is working on a plan for the business, his customers, and even the house. We'll move to Newton. To my childhood home. Next August, after the ag fair, we'll move, and you'll be all settled by the time the new school year starts."

I look over at Melissa as she says this. A plan. That's an overstatement. There are so many moving parts. I need to make sure I keep my customers on board, create a succession plan, and hopefully make sure we can secure some money to start our new life in suburbia.

At this point, everyone is crying. River has come over to the couch and is showing real concern. Ilana is hugging her so tight I think River is going to yelp. But she doesn't. She's such a good dog. The girls continue to listen. They continue to raise their objections, which Melissa deftly fields and turns into positives.

We don't touch on the island's toxic nature and how much we fear for their emotional future if we stay. My back problems and Melissa's desire (fictitious or otherwise) to get back in the workforce as a web developer is what we stick with as arguments. They are somewhat real. But, the real, real is not touched. We keep our 'adult problems' with the island off the table. The last thing we want is to tarnish the girls' love of their island and have them second guess their happy childhood.

We talk for hours. We're all exhausted. Melissa ends with the carrots. "Each of you will get to decorate your new rooms. Sasha, since you have the tiny room here on Chappy—you will get to pick your room first." This is good. I'm totally on board. Sasha has always taken a back seat to

Ilana's special needs and wishes. She often feels forgotten. Hopefully, this will give her some confidence that we are thinking about her in this move. And we are right. She does brighten a little at this suggestion. If only a little.

Melissa smiles and continues. "And here's a gift card for each of you to Pottery Barn. You can use them to buy whatever knickknacks you want for your new rooms. This is a whole new beginning."

Ilana is already coming around and thinking about the Red Sox games she can go to, shopping excursions she can go on, and city life in general. The planning has begun. In the coming months, she'll pack and unpack bags even though the travel date is months away. She'll scour websites and find the perfect dresser to go with the bed she has picked out. Ilana is nesting. Ilana is trying to plan so her new world can be familiar, manageable, and controllable.

Sasha is another story. She was quiet when we started this conversation—more timid. She is our Buddha baby. Always so happy and carefree. But we have flipped a switch in her brain. The words, "You have ruined my life," get repeated each day. Sometimes multiple times a day and at high volumes. "I have put up with Ilana this and Ilana that my entire life. And the only thing that gives me happiness is my friends, Chappy, and our home here. You are ruining all of that."

My heart breaks for the umpteenth time. She's right. But is she? No, this is for the best. The arguments go back and forth in my head. Over and over again. Melissa doesn't have this dilemma. She's done. She wants out. Just like the sailing adventure to Cuttyhunk—she didn't sign up for this shit. Boston is her home—where we can have a normal life. Period.

I can't think about this anymore. I need to plan our escape.

Not So Quickly

OK, we're going to do this. We can do this. But I need to make sure Chappy Unlimited lives on. I want to make sure my customers are protected and cared for. The word legacy comes to mind. I've worked too hard for too long to get my customer's homes and summer lives on remote control to have it all just go away. We walked away and closed down the stores of World View Graphics when my brother and I dissolved our clothing company. They were successful, but we just walked away. Too hard to find someone who could do what we did—care for our designs and our customers the way we did. That was our mantra—our rationale. Now I regret it—so much work—so many relationships cultivated. The creativity and breadth of artwork shelved. I look back at our non-legacy and feel empty. It's almost like it never existed.

I want it to be different this time. So, I make a list of people that might be able to take over Chappy Unlimited. I check it twice and all that. It's a small list—a ridiculously small list. I need someone to steward my behemoth of an operation, keep my crews from falling apart, make sure they're cared for and productive. I need to do all this and make sure my customers stay onboard for the switch. First,

I put names on the list of people all over the island that are competent to do this, don't already have a company of their own, and don't hate Chappy. But then I crumple it up. The reason companies have such a hard time with Chappy is because they're not here. They don't get the rhythm of the island or want to. They're not on-island at two in the morning when emergencies happen, or heck in the middle of the day, like when the ferry breaks down. So I make a new list—one with people from off of Chappy that love it and would potentially move here and then another list with Chappy residents that could do the job. I look at the two pieces of paper and am not reveling in my undertaking.

Over the next few weeks, I talk on the phone and meet up with various people on both lists. I don't tell them specifics. Never mention I want to sell Chappy Unlimited. Just trying to feel them out. Do they want to own their own business? What are their long-term plans on the island? Questions about Chappy and housing. The answers don't fill me with confidence in my task at hand—new promotions at their current job, confidential wishes of their own to leave the island, and then the Chappy specific utterances that make me wince. It doesn't look good. I only have three names left. One from off Chappy and two on.

Melissa understands that I don't want to publicize the move—all the questions and objections from friends. But she asks, "Why not advertise the opportunity off-island. People are constantly looking to relocate here—to get out of the rat race."

I already thought about this. "I'm not looking for a quick payday. I don't think they'll last on Chappy—coming to it cold. It's not for everyone. Hell, it's not for most people. I need someone Chappy tested. I think you know that."

We talk more. It goes on for days, weeks. I talk to more people on-island and off. The list doesn't get bigger. People who have their act together already have a company of their own. Others are worker bees for a reason. I see very little drive in them to advance or succeed. Or worse, they have drive, but continually shoot themselves in the foot—make bad decisions, so it makes succeeding harder. Their lives have become so complicated and dysfunctional due to their choices. They don't have the bandwidth to deal with anything more than what's directly in front of them at the moment.

I struggle to connect, manage, and be there for one family. I don't understand how people with multiple ex-spouses and children with various partners hold it together. Add in the drugs, other illegal activities, and you get a fragile balancing act for people that don't have the resources, stable footing, or support system to advance. I'm painting a bleak picture. It's not pretty. That's precisely why we're leaving.

In the end, it comes down to one name... Rich. He's always been in the back of my mind. I think that's why I kept telling him not to worry about housing. I just needed to come to terms with what my head already knew. But he has so many of the same flaws that has made me cross others' names off my list. An ex-janitor who has not managed anyone doesn't have the skills for most jobs and barely has enough money to exist each month—let alone buy a company. Yet he's on Chappy. He's so eager to please. He already knows my crews, the procedures, and the clients. And Missy can be his co-pilot. The two of them combined just might have what it takes to run Chappy Unlimited and secure a financial future for their family. Rich doesn't need to be a rock star at the work. He's not me. He only needs to not fuck things up. And besides, Rich and Missy need a place to live, and my home has just become available.

The Bombshell

It's the day. Honestly, I have been putting this task off for months. It's springtime again, and we're so busy, but I can't wait any longer. If I don't put my plan for Rich in motion, if I don't put the facts out into the world, then it's not real. Something in my head, no matter how well thought out, is still only in my head. But not today. Today, I change everyone's life in more ways than even I can comprehend. Today is the day I give Rich the keys to the castle.

He arrives at my house after work. He's all sweaty and tired. This is a good thing. He's in the swing of the business. He still isn't a rocket scientist when it comes to the skills of all the jobs he helps the guys with, but he is a serviceable cog in the wheel. And all the customers seem to like him. That's what counts. I tell myself all this so I can feel like I made the right decision, but the bottom line is there was no one else to groom as a successor. The island gave me no other choices. And honestly, I feel like I have created a bulletproof transition plan.

I yell to him from the house to clean up as best he can and meet me inside when he's done. Rich is busy brushing off all the wood chips and grass clippings from his socks and pants when I find him on the front porch. He places his boots neatly in the corner behind the door and follows me into the house. Unaware that his life officially changes... now.

We sit down at the kitchen table in a nook off our dining room. I get Rich a glass of water, and while he's taking his first sip, I blurt out, "Well, I have it all set up so you will not have to look for a place to live for a long, long time. And there's so much more."

He slowly puts the glass down. His eyes go wide, and he waits. I rip off the Band-Aid like my wife did with the girls just a few months earlier and tell him, "You are going to live in my house."

Rich is just staring at me. I'm apparently being too vague. I just need to say it. "I'm going to set you up as the new owner of Chappy Unlimited, and you will rent my house and live in it with your family."

Rich nervously laughs and says, "OK, what? Nooooo? Where are you going? Noooooo?"

I slow it down and tell him about my family's plan to move off-island. I tell him vague stories about my health and our desire to get better quality sensory help for Ilana off-island. I leave out all the parts about our disillusionment with island life. It doesn't help to tell the animals staying behind that they live in a dysfunctional zoo with little hope of a healthy life for themselves or their kids.

"Rob, I can't run your business."

I take a breath and tell him to slow down. I need to slow down. "We can get into the weeds about running the business another time. I have already spent the last month creating a manual for every customer's house, so you'll be on top of it all. It runs something like 300 pages at this point. And you have all the employees that will have your back."

"Wait, you know I have no money. How am I supposed to buy your business or pay the rent on your house, for that matter? This place is insane," Rich screeches as he paces the dining room.

"Don't worry about the rent," I say a little too loudly. "I'll make it the same as what you are paying now." Honestly, it will be a huge haircut on what I could get, but it'll still cover the mortgage, and that's all I care about at this point. I talk as I show him around the house, room by room. I realize as I watch Rich peering in every corner that I have never had Rich in the house farther than the mudroom.

He's still a guy I have never been able to connect with on a deeper level. I once again begin to think about him and his shortcomings. But then pull back. Rich is not me. No one is going to work at this business the way I did. Looking back, I don't know how I did it. The fact is I grew into the job. Hell, I didn't know what I was doing when I started. Rich is just me sixteen years ago. I'm giving Rich the tools to succeed and have a better life. He can do this. I can do this.

We start to talk about the business. Rich again talks about money and his lack of any. "Don't worry," I say. "I've been thinking about this, and I have it all worked out."

Rich eyes me with a sheepish grin. He still thinks I'm pulling his leg. Not too late for me to tell him, "Yeah, it's a joke. I was just testing you." But I plug on and go deeper into my plan.

"I'll stay on, and we'll co-run the business for the next three months. I'll pay all the bills and collect the money, and it will go into a new checking account for your new business. Eventually, I will take some of the profits out as you get comfortable in your new role as payment for buying the business. But only when you're ready." I explain this will create a good nest egg for him to feed off and solidify his financial stability. Rich doesn't get it. I talk more.

Tears stream down his face. He still can't wrap his head around it. "What? Are you really leaving? Why not stay, and we can conquer Chappy together?" Rich still wants to be my best buddy. Why doesn't he want this? Why isn't he seizing this opportunity for himself and his family?

"Rich, you're not listening to me. I have already conquered Chappy. I'm done. Now it's your turn. I'm going to help you make your mark and set up a future for you and Missy and the kids." I realize with the same questions coming back over and over again that I'm not getting very far in the synopsis of this plan. So I cut it short and tell him to go home and talk it over with Missy. We have plenty of time to talk this all out. I tell him not to tell anyone in the meantime. He shakes his head as he puts on his boots and promises not to say a word.

Leaving Paradise

I'm sitting in my seat on the top deck of the *Island Home*, a massive three-decked vessel that transports people and cars between Martha's Vineyard and the mainland. I say the ferry's name over and over under my breath, *"Island Home, Island Home."* Not anymore, I think.

The salt air paints a picture. There's laughter and talk of journeys taken all around me, but all I can do is concentrate on the hardened piece of pink gum under the seat in front of me. It feels too Herculean to lift my head and watch the shoreline of the Vineyard recede into the distance.

I've accomplished so much during this chapter of my life. I've checked off so many boxes and gotten so much done. I feel a breath of fresh air as my to-do list for once is blank, and there are no messages on my phone from customers. I tell myself it's time to forget the past, all of it, and concentrate on the future.

Our belongings are already in our new suburban home, and we are finally leaving paradise for good. I have to say it again as I don't believe it or comprehend it, for that matter. We're leaving paradise. It's been six months since Melissa and I started to make this idea real and dropped a bombshell on our whole way of life.

It's summer again as I sit on this big boat ferrying us away from our island home. The bleak and hopeless feeling of winter is far behind us. The air is warm and moist. Our plans and resolve are still in place and sailing smoothly. Rich is set up in our house. The business is running efficiently with all my old, valued employees in place. And we are making our move.

The ferry is crowded. People are happy. They have just experienced what they think it might be like to live in Shangri-La. But for us, we're rejecting that narrative. I want to tattoo on my ass, "The grass is always greener..." And at the same time, I know I'm throwing away a dream reality.

I have come to realize that by living on islands for so long, we're among those who missed the boat—Noah's rejects. So distant from mainstream life. Proud of it for many years but tired of it now. This is all swirling through my head. The stories you have just read are swirling through my head.

I have always been so sure of myself—confident and fearless. But now, not so much. Choosing the road most traveled has always seemed less fun than driving off that cliff known as civilization. A childhood spent watching my father skirt the norms and rules and succeeding paved my way.

I did the same and always seemed to have more fun than those around me. Starting fun businesses, never wearing 'big boy pants', and living on islands became the natural progression of my efforts. I have loved the ride. I have come to love and feed off the natural beauty of the islands. One minute serene and quieting to the mind and the next exciting and raw as Mother Nature unleashes her fury. And yet I see up ahead parallel roads and even perpendicular roads I might want to be on in the long run. But can I get there? Suburbia and its conventions are so constricting and plain. Do I really want to get there?

I concentrate on my family sitting next to me. Melissa is happy to re-enter the real world, Ilana is always looking for a better place to fit in, and Sasha is seething as she tells me for the umpteenth time that I have ruined her life. Have I? Too late. I'm going to jump. We're going to jump. Jump off this rock and start anew. My DNA says that jumping should not be a problem. But then I think about the dysfunction of my fellow Noah's rejects on Chappy—and the ones that tried to break ranks and move off-island. What makes me so unique or in possession of the ability to survive in the real world? I don't know. But like in my past adventures, I'm ready to find out.

Repercussions

It has been one year since we left Chappaquiddick. It has been one year since we left our rock off a rock to move here. And by here, I mean Newton, MA, suburbia USA. It's on the fashionable western outskirts of Boston. It has a nationally ranked school system for the kids. Melissa can go to one of two Whole Foods in the neighborhood, and the Apple Store is a mile from our house. Our new life experiment is underway.

Routines are a healthy thing. It's 7:40 a.m., and much like on Chappy, I'm walking my girls to the bus stop. Sasha has not yet told me I have ruined her life this morning, but there's still time before she gets on the bus. Ilana is like a pig in shit. She holds my hand, she plays with River on the sidewalk, and the only thought in her head is whether the Red Sox will go all the way this year. She wants to go to her first World Series game. Ilana has already been to four games this season and is an avid member of Red Sox nation. Sasha hates sports. Hated them on Chappy and hates them in Newton.

I just let it all flow over me. I'm not taking any of this personally—the good and the bad. It's too early in the experiment to make any judgments. I don't even know how

I fit in yet. I'm trying to reinvent myself. It takes time.

The thoughts about the move reel in my head as I walk back to our 'home' with River after depositing the girls on their school bus. I refuse to put a leash on her. She's a free spirit. Putting a dog on a leash is so domestic. River wants to run and play and jump. Plenty of people remind me of the leash laws in suburbia, and I thank them and walk on. It was hard at first, but she's a lab and smart. She now sits at crosswalks before crossing and waits for my signal. The squirrels were a tough temptation at first, but she now ignores them when she sees them across the street—unless I give her the OK, and then she pounces. Good dog. Smart dog. River is acclimating to the grass on the other side of the street quite nicely. It's a start.

I head to the Newton Library. I spend one hour looking for job opportunities online, another one hour looking for start-ups that might need my help as a co-founder, and then another three hours writing the book you're now reading. It's a ritual. It passes the day.

It's hard on my ego that no one wants to hire me. I accomplished so much as a business owner. I was successful in every endeavor I undertook. But I'm fifty-two. I'm perceived as a lone wolf. I have not hit a round peg through a round hole countless times for the specific job I'm applying for. I get that, and at the same time, I know the 'real' reason I'm not gaining any traction. It's just like my fears as I walked on the side of the road in my dad's posh town. The people know I don't belong.

Melissa calls me from her office. "How's your day so far?"

"It's going as planned. I'm going to a conference on start-ups tomorrow, and maybe I'll meet some founders there."

"Great. But be home early. We have tickets to see First Aid Kit at the Orpheum. Remember? As a celebration of my first raise?"

"Oh yeah. Very cool. I might just go directly to the concert. The girls can make mac and cheese for dinner if you want to meet me directly from work."

"We can figure it out tonight. I have to go. My calendar has me booked up for the rest of the day. Crazy! Love you."

I tell her I love her back, and we hang up.

It's now 1:00 p.m. and time for my yoga class at the Jewish Community Center (JCC). It's like a YMCA but has yet to give up its religious component. The class is OK. I'm spoiled with the level of instructors we have on the Vineyard. I miss my power yoga sessions at the Y, but it will do. Except today my ritual is interrupted. A situation arises that I'm not used to. It seems that people in the world, not just the Vineyard, don't particularly like Jews. Go figure. And one of these people, or a group, who knows, decides to call in a bomb threat to the JCC where I'm stretching and sweating. The childish anti-Semitic jibes of a ten-year-old at Ilana's school seem nostalgic compared to the terror I currently feel as I run next to a mother holding her baby through the halls of the JCC. You can run, but you can't hide.

My hands are still shaking as I pull into our driveway. I see and wave to my neighbor. He's Asian with two kids, and I think his parents live with him. I don't know his name. I don't know his politics. My smile and good nature toward him are wrapped up in the fact that I have no idea who he is. This is what I signed up for. The same is true of the hermit in the house on the other side of us. Yes, I pull her trash bins in for her after the garbage truck has gone by. But this is where it ends. I don't know if she needs medical care. I don't know if she has friends or even family. It feels good to be anonymous. It feels so light not to know the facts about my surroundings.

Sasha is pouting when she comes into the house after school and throws down her backpack. "Why can't we just go back to Chappy?"

OK, here we go. I ask her to explain.

"The kids care so much about money. They care about what you guys do for a living and where we live. Why should they care?"

I shake my head and don't have an answer. I talk about class and structure and the necessity of placing people in manageable, well-defined boxes. But it's all bullshit. I don't really get it myself.

"On Chappy, we went to school with Brazilians, like Juanita's daughter. They had it hard. I know it. But no one ever threw it in their face. And Annie, I knew the first time we went to her house that they were rich. But it was never a thing. No one ever talked about it or cared about it. We just played."

Tears run down Sasha's face as she can't catch her breath. Is it wrong to want Sasha to learn these truths about the world while she's young? Is it wrong to burst her idyllic bubble at such a young age? I don't break down even though I want to.

I can't fix this. I'm the one that caused it. I need to keep calm as we ride this out. At least she doesn't know about my day at the JCC. But I'm wrong. It only took ten minutes for the cell phones at Sasha's middle school to start blowing up with news of the bomb threat.

"What the hell," she blurts out when she remembers the fact a few minutes after finishing her first tirade. "Why do people hate so much? What's their deal? We've never done anything to them."

Again, I don't have an answer. I talk about the Spanish Inquisition. I talk about the Holocaust. I get blank stares. I'm not prepared for these conversations. I should have been more prepared. I feel guilty that I caused this.

I dial my dad's number for advice and assurances but only hear the familiar refrain. "The number you are calling is not in service. Check the number and dial it again." My dad's not there. He's not anywhere. Jerry is dead. He took the move hard. But not in a Jewish guilt-ridden nagging kind of way—in a Jerry way. Stoic—matter of fact—calculating the future. He didn't ask me the standard questions like, where will you move to? What will you do? Will you sell the house on Chappy? He believed I'd thought of all of those things. He assumed I had a plan. Jerry had raised me to be ready for the unknown, the chaos. Instead, he jumped to the end game.

The 'conversation' in his apartment was quick and to the point, like Jerry. "The girls will be better prepared for the world living in Boston. Melissa is all about the kumbaya Vineyard ecosystem, but being in a city will bring into focus the need to know about money, the stock market, trade-offs in life, and that most people hate us as a people."

I sidestepped Melissa being over the façade of living in a utopian, crunchy granola island and focused on the easier issue. "Come on, Dad, they're still little girls." But as the words came out of my mouth, I understood my words were his words. I had learned everything and nothing at all.

He told me for the umpteenth time, "I had three jobs by the time I was a teenager—a paper route, working for the city on a road crew, and driving a ding dong cart. Never too early to know what the world is all about."

Sometimes I wondered if he realized how many times

he'd told me the same things over and over again. I didn't want to listen to them again but knew that soon I would only be hearing them from the earpiece of a phone. So, I indulged and egged him on. The hardship, the post-depression era, the anti-Semitism, and the cold bosses all played their parts in his stories. And I just sat there, soaking in every depressing minute of them. But not depressed. Instead, I'm already nostalgic for the loss of having my dad in my daily life—porn-ridden computer problems and all.

My dad talked on. He never let on that he understood I'd heard it all before. While I listened, I looked around at the inches of mess on the floor around his apartment. Who was I kidding? There were places where there was a good foot of debris in the kitchen area. It didn't have to be this way. But it really did. I had come to terms with that. Jerry was Jerry. Me being here or not being here was never going to change that.

The stories came to an end, and I cut in. "You going to be OK without me?"

"Sure. You don't have to worry about me. I have my routine. The nurses at dialysis take good care of me. I love it here. What would I do anywhere else?"

We're not big on going deeper. The one time my dad let his guard down and openly wept was when he had an operation on his feet due to diabetes. It left me paralyzed emotionally. Not that I couldn't handle it in theory. Just that I had not seen an emotional side of my dad... ever. I tried to confide in my brother about the incident, but we have a similar relationship. I stopped, barely after I started.

So Dad knew. I buried deep down how much my dad depended on me and convinced myself he'd be OK. He would go on creating and telling Jerry tales.

But in the end, he wasn't OK. A raw outburst on the phone to me from the hospital after a fall off his moped said it all. "I can't take this anymore. There's no use living."

So you would think his plan to lock himself in a hotel with hookers and a carton of Max 120s would kick into gear. But he didn't have the strength or courage for that. Depression hit him hard as he saw a nursing home in his future and knew he no longer had the bravado to go out in style—his style.

I gave Jerry an out. I don't know if it was to ease my pain or his. That one true emotional outburst from him in the hospital was too much for both of us. I saw how pained he was after being so honest. I know how hurt to the core I was for not being emotionally closer to him—not to mention physically closer. So I made it easy for both of us.

"Dad, you don't have to be here if you don't want to." I paused, unsure if I had the guts to go on. I had talked to Andy about this idea, and he was dead set against it. But he wasn't in the room. He hadn't seen and known Dad on a daily basis the way I had.

I ripped the Band-Aid off. "You're on dialysis, but you can stop at any time. Your body will take care of the rest."

His shoulders went slack, his face smoothed, and he relaxed back into his chair as the idea and ramifications took hold in his head. I was relieved by his reaction and mushed on.

"Your body can't process the waste, and eventually, the toxins will back up in your system and make it shut down. They would give you drugs so there would be no pain as this happens."

And just like that, Jerry started making plans. Car in Rob's name. Check. Make sure beneficiaries for the different Fidelity accounts are set. Check. Paperwork filled out and ready for Andy and my signatures for Social Security death benefits. Check. Check. Check, and more checks. He wanted to control it all and did. Jerry's death was so well thought out and matter-of-fact that it robbed me of the messy clumsiness of a sudden loss. My constant calls to his defunct number remind me I was not really ready. I'm still not ready. Why doesn't he just pick up?

Time passes. I call my brother more often than usual, just to say hi. He's my only connection to Dad now. We plan to rendezvous on Noah's Rejects this weekend. Andy was nice enough to adopt the boat and put her in Newport, where we both could use her. She's still my escape. It just takes me a little longer to get to her.

My daughters become moody teenagers. This is normal and expected. They have their secrets. They begin to make friends in suburbia. I don't know much about them or even their parents' names. I should know their names, right? Sometimes I think I'm taking this anonymous thing too far.

I'm getting used to suburbia, but the lack of nature and wilderness is like a straitjacket around my heart. I don't wake up every day to smell the nature that surrounds me. My first sounds of the morning are passing cars or a fire engine on the busy street below and not a robin or blue jay singing outside my window. Nature has been a constant theme in my adult life. Not anymore.

The other constant that I left behind is my business, Chappy Unlimited. Or, so I thought. It's falling apart. I just wanted my legacy to live on. I wanted my customers to stay happy. But they are not happy. I thought I sold the business to a young guy who just needed a break, to a family who needed some security. I felt proud of myself. I literally gave Rich the keys to the castle.

But customers are calling me, pleading with me to

come back, and asking for advice. I try to be helpful and stay out of it all in the same instant. It's hard.

Rich has fired customers because they don't say thank you when he finishes a job. He's stealing money from them. He's telling people his mother has died when he falls down on the job as an excuse. His mother isn't dead. What am I supposed to do? I'm trying to start over in suburbia.

It's all coming to a head. Rich's wife kicks him out and gets a restraining order. He can no longer work out of the house—where all the tools are. This is ending badly. Within another year, he will have absconded with all the money his customers loaned him... and fled to Africa. He owes money all around the island, ruined the name Chappy Unlimited, and left his wife and children alone in my house with no resources to survive.

Who does that? How did I not see that? Did I not want to see that? This was not the clean exit I was hoping for. My legacy and big payday are gone. I feel like I'm in danger of being sucked back in.

Melissa talks me off yet another ledge and tells me to let it go. We knew the odds of Rich succeeding. It didn't matter how turnkey the operation was. Rich is an islander. It turns out he's just another guy who can't get out of his own way. The keys to the castle are useless if you're too drunk to find the lock.

It would be so easy to just run back to Chappy. I knew it was a possibility based on the track record of many of my fellow rejects. Maybe it would be for the best. I have yet to find a purpose in my new life. I know why I left. I'm proud of our decision. It was a courageous one. But I'm not happy yet. Everyone can see it on my face. I'm a puma pacing back and forth in a fabricated habitat at a local zoo. I'm planning my next move, planning my escape. The stakes are so high. I can't panic. I can't panic.

And I won't panic. It's not in my nature. This is just another emergency situation. For right now, that's OK.

I'm not going back. I won't go backward. I'm putting my family first, above the pull of my customers and employees for once. This move has been a healthy one. It's just going to take time. And as I write this epilogue, it has been three weeks since Sasha has said she hates this place.

In truth, I'm beginning to embrace my moniker as a Noah's reject among the animals in my new zoo. I'm unique. I'm a snowflake. I'm not merely a cog in the wheel of society. Will I be able to live as a Noah's Reject in the belly of suburbia and the greater society? This is another story. I have no idea. I want to know the answers now, but I have to wait—come to terms with who I might want to be. I have to live it. Breathe.

Acknowledgments

I would like to thank Melissa, Sasha, Ilana, River, and all my friends (on-island and off-island). Thank you for putting up with me through this writing process. To Andy, who has been by my side through it all and then some. To my Mom, who has always had faith in me to accomplish anything. And to Daddy-Len, who is the sweetest, nicest guy and most deserving of a do-over.

I would like to thank Niusmar, Chris, Mark, Raphael, Adulto, Luge, Linda, Line, Lorna, Branco, Sergei, Hekuran, Besart, and the hundred or so other employees over the years that had my back and were also struggling to survive on our rock.

I would like to thank my customers for being my customers, letting me come into your world, and giving me the bandwidth to live and grow on Chappy. In the end, we are all family.

I would Like to thank the writers who have always inspired me—Gonzo journalists: Joan Didion, Ken Kesey, Tom Wolfe, Jimmy Breslin, Spalding Gray, and of course, Hunter S. Thompson. The only way to produce an objective piece is for your audience to know you wrote it subjectively. "Subjectivity is objective."

I would like to thank humor for always being a part of my life. More specifically: Mel Brooks, Carl, and Rob Reiner, the original, "not for prime time" cast, David Letterman, Larry David, John Stewart (and cast—Rob, Jason, Lewis, Ed, John O., and both Stephens), Gary Shandling, the creators of Loony Tunes, Berkeley Breathed, Garry Trudeau, Bill Waterson, and Gary Larson.

I would like to thank the best poets of our time: The Rolling Stones, The Beatles, Bob Dylan, The Avett Brothers, Elvis Costello, Joni Mitchell, Carole King, Elton John (Bernie Taupin), Cat Stevens, Stevie Wonder, Sting, Rickie Lee Jones, Simon and Garfunkle, and of course – ENTRAIN (our wedding band). There is so much meaning in each sentence. How do you venture to write a book when competing with the compactness and elegance of a song?

I would like to thank the Newton Public library, which has been my working home during the writing process of this book. Please support your public library. The books, the space, the kindness... it's all good.

Finally, I would like to thank the early readers of this book for suffering through my indulgences and terrible writing: Karen King, Linda Cohen, John DiCocco, Howard Odentz, Christine Giraud, Jana Eisenstein, Patty Caya, Leah Berkenwald, Mayam Keramaty, Kathleen Tumminello, Barbara Nelson, Elle Williams, Bre Power Eaton, Marie Coleman, Miriam Glassman, Bill Barton, Kimi Ceridon, Megan Brake, Shannon McFarland, Jesse Liberty, Prassede Calabi, Deborah Lapides, Barbara Adelson, Sue Hollister, and Kimberly Hirsch.

About Atmosphere Press

Atmosphere Press is an independent, full-service publisher for excellent books in all genres and for all audiences. Learn more about what we do at atmospherepress.com.

We encourage you to check out some of Atmosphere's latest releases, which are available at Amazon.com and via order from your local bookstore:

Ghosted: Dating and Other Paramoural Experiences, a memoir by Jana Eisenstein

Dancing with David, a novel by Siegfried Johnson

The Friendship Quilts, a novel by June Calender

My Significant Nobody, a novel by Stevie D. Parker

Nine Days, a novel by Judy Lannon

Shining New Testament: The Cloning of Jay Christ, a novel by Cliff Williamson

Shadows of Robyst, a novel by K. E. Maroudas

Home Within a Landscape, a novel by Alexey L. Kovalev

Motherhood, a novel by Siamak Vakili

Death, The Pharmacist, a novel by D. Ike Horst

Mystery of the Lost Years, a novel by Bobby J. Bixler

Bone Deep Bonds, a novel by B. G. Arnold

Terriers in the Jungle, a novel by Georja Umano

Into the Emerald Dream, a novel by Autumn Allen

His Name Was Ellis, a novel by Joseph Libonati

The Cup, a novel by D. P. Hardwick

The Empathy Academy, a novel by Dustin Grinnell

Tholocco's Wake, a novel by W. W. VanOverbeke

Dying to Live, a novel by Barbara Macpherson Reyelts

About the Author

Rob Kagan is an islander at heart. He's lived in Newport, Rhode Island, St. John, USVI, and Chappaquiddick for twenty-eight years until ultimately relocating off-island. Reinventing himself from an entrepreneur to a customer experience professional allowed him to fit into a new type of zoo—suburbia. He currently lives on ZOOM (0-2-1-3-4).

Made in United States
North Haven, CT
03 May 2022

18819073R00214